Praise for *The Unfinished Leader*

"Leaders in all organizations—whether companies or governments—are faced with messy challenges every day. *The Unfinished Leader* accepts these paradoxes as a fact of life and offers useful advice and real-world examples so every leader can respond more effectively to these challenges."

—**Alan Webber,** founding editor, *Fast Company*

"*The Unfinished Leader* is a fascinating and provoctive book which makes a strong case that leaders are always 'becoming' rather than reaching a destination. In particular, the authors focus on the paradoxes that characterize organizational life and how leaders can learn to confront, live with, and ultimately leverage those paradoxes. The book is a compelling combination of counterintuitive theory combined with a tremendous amount of very practical and pragmatic advice. Leaders at all levels, facing the increasingly paradoxical nature of leadership and organizations, will benefit greatly from this work."

—**David A. Nadler,** principal, Nadler Advisory Solutions, and retired vice chairman, Marsh & McLennan Companies

"Leadership dilemmas are an opportunity to inspire innovation and creativity if you approach them with the right tools and mindset. Full of invaluable insights from international CEOs and senior executives, *The Unfinished Leader* provides practical advice on how the best leaders turn obstacles into opportunities to inspire innovation and creativity."

—**Marvin Chow,** marketing director, Google Inc.

THE UNFINISHED LEADER

*Balancing Contradictory Answers
to Unsolvable Problems*

David L. Dotlich

Peter C. Cairo

Cade Cowan

JB JOSSEY-BASS™
A Wiley Brand

Published by Jossey-Bass
A Wiley Imprint
One Montgomery Street, Suite 1200, San Francisco, CA 94104-4594
www.josseybass.com

Jossey-Bass books and products are available through most bookstores. To contact Jossey-Bass directly call our Customer Care Department within the U.S. at 800-956-7739, outside the U.S. at 317-572-3986, or fax 317-572-4002.

Wiley publishes in a variety of print and electronic formats and by print-on-demand. Some material included with standard print versions of this book may not be included in e-books or in print-on-demand. If this book refers to media such as a CD or DVD that is not included in the version you purchased, you may download this material at http://booksupport.wiley.com. For more information about Wiley products, visit www.wiley.com.

Library of Congress Cataloging-in-Publication Data
Dotlich, David L. (David Landreth), 1950–
 The unfinished leader : balancing contradictory answers to unsolvable problems / David L. Dotlich, Peter C. Cairo, Cade Cowan.—First edition.
  pages cm
 Includes bibliographical references and index.
 ISBN 978-1-118-45509-8 (hardback); ISBN 978-1-118-86711-2 (pdf); ISBN 978-1-118-86714-3 (epub)
 1. Leadership. 2. Decision making. 3. Work and family. I. Cairo, Peter C., 1948– II. Cowan, Cade, 1972– III. Title.
 HD57.7.D678 2014
 658.4′092–dc23
                                        2013046389

Printed in the United States of America
FIRST EDITION
HB Printing   10 9 8 7 6 5 4 3 2 1

One must not think slightingly of the paradoxical
. . . for the paradox is the source of the thinker's
passion, and the thinker without a paradox is like a
lover without feeling: a paltry mediocrity.
—Søren Kierkegaard[1]

CONTENTS

FOREWORD

Stephen H. Rhinesmith

Most people are so used to hearing about the complete leader, the whole leader, and the balanced leader that it probably brings you up short to think of the unfinished leader as a role model. But that is what this book is all about.

When could an unfinished leader be good? Well, it might be in a complex world in which there are no easy answers. In a world where leaders need to see themselves as constantly open to new possibilities. In a world where leaders are willing to jump on new ideas and accept that they probably don't have all the answers—and never will.

A leadership model that posits that the ideal leader is *finished*—complete and self-sufficient—has several inadequacies in today's world. First, leadership is becoming a collective experience as the world becomes more complex. Few leaders today can manage the challenges of a complex, technology-driven, connected marketplace by themselves. The increasing numbers of books on collaboration underscore the need for leaders to achieve their organizations' objectives in a way that moves them beyond whether they personally are finished leaders.

This coincides with a trend in leadership research to identify effective leaders as authentic in their relations both with others and with themselves. That means acknowledging strengths and weaknesses and ensuring that the best skills are applied to manage the most important challenges. This again requires moving beyond thinking about one individual as an independent, finished actor.

The leadership literature today also stresses the concept of effective leaders as self-aware. And being self-aware in today's world also means being aware that you can't consider yourself finished as a leader. We are all destined to be unfinished as we continue to learn and develop for ever-changing challenges.

But we need unfinished leaders for yet other reasons. As the authors point out, we will never finish the most important personal and professional challenges. This is because more and more of our problems are not puzzles to be solved but paradoxes to be managed on a continuing basis that has no end. This turns the image of an effective leader as decisive problem solver on end. Effectiveness in a global, interconnected world depends on leaders who accept not only that they will never be finished but that the world around them will never be finished. Many of the most important challenges we face will never be solved once and for all.

This does not mean there cannot be temporary solutions, only that fewer solutions will last. The Chinese for centuries have believed the world is on a continuum between yin and yang. The pendulum stops for a split second only before it starts swinging in the opposite direction. I was interviewing a leader in Shanghai a few years ago, and he said with pride that his business had been very successful in recent years. As a result, he was working hard to anticipate a future downturn, because he knew life was never one-sided. The swing of the pendulum would require him to "manage the other side."

Many leaders operate as if they fail to see the other side. They believe they have found the solution—the best product, the best market, or even the best niche to ride "just for the next year." But anticipating the other side of success is a basic skill of an unfinished leader, who understands that no victory comes without the shadow of the next wave of innovation.

One could posit that all effective leaders are unfinished—in their work and in their own development. That is the contention of the authors of this unusual and important work.

The authors point out that paradoxes, unlike puzzles, have more than one right answer, and more important, they do not have an ending. Paradoxes are not susceptible to being finished. The only way we can successfully manage paradoxes is to understand that we as leaders will never be finished. Never finished in our solution to all problems. Never finished in our achievement of all goals. Never finished in the development of ourselves.

In our businesses and nations, we are daily becoming more globally entwined. This is leading to new innovations, increased productivity, growing GDPs, and a better quality of life for a majority of the people in the world. It is also opening us to the threat of pandemic diseases, terrorism, and outsourced jobs that will never return.

This sounds a like a bleak picture. And it raises many complex problems. Complex, yes, but not necessarily bleak.

Leaders who strive for final solutions will never be successful. The essence of future leadership will be the ability to manage a world of contradictory demands and needs. It will demand weighing each and ensuring that over the long term all critical needs are addressed. This is not to say that there are not challenges to be overcome, goals to be met, and victories to be claimed. But the world is filled with those conundrums we call paradoxes—the issues that demand that we choose between right and right, where one solution is never final, only temporary. No paradox can be finished once and for all. Only leaders willing to accept that the world is not simple and cannot be tidy will be effective.

There is an old saying: "For every complex problem, there is a simple answer—and it is wrong." Working with that belief, the authors posit that successful leadership in the future will depend on *mindset—a way of looking at the world that allows one to weigh opposing and contradictory demands and manage them on an ongoing basis.* This in turn depends on how we live and lead others to "jump over the line" from puzzles to paradoxes, and from certainty to openness. The best leaders are those who can see the bigger, broader picture on a global basis and not be overwhelmed by the world's variety of values, viewpoints, and needs.

Developing an open mindset is more important now than ever. We can see how closed mindsets are creating turmoil throughout the world. Fundamentalists of all stripes—political, economic, religious, social—are claiming they have the answer to one side of a paradox. Remember, for every complex problem there is an easy answer—and what most fundamentalists have to offer are simple, easy answers that represent only one side of the right-versus-right conundrum posed by the world's paradoxes.

F. Scott Fitzgerald once noted, "The test of a first-rate mind is the ability to hold two opposing ideas in one's head at the same time and still retain the ability to function." Too few people today are passing that test. Instead, they retreat into ideologies or interest groups that have no interest in reconciling differences because they do not acknowledge the rightness of the other perspective.

Each of us has a personal as well as professional journey to cut through a diverse, ambiguous, and uncertain world. In the process, our ability to reconcile differences and develop new mindsets for paradoxical thinking will be critical—critical not only to our own happiness and development but to the capacity of the world to deal with its uncertain and unsettled future.

PREFACE

Perhaps you remember the first time you heard about the prisoner's dilemma. Someone told you the details: Two prisoners, accomplices in a robbery, are stuck in solitary confinement. The police, short on evidence, try to tempt each of them to rat the other out. If both comply, they will both get two years in jail. If both deny the crime, they will both get one year. If only one denies and the other rats, the rat will go free and the denier will get three years.

So what should they do? If you're like us, when you first heard of the dilemma, you thought you could solve it, and yet round and round you went and in short order you realized you couldn't. Fact is, there is no right answer because you get different answers based on your view of things like loyalty, cooperation, rationality, and retribution. What's right just depends.[1] Still, you probably remember your consternation as you twisted your brain into knots considering the alternatives.

You might be surprised, but we encounter this same kind of consternation all the time when we teach executive leaders in large and small organizations. As part of Pivot Leadership, we work with top executives around the world, and are often called when leaders are debating an important new decision. They're all looking for the *right* solution, but enough factors come into play that they're tying their brains into knots coming up with it. The knots are a signal: There is no correct solution.

So then we do our job: We point out they're not facing a simple problem with a fixed solution that everyone can agree on. They're facing a paradox, usually a problem complicated not by just a single set of contradictory forces but by many. It's hard for them to see this because of the problem's complexity and their immersion in the details. The problem has many solutions, and although the stakeholders probably can't all agree on one, if they can accommodate some healthy dissent, they can come to a consensus decision on the right way to act.

When we point this out, we hear a big sigh of relief—so big that it's often audible around the room.

You might be puzzled. How could some of the world's top leaders—often from the biggest and most profitable companies on the planet—have trouble seeing the distinction between simple problems and paradoxes? It turns out that the distinction is hard to detect until you're trained to do so. Second, how could those people value our revelation so much? The answer is that we helped them unfreeze a paralyzed decision-making process. People could then manage problem solving in a new way and act more swiftly, intelligently, and confidently.

Our coaching has elicited this sigh of relief so many times that we decided we had to write a book about it—or rather, about what causes people's misunderstanding of paradoxes and how to overcome paradoxes once they're recognized. Indeed, although we have been consulting with top companies for decades, the problem of paradox paralysis comes up more often with every passing year. Especially in the last five years, we have seen paradox-related consternation grow quickly, and we decided the time was right to put a book in your hands.

A lot of the insights in this book come from our work as strategy consultants and teachers of executives, which we have collectively pursued for more than thirty years. Our clients have included leaders at firms like GlaxoSmithKline, Deutsche Post DHL, AbbVie, Nike, Colgate-Palmolive, BlackRock, Thomson Reuters, Becton Dickinson, Ericsson, Johnson & Johnson, Aetna, National Australia Bank (NAB), the private equity firm KKR, Avon Products, Time Warner, Boehringer-Ingelheim, Citigroup, and Illinois Tool Works (ITW). In the typical situation, we get a call from a CEO for advice on how to transform a company or its leaders to meet a new strategic challenge, and one thing leads to another. Inevitably, the conversation turns to the significant paradoxes that are confronting the organization and how to manage them. Often these conversations result in efforts to drive an understanding of paradoxes more deeply into the organization. In one case, we consulted with a CEO, and after we pointed out the nature of paradox management, he wanted us to train his top 150 leaders in our approach.

Many other insights in our book come from our research. Specifically, we launched an effort a year prior to writing that we called The Pivot Paradox Project. We interviewed a hundred CEOs and top leaders from a wide range of companies about the paradoxes they face. These leaders included Frank Appel, CEO of Deutsche Post DHL; John Veihmeyer, CEO of KPMG; Henry Kravis, co-CEO of KKR; Ian Cook, CEO of Colgate-Palmolive; Cameron Clyne, CEO of NAB; Alex Gorsky, chairman and CEO of Johnson & Johnson; Bill Weldon, formerly chairman and CEO of Johnson & Johnson; Larry Fink, chairman and CEO of BlackRock; Andrea Jung, former chairman and CEO of Avon Products; Andrew Thornburgh, CEO of Bank of New Zealand; and Scott Santi, CEO of ITW. The research provided us with insightful stories and perspectives on paradoxes that exist in organizations today.

One of the valuable lessons from the project was that paradoxes come in many forms, and they occur everywhere. In fact, we found that much of our advice applied to people in their personal lives as well as their leadership roles. If people solved some of the more universal personal paradoxes—for example, the conflict between making money and finding meaning or to achieve the right balance between work and family—they developed the skills and perspective to deal with them better as leaders in their organization. We hope that as you read the book, although we speak directly to you on the job, you will see that we're also addressing you as an individual facing paradoxes at home, in the community, and as a citizen.

Many clients and friends contributed to our understanding of paradox in organizations and are an important part of this book: Ken

Meyers, Nicole Cipa, Mary Lauria, Tim Richmond, Kristin Weirick, Monique Matheison, Mike Tarbell, David Ayre, Kim Lafferty, Carolynn Cameron, Rolf-Dirc Roitzheim, Joan Lavin, Kevin Wilde, Mary Lauria, Peter Fasolo, Arturo Poire, Selina Milstam, Andrew Kilshaw, Annie Brown, Dan Johnston, Kristy Matthews, Kim Lafferty, Roger Cude, Vicki Lostetter, Jeff Smith, Mark Wiedman, Fabian Carcia, Daniel Marsili, and Angela Titzrath.

We couldn't have completed the research for the book, or articulated the insights, or gotten it written without the support of many people. At Pivot Leadership, our team included Ryan Fisher, Stacey Philpot, Albertina Vaughn, Ron Meeks, Kathleen Olsen, Antoine Tirard, Julie Aiken, Julie Roberts, Anesu Mandisodza, Brenda Fogelman, and Michaelene Kyrala. Bruce Wexler assisted with an early copy of the manuscript, and Bill Birchard as editor and coach was superb in guiding this book to its destination.

We especially want to thank the many people whose stories provided details and background for the book. Some of them we name; others, for reasons of privacy, we do not, and we have disguised them by changing identifying facts. Still others provided only background for the book—we couldn't fit everyone's story into its pages and had to make hard decisions of what to (and not to) include. All these stories come from our research or recent consulting work, and for that reason we do not note any of them at the end of the book. In any case, we want to thank all the people who allowed us to interview them. Their stories, all true, are what make it possible to convey this crucial yet subtle element of leadership practice so clearly.

We also want to thank our wonderful editors and support team at Jossey-Bass, whose patience and belief in this project sustained us through multiple rewrites: John Maas, Susan Williams, Clancy Drake, and always Cedric Crocker.

Finally, we want to thank you as a reader. Presumably you are a leader or would-be leader in some capacity. It is the response of people like you, upon publication of this book and our previous ones, who inspire us to do the hard work of authorship. We see much consternation in our line of work, and our most earnest hope is to release people from that prison of indecision that comes from wrestling with paradoxical problems without having the tools to manage them. With this book, we hope to help many take that first step in mastering a new leadership practice.

February 2014

David L. Dotlich
Portland, Oregon

Peter C. Cairo
New York, New York

Cade Cowan
Atlanta, Georgia

THE UNFINISHED LEADER

INTRODUCTION

Stepping Up to Complete Leadership

Perhaps no other animal is so torn between alternatives.
Man might be described fairly adequately, if simply,
as a two-legged paradox.
−John Steinbeck[1]

In a book about how to manage paradox, we will start with one that applies to you personally: The only way to become a finished leader is to remain an unfinished one. There you go. You thought we were going to distill the many insights in our book into a clear axiom. And instead, well, we made a statement that sounds complex and ambiguous.

Although this is a risky way to start a book, we want to make a point: If you're a leader—or an aspiring one—you can't afford to be scared off by complexity or ambiguity. You have to hunger to thrive in their midst. And if you're that kind of person, this book is for you. Step by step, we show you how to make better decisions and act more decisively in a complex world—practices that will prove useful even if you already recognize that you live in a world of paradox and have found ways to work with it productively.

Many people believe the way to solve complex problems is to reduce them to something simple. This is not our approach. As Albert Einstein was quoted as saying, "Everything must be made as simple as possible, but not one bit simpler."[2] We agree. If you're too much of a reductionist, you end up glossing over the rough edges that make most difficult problems so prickly.

And "as simple as possible" is getting more complex by the day. In fact, the most important problems we face—at home, in the office,

1

in the factory, in the community—have increasingly taken on complex new forms full of illogic. Especially when it comes to leading people. Problems of the past were two-dimensional in comparison. As Chapter One explains, we call these simpler problems *puzzles*—straightforward, single-solution problems you can solve once and for all.

But these two-dimensional puzzles have morphed into multi-dimensional paradoxes. They bristle with contradictions. They pit the forces of one interest against another. You can't solve them once and for all. In fact, you can't always solve them *at all*—although you can manage them.

You may believe you can simplify every complex problem into an uncomplex essence. Then you can tirelessly work to find the single right solution for the problem in question, then close the book on that mind twister, pat yourself on the back, and declare: Mission Accomplished!

But with leadership paradoxes, you can't arrive at a single or right or definitive solution. The paradoxes may trick you into thinking you have to give in either to one opposing choice or to the other—the long term or the short term, for instance. Or they may tempt you into trying to turn every set of contradictions into complementarities. But they will confound you if you approach them this way, and instead of patting yourself on the back, you may want to tear your hair out and proclaim: Mission Impossible!

One of our consulting clients is CEO of a big company that faces an uncertain future. The company has thrived for many years with captive customers, stable technology, and seasoned management. But as the Internet has changed the product set, and as customers enjoy more choices from firms breaking down industry boundaries, he has decided the ability to thrive in the future will require new capabilities. He has also realized that nobody on his senior team has those capabilities, nor can anyone quickly learn them. So what does he do? Does he fire all of them? Does he send them to training? Does he hire young MBAs to work with them to understand and master the challenges of a suddenly alien business?

He has worked hard to build the company, and he wants to secure his legacy. His goal is to position the firm as sustainable for decades. So what's the best way to solve that problem? Does he decide based on people performance or company performance? Does he reward loyalty or skill? Does he think about the welfare of his colleagues or the entire employee base? Does he think about the short term or long term? The decision is full of contradictions. What do you think? What would *you* do?

After much thought about the paradoxes built into his dilemma, he reshaped his organization around the talents (and deficiencies) of his people. He came up with an innovative regrouping of products and services, highlighting the strengths of his key players, reducing the role of some, and positioning others for greater future responsibility. He added new people to his team, and removed one or two of the old ones. In short, he faced into paradox and rather than decide between either/or alternatives, he used paradox to spur innovation in his thinking and then his decisions.

We have been helping people like this CEO make difficult decisions for years, and we have found that these paradoxical situations have come up more and more. In fact, top leaders face paradoxes all the time. And the number of paradoxes they are facing has exploded, along with the numbers of choices in every aspect of business—new ways companies compete for customers, new technologies embedded in products, new ways to work and collaborate, new global marketplaces, new competitive players, and so on.

We have discovered much about how to help people faced with paradoxes. Confounding as the contradictions are, they can be managed if you approach them the right way. You cannot master this approach in business school, nor through traditional management experience. You have to learn it through direct experience in struggling with paradoxical problems, acknowledging them, sorting out the contradictions.

We help you get started with this book, offering a range of content to highlight an approach that works. We tell stories of leaders who are struggling with paradoxical questions. We summarize research to show you how the world has changed and how you can react effectively. We itemize our processes and tools for moving one step at a time to solutions. We base all of this on our decades of experience, in which we have observed patterns of dysfunction in handling multiplying paradoxes—and how to move beyond them.

We agree with many of the books on leadership today. They offer lots of good tips and techniques, from recruiting to motivating to inspiring. But this book adds something vital to the leadership bookshelf: It singles out skills that most leaders desperately need today but don't have—especially veteran leaders who earned promotions when organizations faced fewer contradictions. It offers advice to these leaders as whole people, without separating the mental skills or personal characteristics needed on the job from those at home or in the community. This is not a book offering another theory. It is a how-to handbook for getting started.

We focus on collaborative problem solving because the heroic approach—the solo gunslinger protagonist going after antagonistic business forces—is not up to the task at hand. We focus on broad-based collaboration, because many people are required to help you out—not just those who sit in offices down the hall. You also need people sitting in other offices, living in your communities, or facing you across the dinner table. A company, after all, is only as smart as its people's capacity to collaborate on paradoxical problems.

You may have noticed that in the world today paradoxes seem to have paralyzed many institutions. Everywhere you look, leaders seem caught in the dysfunction of seeing problems only as offering either/or solutions, one extreme or the other. One side will not acknowledge the validity of the other side, creating problems that seemingly can't be addressed and get worse through inaction. The U.S. Congress leaps to mind here. But many business organizations are also slowed or sometimes stopped by paradox generated through matrix organizations or line-versus-staff, global-versus-local, product-versus-service conflicts, all of which are really paradoxes awaiting management.

Students of human organization patterns used to think that only the most senior leaders dealt regularly with paradoxes, but in today's organizations full of empowered people, just about everyone does. This book can help you begin the conversation on how to deal with them. How will your team, peers, boss, and even spouse manage amid so many contradictions? How can they become collaborators in bringing the toughest ones to resolution? When you wrestle with others over paradoxes, you will have a new insight: While contradictory forces can drive a wedge between people, you can also use those forces to unite people. Although paradox can spark strife, it can also spur possibility.

The advice we give in this book expands on our advice in earlier books, in which we called for the development of "head, heart, and guts" leaders. You use your head as an analytical tool. You use your heart to listen to and empathize with your collaborators' and stakeholders' points of view. You use your guts to summon the courage to act in the face of complexity and ambiguity. The CEO we described earlier found that his head, heart, and guts were telling him different things. You will find the same thing in the paradoxical challenges that are common today.

To deal in this world, it takes a specific approach, which we describe here: First, in Chapter One, we urge you to draw a distinction between straightforward puzzle-like problems and complex paradoxical ones. When you can identify the beast you're going after, you're more likely to succeed in subduing it. There's an old story about a rookie hunter who arrives at a game station bragging about the cow moose he shot. The wildlife officer retorts, "That's some poor honest farmer's mule!" The lesson, of course, is that knowing the size and shape of the problem you're going after makes all the difference.

Second, in Chapter Two, we urge you to recognize the human strengths that help people to solve puzzle-like problems but hinder their work on paradoxical ones. We highlight the natural human drives for control, consistency, and closure, for which most leaders have been rewarded over a lifetime. Who wants a leader who doesn't want to control events? A leader who doesn't act consistently? A leader who can't bring about closure? But with paradoxical problems, these drives get the problem-solving plane down the runway but fail to give it sufficient lift to take off. Leaders need to understand how to use control, consistency, and closure but also how to give away control to others, to tolerate inconsistency, and to accept a lack of closure.

Third, in Chapter Three, we urge you to take stock of the limitations the organization puts on managing paradoxical problem solving. Ironically, many things that make an organization run efficiently are antithetical to managing paradox effectively. Matrix organization creates multiple internal advocates for either/or choices—either theirs (good) or their rivals' (bad)—instead of a range of more reasonable options. Strategic planning assumes you can predict and control the future rather than act, react, and adapt. Performance review systems reward people for solving puzzles and, as an unintentional consequence, ignore most good work on paradoxes. Added to these organizational dysfunctions are personal ones such as arrogance and aloofness and perfectionism, and we discuss many of these in Chapter Three.

Fourth, in Chapters Four through Six, we urge you to start on the path to dealing with paradox by changing your thinking. By reworking the mechanics inside your head, you can engineer fresh perspectives that facilitate the collaborative search for solutions. We recommend practicing three mindsets, each helpful in different situations: the purpose mindset, the reconciliation mindset, and the innovation mindset. To oversimplify a bit, the innovation mindset calls for out-of-the-box thinking; the reconciliation mindset, inside-the-box thinking; and the purpose mindset, above-the-box thinking. They foster, in turn, invention, negotiation, and aspiration.

Fifth, in Chapters Seven through Eleven, we suggest five time-tested tools that we have found especially helpful in resolving paradoxical problems: scanning the environment, scenario thinking, stakeholder mapping, dialogue, and conflict management. These tools are not new, but as with tools in any trade, you can apply them in specific ways to fulfill particular objectives. We aim to show how to use them to engage in broad and deep conversations, allowing you to work with groups of people in an unbiased way. We have found that many people, even when they recognize paradoxes, feel overwhelmed and unable to deal with them. These tools break the paralysis. They get you to advance your thinking and to act in the face of ambiguity.

Finally, in Chapter Twelve, we show you how to develop your personal skills as a leader intent on mastering the paradoxes of our time. We focus especially on human weaknesses and how to identify and mitigate them. We hope in the process to give you permission to accept that, however hard you try, you will sometimes let the quirks of your personality thrust monkey wrenches into the spokes of smooth collaboration. You will sabotage your own best intentions, but you can often head off your self-destructive tendencies. We offer ways to help keep to your chosen path.

All this brings us to our opening paradox: "The only way to become a finished leader is to remain an unfinished one." Becoming a finished leader means you have developed exceptional leadership skills, and you constantly upgrade them as you recognize your failings. But practice does not make perfect. None of us is perfect. So keeping a sense that you're unfinished keeps you fresh and makes you better.

Along with engaging your head, heart, and guts, your unfinished attitude makes you a complete leader. Your attitude of humility helps you to drive every day toward mastery, while accepting that you can never quite get there. You accept that your task is to keep trying— diving deep inside yourself, reaching broadly out to others, and embracing complexity without denying it. That's how you will find ways to act effectively in a world of paradox.

PART ONE

THE CHALLENGE
OF PARADOXES

1

Puzzles and Paradoxes

*Par-a-dox: noun, def. 3: one (as a person, situation, or
action) having seemingly contradictory qualities or phases.*
—Merriam-Webster[1]

You often hear of top-flight managers who do so well at one company
that another firm woos them away for a tidy sum—only to turn into
losers at their new jobs. And you often wonder: How could wunder-
kinds in one company so quickly become bona fide duds in another?

We can't tell you all the reasons why, but we know one of them.
It relates to how people solve problems. As a way of explaining, let
us tell the story of Ron, a client and the former hotshot leader at a
media and technology company. Ron, who made his name as a brain-
iac overachiever, could absorb, integrate, and act on vast mountains
of data about consumers and market trends. With a team of geeks and
creatives, he developed breakthrough marketing strategies, created
brilliant ad campaigns, and delivered rapid market growth.

After great success, Ron was tapped to become COO of another
company. He took the same approach there—and it didn't go well.
Almost too late, he realized that the real problem he faced was not
solving an analytical puzzle about global marketing. It was figuring
out how to work with others in a matrix organization.

Ron and others at headquarters wanted one thing. People in the
field wanted another—and both sides had good reasons. Ron was
caught navigating between contradictory organizational forces. In
spite of his intellect, he was skewered for arrogance by regional salespeople, who shunned him as cold and uncaring.

Ron was proving as ineffective in his new job as he'd been effective in the old one—so much so that his boss threatened to let him go. It didn't matter that Ron, based on his exhaustive analysis, *knew* how to build bigger market share with a bigger and smarter brand, offering customers a new website, new loyalty programs, and new amenities. He could even prove in meetings that he had the right answer: He had irrefutable numbers and logic.

And yet Ron's inability to deal with contradiction became the problem itself. Ron was one man in one unhappy job, but we have encountered people in the same circumstances in other companies. In fact, he may remind you of someone you know. Or maybe you, yourself. Because the fault he revealed at the conceptual level was common among leaders: thinking of every problem as an analytical one—and acting on that thinking so single-mindedly as to remain blinded to the reality that the make-or-break problem may actually be a paradoxical one.

When we use the term *paradoxical*, we do not mean paradoxical as in literature. We mean paradoxical as in bristling with opposing forces—forces that seem contradictory or even absurd in juxtaposition. Forces that cannot be muted or ignored. In Ron's case, that meant forces that pushed a headquarters solution on one hand and a regional one on the other. Or put another way, forces that required acceptance of a solution at the headquarters level versus acceptance at the regional level. Achieving ownership at both levels—a contradictory task—was key. If salespeople didn't *feel* that ownership, they wouldn't take action in spite of Ron's appeals to the CEO to force compliance.

When leaders don't see the paradoxical nature of problems and solutions—when they think they can solve every problem as an analytical puzzle, as Ron did—they fail at some of their hardest challenges in management today. Especially the people challenges. They get stuck on one side of the line separating straightforward problems from complex ones. And their decision making then perplexes, angers, and alienates people around them—bosses, subordinates, partners, even family.

We tell more of Ron's story later, because he did ultimately transform himself to overcome the challenge he faced. He began to think about how he could change his own behavior, rather than fix his new organization. He decided to learn before he leaped, and listen before he led. Over time he was accepted by the new organization, which began to appreciate the value he could provide.

But first we look deeper at the ability he initially lacked: to recognize the difference between problems with pat answers, what we classify as puzzles, and problems with no pat answers—and no promise of ever having them—which we classify as paradoxes. Life can be miserable—as Ron learned, in spite of his devotion to a quality analytical solution—if you don't make this distinction. It's essential to jump over the line and work with others to handle paradoxes.

If you don't make this distinction, you make another error—an error we see in leaders all the time—thinking the skills needed for resolving one kind of problem are adequate to handle the other. They aren't. And the deployment of the wrong combination of mindsets and tools explains why leaders who excel in solving puzzles flail and fail with paradoxical problems. Only by jumping over the line (and when appropriate jumping back) can they manage the complexity that life throws at them today.

Jumping over that line is no small task for many leaders, but it is well worthwhile. Obtaining this ability is what sets them up for functioning at much higher levels of performance. It also sets them up to function at the highest levels in the organization, since the higher you go the more paradoxical the problems become. Managing those problems effectively enables you to avoid frustrating others while eliciting unparalleled levels of energy from your people.

It can also do something else, and that is prepare you to see that dealing with paradoxical problems often raises, in turn, paradoxical solutions: The way to compete in the long term is to compete in the short term. The way to compete globally is to compete locally. The way to create stability is to create change. The way to serve yourself is to serve the team. The way to gain power at the center is to give power to the periphery. The way to achieve cohesion is to champion diversity. These solutions result from first seeing the basic distinction Ron missed entirely.

The Problem Continuum

Everyone implicitly knows but rarely stops to consider one core truth: The kinds of problems that emerge in an organization do not all come from the same mold. In fact, they don't even come in just two varieties, puzzles and paradoxes, as we have implied. They vary along a continuum. From quantitative problems to policy problems. From questions of achieving factory efficiencies to conundrums in making investments. From sticky situations in customer service to the quandaries over balancing stakeholder claims. From snags related to regulatory rulemaking to predicaments of centralizing versus decentralizing organizational authority.

On one end of the continuum are problems with solutions built on uncontestable facts. On the other are ambiguous problems raising a muddle of alternative solutions wherein every element is contestable. Fortunately, you don't need a whole taxonomy of problems to further your leadership skills. It's only necessary to distinguish between black-and-white puzzle-like problems and unresolvable paradoxical ones, and to recognize that puzzle-like problems amenable to a single solution differ from paradoxes with no fixed and enduring solution— and to accept that what look like easy, win-win puzzles can evolve into chronic no-win paradoxes.

We've seen a lot of misery among corporate leaders as they solve problems—a lot of it self-inflicted, and much of that starting with failure to make the puzzle-paradox distinction. That's of course what happened to Ron. He could analyze complicated markets and come up with a rational and defensible approach to what needed to be done. He could not so easily solve the complex paradoxes posed by conflicting forces in the matrix organization in which various factions competed with one another. Regional sales chiefs, the dukes of their own lands, refused to simply bend to his will.

Puzzles We Know

Today's leaders have invariably received plenty of training in solving problems with puzzle-like qualities. With persistence and ingenuity, using analysis and rigorous logic, they have become accustomed to arriving at a right solution. The analysis, of course, depends on facts and data. And the facts and data point to insights. The insights in turn allow the leader to wield a set of known tools and procedures to launch a frontal attack that promises a certain solution to the problem.

The classic puzzle in management is the "traveling sales rep problem." What's the shortest route for someone to drive or fly to a fixed number of cities and return to the original city? The problem, even once you get to a large number of stops, has a definitive answer, even if not easy to determine. The same is true of many analogous questions of optimization in planning, logistics, manufacturing, and other fields. The traveling sales rep problem is a favorite of mathematicians.

Solving puzzles like this brings a lot of satisfaction to most people, and it's easy to see why. As in crossword puzzles, picture puzzles, or chess, so in operations management, product development, and customer service, people have learned again and again to win—and feel like a winner—with a fixed solution.

Note that by referring to puzzle-like problems, we don't imply simplicity. Many problems with what appear to be straightforward solutions are complicated and difficult. For example:

- Determining the lowest-cost providers of materials for manufacturing.
- Determining the impact on margins of currency fluctuations in non-U.S. businesses.
- Identifying the technical training requirements for operating new logistics software.

- Determining consumers' level of satisfaction with a new product launched in Asia.
- Determining the impact on client portfolios if the yield on municipal bonds drops.
- Forecasting price points based on shifts in commodity markets.

These are tough puzzles to figure out. They have many parts, and the parts interact in many ways—and yet as complicated as they are, they still have single best solutions. And they can still be solved most of the time by just one smart person. As an example, the head of a health care business we know, an executive with lots of experience, had to develop a strategy to resuscitate a money-losing hospital device business. Competitors had invented new technologies and lowered costs, squeezing her unit's margins. Hospitals were replacing some of her business's core products in surgical devices.

The first step for this executive was to come up with a new strategy. She faced some complicated questions: Which segment of the market was growing the fastest? Which customers had the most money to pay for supplemental surgery and medical devices? Which governments reimbursed the most for medical procedures? Which competitors' technology was declining? Which was most promising? Questions like this go on and on. But each has an answer, and she could formulate her strategy based on an analysis of the facts at hand. Coming up with the strategy was still hard, and it was important. To grow her business at that point, the most important challenge was to get the strategy right. But she was facing a puzzle, albeit a complicated one, nothing more.

Like other authors, we contrast complicated problems with complex ones.[2] A *complex* problem has no straightforward solution, defies purely logical analysis, and never yields to one answer. Complex problems are paradoxes. Distinguishing between *complicated* and *complex* is another way of distinguishing between puzzles and para- doxes. That many leaders don't make that distinction goes a long way toward explaining why company leaders so often ask us to come in and help them—and why we often trace their challenges to resolving paradoxes.

Paradoxes We May Not Know

It's useful to define paradox, as often used in management, in more detail. Leaving aside its literary uses, we define *paradox*, first, as a problem requiring leaders to recognize and fulfill two or more competing demands at the same time—for instance, winning at global and local levels simultaneously, as in Ron's case. You can single out what factors are under tension—and will always stay that way—almost like the poles of a magnet. In other words, paradoxes press leaders to serve one need while serving its opposite. That's hard enough on its own, but leaders are always facing multiple paradoxes at the same time and trying to find a way to proceed—when all the ways with a chance of improving current conditions are apt to seem illogical if not irrational when viewed from different perspectives.

Second, management paradoxes do not have a single right solution. They may have many solutions. Whereas in puzzles, two informed people will agree on a right and wrong answer, in paradoxes, they will rarely agree on either. The health care executive and her colleagues could agree on a strategy, because it posed a puzzle. But as it turned out, they could not easily agree on something else, because they faced a common paradox—how to create change in the organization while maintaining stability. More specifically, the challenge was changing people to fit the new strategy. It turned out that she had to fire and hire to form a new winning team without disrupting the company's focus on performance.

Third, management paradoxes never get solved; they only get managed. Ron could choose to focus on just one competing demand—pressing ahead with a global marketing plan. But that solution would not—did not—last. In paradoxes, choosing to give priority to one opposing force does not eliminate the other. If you push for a global solution, local interests come around and hit you in the back of the head. If you push your solution down through the hierarchy by appealing to central authority, the decentralized authorities come from behind and trip you up if they don't agree on the solution. For example, if you get the CEO to champion your cause, the heads of functions, product units, and geographies who run the company can block your success. And so this year's solution, as the wheels of time turn, inevitably becomes next year's dud.

Solutions to puzzles are forever, rain or shine. Solutions to paradoxes must be monitored over time. They can change with the seasons.

The difference between puzzle- and paradox-like problems—and the need to distinguish them—has gotten plenty of study both inside and outside business. As far back as 1973, Horst Rittel and Melvin Webber, professors at the University of California, Berkeley, described problems of social policy as either "tame" or "wicked."[3] Rittel and Webber referred to what we call paradoxes as wicked problems, in the sense of devilishly hard to resolve. They referred to puzzles as tame problems. And they noted that searching for rational, scientific bases for solving wicked problems was futile, owing to the difficulty of defining the problems, knowing correct from incorrect solutions, accommodating different perspectives of people involved, lack of definitive answers, and so on.[4]

"Proposed solutions" to paradoxes, they wrote, "are expressed as 'good' or 'bad' or, more likely, as 'better or worse' or 'satisfying' or 'good enough.'" No true/false or right/wrong answer was possible, they argued. "The one best answer is possible with tame problems, but not with wicked ones."[5]

Even seasoned leaders get trapped into puzzle thinking, looking—as if in a multiple-choice quiz—for the correct answer. One CEO who had gone through many yellow legal pads filled with checklists told us in our research, "One day I looked at my list of problems to solve and realized I couldn't put a check next to any of the items on my list. Some of them had been on there for months, and I had one of those 'aha!' moments. I realized my list of problems were really paradoxes and they were never, ever going to be solved."

What are some examples of the paradoxes a company leader would encounter? The following list gives the most common competing forces we've identified. Notice how we break these out as sets of single contradictions, in keeping with the way most of us think, although paradoxes may actually present three or more facets.

- Long term (investments) versus short term (profitability)
- Company versus function
- Local versus global
- Stability versus change
- Hierarchy versus flat structure
- Diversity versus meritocracy
- Core growth versus innovation
- Control versus delegation
- Honoring people versus demanding performance
- Work versus family

For example, determining what marketing decisions should be made in subsidiaries instead of at the corporate or division level would be a specific paradoxical problem. So would determining the right balance between investment in new versus existing products, devising a system to reward team versus individual performance, or figuring out how to achieve your career ambitions without sacrificing your commitments to your family.

Some paradoxes are strategic, such as long term versus short term or core growth versus innovation. Some are structural—hierarchy versus flat. Some are a matter of style—control versus delegation. And some are personal—work versus family. In all types, at least two opposing forces fight for air, and it seems impossible to give any of them the oxygen they need. Deprive one side of the paradox of priority and it will come back to fight doubly hard. You may tell yourself, "There must be an answer to all this!" Or you may berate yourself, "I should be able to fix this once and for all!" Odds are, there isn't, and you can't.

When Ron started to come to this realization, he finally set himself on a course for success. He saw that he was ineffective because he couldn't get anything done. When he focused on the global forces, he ended up appealing to his boss, and he soon found that issuing commands from the top down didn't work. And even if it did, Ron risked looking weak and dependent. He wanted to control the organization, but he couldn't—even the CEO couldn't exercise complete control. He couldn't get the sales force to implement his ideas, and in turn he could not rack up a list of accomplishments, or any accomplishments at all. And so Ron had to see a paradox for a paradox, and he had to take a new tack to implement his ideas in collaboration with others. When he finally gave more thought to the local forces, he made rapid progress.

Paradox Litmus Test

When you wrestle with an issue that comes across as a basic problem, and yet you're not sure that it is, how do you know you have a complex, paradoxical one? Here is a litmus test: Ask yourself, *Is there negative fallout from the solution you are trying to implement?* Or as professors Rittel and Webber write, have you found that "what comprises problem-solution for one is problem-generation for another"?[6] Do the original opposing forces resurface in a different form as you attempt to make your solution work?

You might notice that the same litmus test works as well in personal as work life. Puzzles stay solved when you have good solutions. Paradoxes resist solutions. Like monsters in a horror movie, they can't be killed. They keep coming back in ugly forms no matter what sword you slay them with. Consider the constant struggle to raise an adolescent. You can't cross paradoxical problems off your list.

As Cameron Clyne, CEO of National Australia Bank, said: "When my executive committee continually rehashes the same issue, I know there is a paradox buried there somewhere." In our work with many top executive teams, this failure to recognize, acknowledge, and manage paradox produces hours of unproductive debate and is the biggest source of frustration in teams.

Approach to Paradox

As a way to further distinguish between puzzles and paradoxes, consider the approaches effective leaders take to paradoxes. One of their most striking techniques is bringing people together to collaborate to find the preferred solution. Unlike some puzzle solvers, they cannot—do not—try to solve paradoxes in a vacuum or by themselves. Managing paradoxes is a joint exercise.

Second, once these leaders get the right people in the room, they rely on logic and analysis without being constrained by it. We like to describe them as people who engage their heads, hearts, and guts, a concept from our earlier books. Paradox leaders use their heads to recognize intellectually that there is no single correct answer with a paradoxical problem, even if there are many alternatives. They use their hearts to collaborate with other people who have divergent thoughts and feelings to develop two or more right answers. They select a solution only after struggling with varying right approaches—none of which include either/or solutions but instead both/and solutions that respond to opposing forces simultaneously. They use their guts to act on a chosen solution without delay, even if they cannot eliminate all uncertainty.

In 2008, professor Russell Eisenstat and several colleagues published a working paper describing the results of surveys of how twenty-six particularly successful CEOs dealt with paradoxical problems. They then described in detail the CEOs' handling of the people-versus-performance paradox in a *Harvard Business Review* article.[7] They confirmed that the CEOs did not view solutions in terms of an either/or choice. Indeed, they didn't see themselves as having to come down on one side of an issue to resolve a dilemma. "The CEOs typically spoke about choice as a non-existing option," the authors observed in their working paper. " 'The task of the role is to be able to reach both outcomes and not choose,' said one CEO."[8]

In other words, great leaders naturally jump over the line to collaborative, both/and problem solving when faced with paradoxes.

That's not to say that if you're a CEO you don't feel torn by opposing forces. But you can engage your head, heart, and guts to find solutions that deftly manage the paradox. Consider the approach of Bassem Bitar, chief strategy officer for Beirut-based Solidere. As the country's largest publicly listed company with a significant national mandate, Solidere has been spearheading projects to revitalize the central business area of Beirut for many years. While the company has succeeded in bringing people back to Beirut to shop, building retail stores and earning profits for shareholders, it has also endured criticism from the people of Beirut. Many people want Solidere to create a marketplace for everyone and preserve green space and traditional businesses.

The paradox, then, is between creating shareholder value and satisfying customers of the central district. If Bitar chooses to focus on profits for shareholders, he risks alienating the people of Beirut and catalyzing sharp criticism and public resentment. If he chooses to please the public by redeveloping the central city in a way that honors tradition and is egalitarian, he will have to sacrifice profit. Bitar is under considerable economic and political pressure to give in to one opposing force or the other, but he and the management team at Solidere have chosen to manage the paradox instead.

The company has done so by reacting to hot button concerns and communicating its sensitivity to them. For instance, Solidere has built green spaces into its plans for further preservation; it has also sponsored community-centric events and rebuilt parts of the city to reflect Beirut's traditional architecture. Bitar and the management team also talk regularly to community leaders and groups about Solidere's longer term time line: Some additional preservation and greening efforts will occur in the future rather than today. Bitar has given the community tangible proof of responding to people's concerns, while noting it will take time to respond to all of them.

At the same time, he has responded to shareholders not only by delivering good profits but by emphasizing how the plan for Beirut unfolds in phases while capitalizing on end customers' needs. For example, at the very center of the company's competitive advantage is its development philosophy that significantly embraces the presence of open green spaces and investment in Beirut's heritage as drivers to create a rich urban environment that people would want to visit, work, and live in. Thus, by reassuring shareholders how and why the company will meet their profit objectives later in the project, Bitar is able to maintain shareholder trust and support. Bitar has indeed managed the dilemma. His method of preserving and rebuilding a city center while delivering profit to shareholders is precedent setting.

Applying the puzzle approach to problems full of paradoxical forces is self-defeating. If you insist on trying to fix a paradoxical problem once and for all, you may end up getting locked into wild swings in decision making and action. You might implement a mandatory cost-control edict, say, and when that fails or people stop traveling to sell products or solve customer problems, you unleash spending. You then issue a new edict. If A isn't the solution, then B must be it; and when B doesn't do it, then you try A again, only harder. The pendulum swings back and forth—and even wobbles from side to side—confusing people.

Andrea Jung, former chairman and CEO of Avon, found herself facing the global-local paradox. About ten years ago, she told us, Avon began a strategic shift to brand management, intent to focus on building consistent global brands. This move was essential to the company's growth. Key stakeholders, including the Avon Board and investors, knew that "going global" was not optional. It was imperative—the only way to drive efficiencies and create strong brands that could be marketed and sold around the world. At the same time, Avon had a long-standing tradition of relying on local leadership to operate the company's traditional door-to-door sales model. General managers in key global markets had the authority to make product decisions based on their understanding of local customers' needs. The challenge for Jung, and Avon, was to drive globalization without alienating local leadership.

The result: "We constantly struggled with the infamous paradox of global strategy and local execution," Jung commented later. "While there was clearly the need to globalize, we may have swung too far too fast without fully understanding the implications. The change had major impact on our business model, leadership roles, and operating governance that presented many challenges throughout the journey." Though local leadership bought into the business rationale and supported the strategic shift, they were too often lacking the capabilities in their organization to execute the new strategy.

More Paradoxes Than Ever

In recent years, problems in work, life, and leadership have come to bristle with complexity. Complexity comes from the greater number of systems that run our lives, the greater interdependence of those systems, the greater scope and scale of systems locally and globally, and the greater number of people—all with their own interests in how the systems should work and what they should achieve. All of this means that leaders need to consider a greater number of outcomes—especially unintended ones—for any solution they develop. The growth in complexity is proportional to the multiplication of paradoxes.

In fact, in industry, you can almost mark your calendar, decade by decade, with the layers of accumulating complexity. After World War II, business aimed largely at building a lot for a little—the imperative was to achieve material and labor efficiency. In the 1960s, the imperative grew to include safety and health for workers. In the 1970s, it grew to include environmentally friendly operations. In the 1980s, world-beating quality systems and products came on strong. In the 1990s, so did demands to deliver unparalleled design, speed, profitability, and global reach. In the 2000s, it became imperative to include transparency, community consciousness, and on-the-job meaning.

We oversimplify, of course. But the layers of complexity have mounted relentlessly, along with opposing forces that can define the paradoxes in management and life. Consider Indra Nooyi, chairman and CEO of PepsiCo. Until recently, PepsiCo, like McDonald's, Kraft, and Nestlé, could focus on creating products that tasted good without being overly concerned about whether they were also good for their customers. They could produce their products without fear of coming under attack from politicians or consumers accusing them of fattening up the populations of the developing world for profit.

No more. When Nooyi took over, she managed a portfolio of products that had long included salty snacks and sugar-filled beverages. But increasingly, activists attacked the company for plying customers with high sodium and sugar, the villains in illnesses like atherosclerosis, heart disease, and diabetes. On top of all the other forces in business today, Nooyi has encountered this new one. She faces a new paradoxical situation, although she doesn't stand as a neutral party. She is chair of the Healthy Weight Commitment Foundation and clearly concerned about obesity, diabetes, and other problems caused by unhealthy eating.

Which direction does Nooyi turn? Does she risk alienating customers by taking the salt and sugar out of beloved products? Does she risk forgoing sales as the company revamps its product lineup? Does she risk losing investors who believe she should stick to her tried-and-true success formula? Nooyi has made a public commitment to create products that are "Fun for You," "Good for You," and "Better for You." Now she has to figure out how to negotiate so many paradoxical forces.

Managing the paradox of good taste versus good health is challenging for many reasons. For one thing, existing products provide the revenue stream the company is using to research and develop healthier products. For another, if Nooyi goes too slowly, she risks political fallout. When he was mayor of New York City, Michael Bloomberg insisted that New York reinstate its ban on super-size beverage containers—and the echo of his message still reverberates nationwide.[9] Third, as a global company, PepsiCo is aggressively pursuing markets in developing countries, which means Nooyi must navigate the complexity of countries with nutritional challenges.

She has taken the first step to managing this paradox effectively: Acknowledging it exists. She recognizes that good taste and good health are opposing points on a continuum—and yet may also be reconcilable. She also believes the choices should be transparent to consumers, allowing them to make informed decisions. As a result, she is trying to anticipate the sensitivities of various groups and approach these dilemmas with a different mindset. So part of her solution is to invest heavily in new "Better for You" products.

We can assume that our problems will only grow more and more paradoxical the way Nooyi's have, and probably not at a slower rate. Unlike their predecessors, leaders of today can often come up with six or eight options instead of just a couple. All may be of apparently equal value. And informed employees and publics argue vehemently for their varied positions, each opposed to one or more of the others and all sure of their own rightness. As outside stakeholders weigh in with more force, no amount of research will clarify the truth—because there is no clear, single truth to be found. Meanwhile, data overload will make it harder, not easier, to locate unbiased information in time to make clear decisions.

The volatility of our times adds to complexity. Consider what happens when, eager to increase flexibility, you flatten your company's structure to foster close-to-the-customer innovation, accelerate decisions, and reduce costs. As you broaden the span of control, reorganize into teams, and encourage participatory decision making, you encounter new inefficiencies. Execution may become bogged down. That creates pressure on you to change processes and thinking, highlighting the paradox of execution versus innovation.

As change catalyzes the need for managing new paradoxes that didn't even exist eight or ten years ago, it will become clear that recognizing and understanding paradox has become a critical skill at any level of the organization. If you approach a problem as a paradox and you really have a puzzle, no harm done. If you approach a problem as a puzzle and you really have a paradox, you will waste untold time and money fighting for a solution that may not exist and an outcome that is not possible.

You may even set in motion unintended consequences that take weeks or months to repair. For example, the decision to outsource operational tasks may seem to require a straightforward, puzzle-like, money-saving calculation. But cutting cost and effort in one part of the company may, paradoxically, increase it in other parts. A company may need new experts, new teams, and new departments to keep up with technology change, managing relationships, and organizational learning.[10] An outsourcing decision may not be a puzzle at all; it may be a paradox rife with contradictory forces.

Becoming Complete Leaders

At this point, you may still wonder: Is all this really new? Haven't paradoxes long been a way of life? And haven't paradox-solving leaders always risen to the challenge of finding solutions to problems with multiple opposing forces? Indeed, yes. In our experience, a top third of leaders, like Bassem Bitar, are naturals. They see paradox-laden problems for what they are. They deploy the proper skills to resolve them. They become role models for other leaders.

Research by Eisenstat and his colleagues, cited earlier, confirms this belief: Top-performing CEOs naturally make the distinction and deploy the skills to treat paradoxes in a differentiated way. They avoid the trap of struggling futilely to choose one extreme or the other, move to one side of an either/or dilemma, favor one stakeholder or business unit over another. They don't commit themselves to a search for a single, rational, clear once-and-for-all-time decision. Further, Eisenstat and his colleagues write, "They are committed to delivering short-term performance while also heavily investing in longer-term leadership and organizational capabilities. They push to increase the diversity of their firm's people, even as they reaffirm the common ground of the firms' shared purpose. These executives . . . discover powerful and integrative solutions to fundamental management tensions that other leaders too often avoid."[11]

Out of every group of leaders, however, only that top third, in our experience, fall into the group of naturals. Another third sense the need for handling paradoxes differently but react to them in a muddled way. And a final third fail to see paradoxes at all. Leaders in this final group are slaves to past training, encouragement, and rewards for heroic problem solving. They see puzzle solving as following a singular set of inviolable tenets of management. They cannot transcend these tenets, and they risk creating solutions that do more harm than good.

Three sets of leaders. Three skills levels. Which group are you in? And if you're not a natural—most of us are not—are you ready to jump over the line?

As the story of Ron shows, that jump starts with seeing the line itself. When you jump over that line, as Ron did, you face multiple opposing forces head on. Ron could control the data and product development on his team, but he could not control the whole organization. He had to open himself to the idea that rational people worked elsewhere in the matrix, and rational people had power and ideas of their own. They couldn't be won over by just being nice and persuading them to his point of view with more data and information. Ron was being tugged in multiple directions, and he needed to honor the opposing forces pulling on him.

At first, Ron's mental model of the organization did not allow an acceptance of dispersed control and heightened ambiguity. It did not allow the idea of submitting to the realities of conflicting power centers in a matrix organization. When his mental model changed, he began to listen to the regional people—at first out of mere acceptance, later out of curiosity about their insights. He began to negotiate as an honest broker. He began to be sought out by some of his peers. He ceased to dominate his boss's staff meetings. The change took six months, but the turnaround was remarkable.

And in the end, by collaborating with others, Ron led the company in developing a new marketing approach, a new website, loyalty programs, and customer amenities. He could sort out corporate and regional tensions, reconcile trust built on stability with trust built on change, and achieve both quality of action and ownership of action. With data mined from customer information, and by adapting the company's global standards to local markets, Ron renewed company growth. The one key to his and the company transformation? Ron points to his acceptance of paradox.

Ron's transformation is not unique. No matter who you are, you can become comfortable operating in an atmosphere of uncertainty, working with others to understand the ambiguity, reaching for consensus in dealing with it, seeking always to listen and innovate rather than speak and operate according to traditional procedures. You can do this at work, and you can do it at home and in the community. This is what makes a head-heart-and-guts leader skilled in the management of paradox.

The next step is undertaking a campaign to understand your deeper beliefs—see what they are, what limitations they have, and when to employ them and when to move beyond them. That's the subject of the next chapter. You can then align your people, transcend conflict, and improve your own and your organization's agility. You become what we call a "complete" leader. And you reap a bonus besides: You willingly, even eagerly, jump over the line in all aspects of life to enjoy, produce, and create in face of paradox and uncertainty.

Complete Leader's Checklist for Chapter One: Puzzles and Paradoxes

✓ Distinguish between puzzle-like and paradoxical problems, between the "tame" and the "wicked."

✓ Recognize that puzzle-like problems present complications that yield to analysis. Paradoxical problems present contradictions that can defy analysis.

✓ Beware paradoxical problems that suggest either/or solutions when they require both/and thinking.

✓ Recognize that puzzle-like problems have a single best answer, and you can *solve* them once and for all.

✓ Recognize that paradoxical problems have several answers, and you need to *manage* them with collaborators and revisit them regularly.

2

Jumping Over the Line

People who honestly mean to be true really
contradict themselves much more rarely than those
who try to be "consistent."
—Oliver Wendell Holmes[1]

We often hear rising leaders lament: "If I can just get to the next level, *then* I can solve this problem." The comment tells us that the speakers believe they will then have the power, authority, and control to implement *the* solution that will work. No more fooling around, they think. With the right hand on the tiller, the ship can be properly steered into port.

But the idea that a promotion, to any level of power, will give *anyone* that kind of control is an illusion. Those who succumb to it believe that all the problems they face are puzzles with fixed, permanent solutions. And they think that as they get more power, they will have the control to solve these puzzles a whole lot better than their predecessors.

But the reality is the reverse. In any organization, the higher leaders get, the *less* direct control they tend to have over solutions and outcomes. Studies even show that CEOs generally have far less control than most people realize. For example, Alison Mackey at California Polytechnic State University used a sample of ninety-two CEOs and fifty-one firms across ten years to analyze how much variance in firm performance was attributable to the industry, firm, and CEO. She concluded: "The CEO effect is estimated as 29.2 percent of the variance in corporate profitability while only accounting for 12.7 percent of the variance in business-segment profitability."[2]

This is a whole lot less influence than you might have guessed.[3] Contrary to what many people believe, CEOs and top-tier leaders are not masters of the universe. In fact, none of us has as much power to control things as we think.

One executive we worked with was reminded of this fact in a blunt way. Barbara, as we'll call her, was CEO of the U.S. unit of a global pharmaceutical company. For years, she ran her own shop and was a great success. And then a few years ago, company bosses in Europe decided to centralize finance, marketing, information technology, and other services around the world. Barbara no longer supervised the key members of her team—the CFO and the heads of R&D, information technology, manufacturing, and human resources—nor the people reporting to them.

This raised a ruckus among her U.S. leaders, who felt decapitated by a foreign power. One of them was outright hostile to her European manager, calling him an idiot and refusing to comply with his orders. Others disliked reporting to their European bosses because of their "management styles"—code for authoritarian. The U.S. head of regulatory affairs responded to an order from Europe by complaining that devising a single regulatory platform that would work in more than twenty countries was nonsense.

We can all become unhinged when we lose control like this, and it is especially likely for leaders who have not jumped over the line, for whom the difference between puzzle-like and paradoxical problems remains a mystery. Barbara was *not* one of them. A natural head-heart-and-guts leader, she knew from experience that she faced more paradoxes than any other kind of problem—paradoxes she could not control and would have to manage as opposed to solve permanently. She coached her reports in doing the same, assuring them that together they would reconcile the contradictory forces of centralization versus decentralization.

The case of Barbara and her direct reports leads to the message of this chapter: After distinguishing between puzzles and paradoxes, you need to take a next step and engage in self-examination. That examination should include a look at three premises that form a touchstone for people who have not jumped over the line. The first is the belief that you can *control* the outcome of all the problems you face. The second is the belief that you can stick with your solution as times change—that is, remain *consistent*. The third is the belief that you must have *closure*—deal with the problem once and move on.

Control, consistency, and closure. Those three premises underpin most people's success in solving puzzle-like problems—problems like that of the traveling sales rep. But when you face the paradoxes that leaders like Barbara confront, a white-knuckled grip on control, consistency, and closure holds you back both from collaborating with people and managing the decision process productively. As you advance to the next level, to manage paradoxes like the world's best CEOs, you have to recognize the limits you have put on yourself by sticking with those premises alone. To be a complete leader, you have to go beyond them.

Desperately Seeking Control

The thirst for control comes naturally to most of us. We desperately seek it to solve any problem. One leader we recently worked with told us that, throughout his career, he thought of climbing the organizational ladder as climbing the floors of a building. He assumed the people at the top exercised all the control. But when he got to the top floor himself, he realized nobody was there. Nobody was pulling all the strings.

The urge for control comes out in different ways. We want to *take control*, for one thing—find a way, say, to fire the idiots who talk nonsense. We want the person in charge to *be in control*—we think, thank goodness the boss knows how to fix the jam we're in. And we actually feel better when the leader reinforces the impression that everything around us is in a *state of control*—the economy is down but our company has a plan to thrive.

In some ways, the search for control is conspiratorial. Leaders and followers are locked in interdependency: The leaders want to be viewed as silverbacks. The followers want the same. Nobody wants to admit to a lack of control, and certainly not to the shortage of skill it implies.

The belief in our ability to control things has a tenacious hold on us—so tenacious that we regularly fall for what psychologists call the "illusion of control." Experiments have long shown that people attribute good results to their skill—something they can control—even when chance plays a major or total role in outcomes (as in gambling).[4] It's human nature to think we succeed because we're so talented, but in fact we always succeed at least in part because we're lucky.

As experts at Columbia and Rutgers Universities recently wrote, "Belief in one's ability to exert control over the environment and to produce desired results is essential for an individual's wellbeing."[5] The researchers noted that studies show the perception of control over stressful situations is a good thing. It actually inhibits the release of stress hormones, prevents immune system suppression, and averts behaviors like "learned helplessness."[6] Their findings suggest a biological basis for the need for control.

The drive for control can serve managers in organizations well until they rise to the position of leaders, where—like the CEO at the top of that building—they can't actually control what happens, both because of luck *and* complexity. At that point they are forced to find solutions to paradox-like problems, and in trying to control them like puzzles, they either fail or cause gross unintended consequences.

We see unintended consequences frequently bedeviling large companies with matrix organizations. In one of them—a major hospital supplier—the CEO fielded complaints from hospitals that had tired of as many as ten different company sales reps making sales calls. One rep might be selling surgical instruments, another hospital gowns, a third diagnostic products. All came from different business units, none coordinated. They each competed for business to meet their own sales targets. The customer would bark: *Can't you just send one rep?*

The CEO held many meetings to set up a new service in which one salesperson would represent the entire company to each hospital. He wanted to make sure that customers would no longer have to face a cast of characters from the same company but different divisions, each with an unrelated menu of products, each driven to fulfill different targets. He hired consultants to prescribe in a thick manual every detail of desired behaviors and rewards. If someone created a lead, they got one kind of credit. If they made a referral, they got another. If they closed the sale, they got a third. After every big sale, the central sales office divvied up credit and commissions among many business units.

The new coordinating service aimed to control the entire sales process to make it easier for the hospitals. But the fight for business by sales reps that once took place in the open at hospitals simply went behind the scenes at the company. People fought over who did what, who deserved credit, how to apportion sales to each unit. People gamed the system. They accused each other of stealing customers. Disenchanted employees left for greener pastures. As it turned out, legislating control became self-defeating. The CEO finally ditched the new arrangement, replacing it with a call to all employees to fulfill a new vision: Everyone in sales would coordinate with others to do the right thing for the customer in the long run.

Desperately Seeking Consistency

Another pervasive unspoken assumption is the desperate need to maintain consistency. The implication is that the actions of a mature personality are forever. Subsequent actions must fall in line right behind the first one. Politicians caught changing their minds like to proclaim: "I'm wiser now than I was then"—which makes sense, even if it is often expressed duplicitously. But the media and pundits rail against this "flip-flopping," bent on holding the leader to consistency with past actions.

The worship of consistency has deep roots. Ralph Waldo Emerson, in his essay "Self-Reliance," referred to people's "reverence for our past act or word, and we are loath to disappoint them."[7] He ridiculed "the man . . . clapped into jail by his consciousness. As soon as he has once acted or spoken with éclat, he is a committed person." He then penned his famous line: "A foolish consistency is the hobgoblin of little minds, adored by little statesmen and philosophers and divines."

Recent research shows just how much we are committed to consistency by human nature. In one set of experiments, people were asked to choose the best restaurant based on six criteria— ambience, amenities, dining guide description, hours of operation, location, and menu. Again and again, they biased their judgment of each successive criterion in favor of the restaurant they leaned toward after examining the first criterion. The same results emerged with people evaluating spaghetti sauces based on three criteria and hotels based on six criteria. Whichever spaghetti sauce or hotel they started out leaning toward, they biased their judgment of successive criteria to stick with that choice—no matter the equivalence of the data.

The results were surprisingly clear, wrote the researchers. "The main result of all three experiments is that the desire for consistency between units of information leads to the distortion of that informa-tion to support the leading alternative."[8] So the evidence suggests we slavishly favor consistency even when no logic supports it.

In spite of Emerson's widely read words of caution, the commit-ment to consistency remains prevalent, whether among leaders or followers. "I hope in these days we have heard the last of conformity and consistency," Emerson wrote in 1847. "Why drag about this corpse?" he asked. But drag about the corpse of consistency we do— now going on two hundred years later.

In our consulting work, we see this regularly. In one case, a manager in a global logistics company was asked by the board to define the ideal leader for the company. What attitudes and attributes should that leader have? What skills and behaviors? The manager brought in a consulting firm, and six outsiders did a six-month study, interviewing 150 executives, studying their behavior, analyzing their comments, preparing a complex model of the ideal leader. When the manager presented the model to the executive committee, the group rejected it out of hand: The model represented current leaders, not leaders the firm would need tomorrow.

The commitment to consistency, solving the *puzzle* of leadership, led the manager to stay the course of thinking in terms of current leadership. But he unwittingly created a prescription for the stagnation of behavior and skills. He made a mistake common among companies doing this exercise: Creating a map to develop more leaders like the current ones. The corpse of consistency was holding him back.

That's not to say there is no place for consistency. Emerson did not write, "Consistency is the hobgoblin" as he is often misquoted. He wrote instead, "A *foolish* consistency." Emerson was for consistency of purpose. If you stay consistent in your principles, you create harmony in the long run, if not a record of predictable actions in the short, he believed.

The result: "There will be an agreement in whatever variety of [your] actions, so they be each honest and natural in their hour. . . . One tendency unites them all. The voyage of the best ship is a zigzag line of a hundred tacks . . . [but] your genuine action will explain itself, and will explain your other genuine actions. Your conformity explains nothing."

Desperately Seeking Closure

The third unspoken assumption that drives people is a desperate need to bring about closure. Social psychologists argue that this arises out of an aversion to ambiguity and uncertainty, as well as a preference for firm, definitive answers to questions.[9] Like control and consistency, closure is a hallmark of effective puzzle solving. Who doesn't want to solve a problem once and for all? Close the door so you can move on.

Arie Kruglanski, a professor at the University of Maryland and pioneer in the field, has found that, in racing to closure, people often go in two steps: "seize" and "freeze."[10] To simplify, you first seize on a certain understanding of a situation, eager to take the shortest route to closure. You then "freeze" on that understanding and become impervious to new understandings. Depending on the situation, *everyone* does this two-step cognitive dance. It is a fact of life, especially at times of high stress and urgency.

Although everyone has a penchant for closure, its intensity does vary by person. Kruglanski and his colleagues even created a "need for closure" scale, using a forty-two-item questionnaire to assess individual differences.[11] The questionnaire grades responses to statements such as "I *like* to have friends who are unpredictable"; "I don't like to go into a situation without knowing what I can expect from it"; and "I [don't] think that I would learn best in a class that lacks clearly stated objectives and requirements."

Follow-up studies have confirmed the individual variability in the need of closure. In one study, studio-art majors rated relatively low on need for closure; accounting majors relatively high.[12] In another study, this one of professionals at Deloitte & Touche, Ernst & Young, KPMG, and PricewaterhouseCoopers, novice accountants generally rated significantly higher than partners.[13]

Over the last twenty years, Kruglanski and his colleagues have found that a need for closure is associated with intolerance for ambiguity, dogmatism, impulsivity, need for structure, and authoritarianism.[14]

In our consulting, we once came upon an unfortunate case of this common rush to closure in an executive we'll call Leanne, the head of a large health care company's consumer business. Leanne was a decisive leader, intuitive, with great judgment. She had the capacity to take complex information and quickly cut to the chase, making smart decisions about global brands, product designs, or even advertising copy. Give her a swamp full of alligators, and Leanne drained the murky water, chased out the problem reptiles, and led her team on a straight line to solid ground for future action. Her strength was closure. In some ways, Leanne was captain of her universe.

As part of her development, Leanne asked us to conduct a 360-degree assessment of her skills. We interviewed her bosses, subordinates, and colleagues. And that's when the bad news surfaced. Leanne remained open to new developments and judgments only to a point. In particular, she was legendary in her rush to closure with people. She thought of people management as a puzzle to solve and dispense with. She weighed people's abilities at the first meeting. If you met her approval, she was protective and nurturing. You were in her in-group. If you did not make the cut on your initial go, she wrote you off.

Members of Leanne's staff talked about being on her shit list, making observations such as "She has a tape she plays on me." They said Leanne would always remember if you screwed up. The tape of your sad performance, even if a rare exception and years in the past, played the same dirge forever.

And that was her Achilles heel as a leader. She didn't allow herself to see change in people. She couldn't recognize that C players could turn into A players. "Leanne stopped knowing me three years ago," one person complained. Leanne was good at making initial decisions but bad at adapting to new information. She would sit in on talent reviews and profess open-mindedness, but she demonstrated such closed-mindedness that her bosses wouldn't elevate her to the top ranks of the company.

All this was unconscious on Leanne's part—and she denied the problem. So as part of our coaching, we asked, "Can you name one person who went from zero to hero among your reports? Give us one example of a person that has made it out of your doghouse." She couldn't name even one. That question cracked her certainty about whether or not she had a habit of jumping to closure in decision making. Did she really know what she didn't know? Gradually, she opened up. She began to see that rather than retrofitting data into her preconceived opinions, she could challenge her opinions based on new information. And with this new attitude, acquired over six months, she refashioned her view of one person who had developed into an A player, and then another.

We could draw a familiar lesson from people like Leanne: "Foolish closure is the hobgoblin of little minds" (with apologies to Emerson). Closure has its place, but it can be foolish in the solution to problems with paradoxical nature—and problems with people almost always overflow with paradoxical elements. Many of us have trouble accepting that closure can sometimes be a bad thing. Keeping a foolish grip on closure—along with control and consistency—prevents would-be great leaders from jumping over the line to managing paradoxes that have the largest potential to improve our lives.

Getting Ready to Cross the Line

If you're one of those people who has jumped over the line to face paradoxes, you have discovered that you start with three more nuanced premises: Let go of total control, value inconsistency in action, and forget about closure. These three givens are the new priorities for leaders who fully employ their heads, hearts, and guts as paradox leaders. A slavish tendency to seek control, consistency, and closure is not an immutable fixture of your personality. You can make yourself aware of these new nuances and, as a complete leader, integrate them in your skillset. You are then ready to transcend puzzle-solving thinking and behavior.

Again, that's not to say you should swear off the three Cs, only that you can learn to apply them in measure and at times when they make sense. Control, consistency, and closure in management are akin to the same in raising our children. Sometimes they are the answer. Sometimes they are the problem. Parents know well that, during their children's upbringing, too much control can backfire. So can too little control. As with any paradox, no single right, enduring answer exists. The best answer on Saturday night may not be the best answer a few weeks or months down the line.

Once people recognize the new ground rules for solving paradoxes, they visibly relax. When we work with leaders, we can see the relief, or as we said earlier, we can almost hear "aha" ignite in their minds. Success doesn't depend on the premises for solving simple problems. It calls for new premises and more skillful leadership. Knowing this gives you more breathing room, more creative space. If you have been holding back on letting go because you didn't know how to cope with paradoxical problems, you can now break free of your shackles. If you felt unsafe even edging across the line, you can now jump across it.

Beyond a Thirst for Control

Barbara, the health care CEO, showed the effectiveness of letting go of control to solve paradoxes. True, she had no choice, but she also had the maturity to recognize the paradoxes she faced. As headquarters severed her direct control over R&D, manufacturing, finance, regulatory affairs, and other central functions, she wrestled with a host of contradictory forces: Centralization and decentralization, long-term versus short-term goals, speed versus responsiveness to customers, product cost versus quality, and simultaneously satisfying both her direct reports and her bosses in Europe.

How did she manage the contradictions? She acknowledged she didn't have control and didn't have all the answers. She shared control for problem solving with colleagues and collaborators. Together, they worked to manage the paradoxes. Barbara couldn't cede accountability or responsibility for performance, of course. She and her team committed to a host of performance measures—costs versus revenues, product cycle time, reduced regulatory challenges, employee satisfaction measures, employee mobility numbers, expense reductions, new product development. But they worked to deliver results as a group, in a consensus-making way.

Conflicts between her European bosses and her U.S.-based team were inevitable, but they didn't have to be debilitating. Barbara took several steps to reconcile differences, even though she no longer had direct control. First, she took care to empathize with the concerns of her former reports, who now reported to her only via a dotted line.

In one case, she appealed directly to the board in Europe for a global change in sourcing policy to ease a burden emerging for one of her colleagues. Second, she persuaded her colleagues to meet as they once did as an executive team, even though she was no longer everyone's boss. She felt that, when people aired their views, they would influence each other in shaping an agenda in which everyone was aligned. They still could function as a team to address those conflicts related to talent, U.S. policy, managing change, and so on.

And this helped when, for example, her CFO in Europe advocated a new global information system. The new system would require new process and investment that would disrupt U.S. operations and hurt profits. Barbara got the entire finance staff in a tense meeting that was nonetheless productive. Together, by focusing on the good of the global business, they saw their way to adopting a new system that was technically complex, would demand long work hours, cost a lot of money, and anger many finance staff people resistant to change. The system would also lead to layoffs of 10 percent of the finance organization.

Barbara played diplomat with her colleagues in Europe, gathering viewpoints in a roundtable discussion, and ultimately negotiating a transition that extended over more time. Her conversations earned her respect from colleagues in Europe and in the United States—even though she was no longer in charge. As Barbara showed, relinquishing control doesn't mean you're out of control. And the rethinking turned out to benefit everyone, enabling fixes of glitches that cropped up in other countries. Barbara showed the mindset that, in today's world, allows leaders to be comfortable in the many situations in which they simply can't master their destiny.

Beyond a Thirst of Consistency

Letting go of consistency also proves necessary for managing paradox. The voices demanding consistency are all around us, of course. In fact, we seem to insist on it in others, although not so clearly in ourselves. Why the obsession with the corpse of consistency? In our consulting with leaders, we have come to a simple explanation:

People too often don't discriminate between different kinds of consistency.

So we have our own obsession: Distinguishing between consistency of principles and consistency of action. The first remains imperative, whether in puzzling or paradoxical situations. But the second remains disingenuous when dealing with problems rife with paradox. Ironically, the U.S. Congress almost always deals with paradox-ridden problems, and yet pushes its members to solve them like puzzles. The public and media crave to see this consistency, but it comes at the expense of our leaders honestly managing paradoxes.

One leader we interviewed who transcends the consistency obsession is an executive from a multinational company based in China, who we will call Chris. Like many leaders in non-Western markets, Chris has confronted a particularly vexing local-global paradox. Leaders in countries like Russia, India, and China talk about local ways of doing business that clash ethically with their organizations' global principles. Chris gives a simple example. He notes that, in China, it is an act of courtesy and respect to offer a gift of moon cakes during the Moon Festival. Yet the company has a policy of no gifts to doctors. In China, failing to offer this gift to their customers would be seen as a sign of disrespect.

"We needed to stop looking at this situation from a black-or-white or right-or-wrong perspective," Chris told us. The approach the company decided on was buying $20 boxes of moon cakes centrally and distributing them to reps with directions to give away only one per doctor. The number given to each rep was limited. This was a good example of consistency of principle—the company certainly respected its customers—but inconsistency in action. Leaders who have jumped over the line see this distinction clearly.

While this decision was a trifle, Chris showed that approaching situations that seem irreconcilable with a new perspective really works. Too often, leaders facing this paradox opt for a rigid adherence to the letter of corporate ethics policy, or worse, they turn their backs on policy and adopt a "when in Rome . . ." perspective. In the former instance, they doom critical projects because they fail to grasp the paradox. In the latter, they lose their ethical moorings, risking harm to their firms. Chris chose a third course, one that reconciled both sides of the paradox.

We all know from our own lives that consistency in the face of opposing forces—forces whose nature and strength change over time—can put us in untenable positions. Consider gradual changes in work-family balance as children grow older. What works when your child is an infant or toddler won't necessarily work for a tween or teenager. This doesn't mean we are flip-floppers. It means we are thinking parents, struggling with contradictions.

Not everyone remains a slave to consistency to the same extent. A series of studies to validate individual differences in the preference for consistency showed that a large percentage (at least half) of college students participating demonstrate no strong inherent preference for consistency.[15] It is plausible the finding wouldn't hold for everyone, since college students often grapple with many paradox-loaded problems in their classwork. But it shows that not everyone is bound by the need for consistency—a subject that should get more press, but one that now gets less understanding than it deserves.

In a 2012 IBM Global CEO Study, CEOs cited "flexible" and "creative" as two of the top four characteristics needed for employee success.[16] A second tier of desired characteristics included "analytical/ quantitative" and "technology savvy." We can infer that the CEOs first want people who can change with the world of business. Only secondarily do they value consistency and puzzle solving. Interestingly, the other top two characteristics cited by CEOs were "communicative" and "collaborative"—just the skills needed, as Chris and Barbara showed, to resolve complex paradoxes.

Beyond a Thirst for Closure

Letting go of closure ranks just as high as a priority for people who want to manage paradoxes. In the same way that a commitment to control and consistency thwarts reconciliation of multiple opposing forces, so does the desire to tie up each problem with a neat bow. Paradoxes just don't succumb to neat solutions. They are messy and impermanent. Each new tide of work and life washes away former line-in-the-sand decisions. We all naturally seek closure, whether we are studio-art majors or partners in accounting firms, but success at bringing about closure always recedes from our grasp in a paradoxical world.

That was what happened with the CEO of the major hospital supplier we introduced earlier. He couldn't, no matter how much effort went into developing a complex pay and reward system, bring closure to the problem of showing a single sales face to the customer. In its place, he called on his people to manage the paradox in the interest of the whole company, making judgments case by case to serve customers.

Cameron Clyne, CEO of National Australia Bank, faced the same issue. He explains how business unit leaders once "owned" their customers—customers in commercial accounts or the private bank, for instance. Clyne worked hard to create processes for sharing credit, cross-selling, and customer tracking, bringing closure to the problem of motivating, evaluating, and rewarding people for work that brought in revenue. But eventually he threw in the towel. He could not bring closure to the problem purely through bureaucratic controls. Like the hospital-supplier CEO, he pressed his people to shift their perspective. Customers don't belong to units, he said. No matter how they come to do business with the bank, they belong to the enterprise.

Clyne brought us in to teach hundreds of his leaders about the paradoxical challenge of meeting both enterprise and business unit needs. He worked to build his direct reports into a team, driven to achieve enterprise goals. He identified intramural squabbling over territory as a paradox rather than a conflict. By getting his leaders to acknowledge the paradox, he opened them up to new solutions.

Though we all seek to see problems through to a happy ending—just as in the movies—we find that both happiness and endings are elusive when the problems are packed with paradox. Most problems in business—and life—defy our efforts to bring about closure. With children, with community, with government, with business, closure of even a limited kind doesn't remain for long, certainly not forever.

The pressures to revisit solutions are relentless. No sooner than you think you've wrapped something up, the neat folds of the packaging unwrap. As people joke: "I was finally getting over being pissed off this morning, and here we go again!"

The Costs of Mishandling Paradox

We incur heavy costs by mishandling paradoxes. When we strive for control, consistency, and closure and can't get them, we get confused and frustrated. This then confounds us, whether at work or at home, and compounds the problem. Delays in recognizing the true nature of the problem lead to many dysfunctions:

- Becoming paralyzed
- Being inflexible
- Getting hit by ignored forces
- Deciding too quickly
- Failing to understand trade-offs
- Failing to be transparent
- Failing to learn

Becoming Paralyzed

Paradox leads to decision-making paralysis when you see that, no matter what you do, someone will say you chose the wrong solution. Unfortunately, that's a fact of life with paradoxes, especially for leaders. Every solution is wrong in some way. You risk feeling vulnerable, being accused of weakness, or worse. And you may hesitate to jump over the line to recognize paradox as a result, which simply turns up the heat, building stress and anxiety and reinforcing a decision to do nothing. On the upside, you might avoid offending or alienating people if you sit on your hands. And you might avoid making an obvious mistake. But you fail to move things forward, essentially offering no leadership at all.

Jan Singer, head of Nike Apparel and former head of Nike Footwear, says, "[Paradox] is energizing if you like change because it may not be solvable and is a challenge. It can be paralyzing if you like things to be solved; for some it may be scary." To solve paradox, she believes, "You cast [paradoxical problem solving] as a place where there is no resolve, but as a place with the openness to think and learn."[17]

Being Inflexible

Paradox can also prompt people to freeze in one position or another, choosing one side of an either/or choice. When you fail to recognize that a supposed puzzle is actually a paradox, you may lock into this either/or thinking. You won't allow yourself to consider other options or to later choose an opposing approach even when the situation demands it. You are like the more rigid novice accountants in the need-for-closure study at the big four accounting firms: You are someone who "truncate[s] the hypothesis-generation task sooner, producing fewer causal hypotheses and demonstrating lower hypothesis quality."[18] In other words, you are someone who comes to conclusions more quickly than others, but at the risk of sloppier thinking.

The leaders of Groupon demonstrated the perils of inflexibility when the company did little to change its business model when entering the Chinese market. Groupon's Western strategy was to lure executives and acquisition targets with large sums of money. In China, Groupon was surprised when one target company, Lashou, refused its offer, despite the rich terms. Groupon failed to understand the market rate of vendor profit split, and it offered a much lower vendor split than was typical. It also imported employees instead of hiring locals, opening in China with only two local Chinese executives. The China unit suffered from inefficiency and high employee turnover. Groupon, caught in the classic global-local paradox, failed by not adapting its business model to the local market.[19]

In our consulting with one company, we learned that the biggest problem was both simple and hard: People's need to be right. After going through the strategic planning process, leaders became closed to challenge, closed to new data, unwilling to say they might have screwed up. They became stuck on the puzzle side of the line, shoes glued to the pavement. They were debilitated by inflexibility.

Getting Hit by Ignored Forces

When you don't factor all the opposing forces into your solution, those forces may come back to bite you in the backside. If as a leader you delay long-term investment, in time your decisions hobble firm performance. Once again, if you solve a paradox like a puzzle, too many factors get ignored in the interest of coming up with a clean solution.

Netflix seemed to ignore the forces of an installed customer base when it decided to solve the problem of an obsolete delivery technology. Its solution was to eliminate mail-in rented DVD movies. All at once it announced a changeover to a dependable revenue stream from digital subscriptions. This was a logical solution to an obvious problem—except the problem was not a simple one of technology. Customers rebelled, venting their rage on the Internet. Netflix stock nosedived. Netflix leaders swung too far, too fast, and they had to backtrack. They missed the implications of the paradox posed by forces of customer stability versus technological change. And in an age of transparency, Netflix paid the price for not choosing better options and involving customers.

Deciding Too Quickly

Freezing in one position or another is an error in the face of paradox, and the tendency to freeze in a hurry makes things worse. Leaders in search of closure may rush to judgment—often in a would-be heroic display of snap decision making. They say X is right and Y is wrong. We have seen countless leaders who would rather not work through the unease and confusion of two seemingly irreconcilable necessities. Instead, they act on their belief in a single solution. Doing *something* may provide relief, but the choices turn out to be ill-considered and the actions premature.

One of the authors (David) experienced this many years ago when he was promoted to supervisor at Honeywell and told to improve the performance of his new group. He was a manager for all of two days before he decided to fire a direct report he'd long felt wasn't performing up to expectations. As a newly minted manager, he hadn't considered the potential legal trouble his actions could create—and, more important, hadn't taken the time to fully assess the situation in his new role as leader. Fortunately, legal problems did not ensue, but more remarkably, the terminated employee went on to achieve remarkable success as an independent consultant. As a leader, David did not take into account the truth that people have strengths and weaknesses, or might change and grow with the right supervision and leadership. He just made up his mind and acted, as if a preconceived solution crafted from an earlier perspective would solve a complex performance problem.

Failing to Understand Trade-Offs

In one of the more insidious dysfunctions that stem from mistaking paradoxes for puzzles, people don't allow for the intricate dance that, in a group of collaborators, takes place between opposing factions. The opposites always remain powerfully linked. Actions suggested by one directly affect the other. But under the surface, we know we are interdependent. By not taking the time to examine the forces vying for primacy, people lose the chance to engage in frank discussions with trade-offs put on the table.

In one bank we have worked with, the head of the digital unit wanted to hire a new manager from a start-up firm in Silicon Valley. After learning the salary expectations of the new hire, the people in Human Resources said "No way." The expectations were so far outside the salary guidelines for the level of the position that paying someone that much would create a unjustifiable precedent and even dissension if it became known.

The head of the digital unit complained to his boss about the HR bureaucrats who were preventing him from growing the online business. The head of HR dug in to maintain the well-established salary guidelines for the bank. The conflict escalated until the paradox was identified: HR's role was to maintain equity across the system. The head of digital's role was to drive business performance, which required hiring the best person at the price required.

Both were right. But identifying their personal conflict as an organizational paradox helped them to see one another's viewpoint and begin to decide how to proceed. In this case, they made much of the higher salary contingent on some performance expectations. The new manager joined and performed successfully, justifying the higher salary.

Failing to Be Transparent

Even when you know you're facing a paradox, you may not want to reveal your confusion over the opposing actions. Rather than share your uncertainty and invite others into the decision-making process, you may go it alone and lose the benefit of outside input. You risk not only closing yourself off to fresh insights but energizing opposition to your actions. To manage paradoxes today, consider transparency as a competitive requirement.

Tony Hsieh, CEO of Zappos, practices this approach by taking transparency to the next level. He shares detailed information about company performance with all employees. He encourages employees to share with others. He invites the public to the company's all-hands quarterly meetings (and now streams those meetings live). He offers free tours of the Zappos offices, where little is off limits for visitors.

And he allows vendors to access data on inventory, sales, and markdowns—data that would be considered proprietary information by any other company.[20] This is the emerging standard by which other leaders are judged, and it is this openness, rather than remaining guarded, that elicits the broader engagement of employees to solve paradoxical problems.

Failing to Learn

Leaders who frame their decisions as choosing between one alternative and its opposite limit learning. If you're sure that option A is right, you have little incentive to learn about option B. The less knowledge you have, the less risk you take. Moreover, if you believe planning is good and spontaneity bad, you hesitate to follow uncertain leads, play hunches, or trust your instincts. This limits the experience you gain from taking action—experience informed not by analysis but from the imperative to act in spite of ambiguity.

Paradox Leadership

Jumping over the line to managing paradoxes is not easy for most leaders. If you're like most of us, you are not a natural in making the jump, and you know that if you stay on the puzzle side you will enjoy the company of the familiar, friendly faces of control, consistency, and closure. On the other side, you see nothing so familiar. This unfamiliarity can provoke fear. Will you get to the other side, lose your bearings, and succumb to uncertainty, depression, and despair?

We believe not. You will recognize the right measure of control to exercise, the right situations for demanding consistency, and the right times to bring about closure. You will know that traditional problem-solving skills have their place, and that paradoxical problems require a place of their own. You will keep constant track of which side the line you're on, and in turn which kinds of skills to deploy. As a complete leader, head, heart, and guts fully engaged, you will gain new bearings and find liberation, not depression.

You simply have to make the jump—just as Barbara did as she gave up power in the hierarchy but demonstrated her power in collaboration. She showed that the way to arrive at smarter solutions to today's toughest problems—wicked, paradoxical problems—comes from giving control to others, committing to consistency of principles instead of action, and seeking closure only by bringing other managers across the line with you. It also comes from avoiding the dysfunctions of decision paralysis, inflexibility, hastiness, and all the rest.

That sets you on the right track as a paradox manager. But of course, that's not the end of our story. As it turns out, you cannot deal with problems full of contradictions solely by changing your own way of thinking and working. The change required is not just internal. You also have to deal with the people and institutions around you, which create other obstacles. We now turn to those obstacles, and show that in tackling them, the complete leader can defeat a range of organizational forces that stymie paradox management.

Complete Leader's Checklist for Chapter Two: Jumping Over the Line

✓ Recognize your drive to control outcomes—and how that hinders handling the ambiguity of paradoxical problems.

✓ Recognize your demand for consistency of both purpose and action—and how the former helps but the latter hinders paradoxical problem solving.

✓ Recognize the universal desire for closure—but how it can lead to frustration when facing a paradox you can't resolve once and for all.

✓ Notice how loosening your grip on the need for closure, allowing inconsistency of action in response to changing circumstances, and accepting a lack of closure pave the way for managing paradoxes.

✓ Help your people understand the differences between paradoxes and puzzle-like problems and why the differences are important.

3

Obstacles to Leadership

Let go of certainty. The opposite isn't uncertainty. It's
openness, curiosity and a willingness to embrace paradox,
rather than choose up sides.
—Tony Schwartz, CEO, The Energy Project[1]

In Bonn, Germany, we once sat in on a Deutsche Post DHL executive committee meeting and watched a scene that often plays out in large companies: a vigorous discussion between corporate staff and business leaders. In this case, the combatants were top executives from finance and key divisions. They sparred not because they were querulous people, but because they had two professional perspectives, worked in two different areas, and had two approaches to the problem at hand.

CEO Frank Appel had assembled the executives to discuss a key issue. The question was: How should we close out the year? Should we take some of the year's anticipated earnings and invest for the future? Or should we hold back some to bulk up the bottom line? This discussion was not unique—almost all companies face the same dilemma as their fiscal year ends. The operations people wanted more investment, the finance people wanted to use the money to report immediate strong financial performance.

Both sides, typical of most companies, wanted the funds to fulfill their view of the proper investment. Division executives wanted to build up cash reserve to start the new fiscal year. They also wanted to invest right away in more marketing and business development for the next year. Finance executives, aware of expectations from analysts and shareholders to beat profit predictions, wanted to use excess cash from operations to bolster earnings. Pressure to do so stemmed from the need to reverse the legacy of the previous leadership group, which had missed expectations.

Appel, in the midst of turning the company around, could easily see both sides of the issue. As in all clashes of this kind in a big organization, each side scored points with persuasive arguments. Each was sure the company's welfare depended on its view prevailing. And as in other companies, the debate became intense. Both sides wondered: "Do you really understand my situation?"

What struck us about this meeting was not that the committee faced a paradox—in this case the contradictory forces of short- versus long-term good. It was that the way Deutsche Post DHL was organized—and more broadly how all companies are organized—can constrain the effective management of paradox. In fact, everything about the way we run organizations can be antithetical to managing paradoxical problems: functional groups, reporting lines, measurements, reward systems, and so on.

At Deutsche Post DHL, divisional and functional silos create inherent boundaries. As in all companies, separate organizations are set up to solve puzzles, not paradoxes, and the silos of professional expertise make sense for that task. But when paradoxes are on the table, functional executives invariably face off against one another, becoming entrenched, unable to cross the line between puzzle and paradox.

There is a grand irony here: Organization is necessary for a company to succeed, but when it comes to solving paradoxes, it can actually block success. The well-oiled corporate system, normally an engine of efficiency, becomes the enemy of effectiveness. It spurs people to insist on pat solutions rather than actions that will help manage paradox. This raises another challenge for leaders. Not only do they need to loosen the reins on control, consistency, and closure, they have to overcome obstacles thrown up by the very organization that sustains them. And if they don't, the obstacles will cripple their ability to reconcile the toughest problems facing them today.

In the end, Appel decided to overcome the factional sparring by changing the perspective of the discussion. He decided not to declare for the short term or long term as if he were solving a puzzle. He would not choose either one answer or the other. He would bring his team together to collaborate on a solution for the whole. He urged them to think about the enterprise first, and then decide together where to invest and where to save. He could step over the line in this way, and so could everyone else, by moving from a parochial desire for control to aiding the entire enterprise.

The Obstacles of Organization

Organizational systems in most companies impose severe limitations when it comes to paradoxes. If we do not find ways to overcome those limitations, paradoxes will divide people, just as they did Appel's team. And everyone will view paradox as the enemy, a troublemaking pest best shunned by anyone who wants to keep the peace. This is an ongoing challenge even for leaders skilled at exercising their heads, hearts, and guts in paradoxical decision making.

One of the central problems is that organizational systems encourage a rational approach to everything, whether that relates to organizing the hierarchy, planning for the future, or appraising and rewarding people. And yet you often need to manage paradoxes in ways that do not take a rational, linear approach. In the following sections, we address each of the common handicaps in turn to demonstrate another increasingly critical skill for the complete leader: Recognizing organizational obstacles for what they are—and preparing yourself to overcome them.

The Matrix

The most potent force opposing an effective approach to managing paradox is the one Frank Appel successfully handled: the silos of management. The strongholds of functional expertise, as at Deutsche Post DHL, are not the only silos out there. The silos of product and geography also act in the same obstructive way. Like special-interest groups in politics, they can drive a wedge between people who might otherwise solve paradoxes together.

In a study of 294 top- and midlevel managers in seven large global companies with matrix organizations, people frequently complained about silo-focused employees. Among specific comments about the matrix, they cited misaligned goals, unclear roles and responsibilities, ambiguous authority, and a lack of anyone responsible for making sure the matrix functioned effectively. The proportion of top managers citing misaligned goals as a dilemma, for example, was 67 percent, but this did not surpass the proportion citing silos, 69 percent.[2] In our experience, these weaknesses persist even as companies try to overcome them.

In most big companies, executives work hard to construct an organizational matrix that aligns people's goals wherever they work in the company. But the breakdown of a big organization into smaller units invariably creates rivalry or antagonism between the groups. If it isn't people in finance and operations going head to head, it's the folks in supply chain and product management. As the authors of the matrix study wrote, "Unfortunately, we found that most employees in large organizations tend to be silo-focused: They view their membership, and loyalty, as belonging to a certain subunit in the organization."[3]

Frank Appel recognized the competition in the matrix, and he took swift steps to address it. We were in the room observing the debate and noticed Appel managing a paradox: Rather than see the decision as an either/or choice, he viewed it from a broader perspective. Appel asked his team to consider the decision in light of the company's larger purpose: connecting the world and focusing on the three bottom lines of customer, employee, and shareholder satisfaction. This gave the team a way to look at difficult choices in a context that stimulated thinking that would yield a collaborative, consensus-like solution.

Some people may continue to think of paradox as an energy sink. But in the hands of a skilled head-heart-and-guts leader, a paradox becomes an energy source. Its potential for sparking breakthrough change inspires people to come together, to think differently, to act earnestly even in the face of ambiguity. That's ultimately what Frank Appel found as the leader of Deutsche Post DHL. After he brought his team together to reconcile their differences in the interests of their stakeholders, they agreed the right action for the entire organization was clear. Instead of overly responding to the expectations of outside or inside groups, they decided their role as "stewards of the enterprise" required them to deliver appropriate earnings to investors while investing the rest of the money for the future.

Strategic Planning

Strategic planning poses another obstacle to helping people recognize and manage paradox. The barrier stems from the planning mentality, which gives the future an aura of certainty. Neither assumptions nor forecasts nor alternatives can be known as valid, and yet the rigor of strategic planning conveys the impression that they are. We think we're dealing with reality. That's why people get stuck on their views of the way things will turn out, and they close down to other views even when contrary data emerge. The strategic plan gets treated like an architectural plan for a building: It's as if the world stands still while we bring in the workers and materials to build it.

University of California Berkeley professors Horst Rittel and Melvin Webber noted this tendency when they first outlined the challenges of wicked problems. "There is the belief in the 'makeability,' or unrestricted malleability, of future history by means of the planning intellect—by reasoning, rational discourse, and civilized negotiation," they wrote. "Many Americans seem to believe both that we can perfect future history—that we can deliberately shape future outcomes to accord with our wishes—and that there will be no future history."[4]

The tendency for people to think they can make the future has not changed in the four decades since Rittel and Webber made the observation. And strategic plans unfortunately continue to block skillful handling of paradoxical problem solving—which requires ongoing collaboration on several solutions that are right and impermanent. Strategic planning is nothing more than puzzle solving writ large, a rational system to produce a single best rational answer. This of course flies in the face of real-world demands, which compel us to deal with an often unrational, paradoxical world.

We need planning: It provides a guide as to how to invest and choose alternatives. But we can get locked into our forecasts— even though, if we take a moment to think about it, we know that all bets are off as soon as the first soldiers hit the beach. "Plans are worthless, but planning is everything," as Dwight Eisenhower once said.[5]

A number of human biases exacerbate the troublesome downsides of planning.[6] Nobel laureate Daniel Kahneman, a pioneer in the field of human bias and decision making, notes a common thinking error: When we analyze data from the past, we almost always conclude that the world is much simpler and more predictable than it is. This stems from the "hindsight bias" and the "outcome bias"—essentially, the belief by humans who, once they know the outcome, believe they knew more about it all along than they ever did. Echoing our themes from Chapter Two, Kahneman writes: "The illusion that one has understood the past feeds the further illusion that one can predict and control the future."[7]

The reality is that plans are best guesses in a world where, as Kahneman has shown repeatedly, luck plays a much bigger role than most people will allow. When we imbue strategic-plan forecasts with oracular authority, we make it harder, not easier, to solve paradox-laden problems. Examples of letting forecasts and plans run ahead of reality are common. After Indra Nooyi took over as chairman and CEO at PepsiCo, for example, she continued the move away from total dependence on sugary drinks and salty snacks.[8] She committed the company to doubling its revenue from nutritional drinks and snacks to $30 billion by 2020.

Nooyi was personally committed to making healthier foods to fight diseases like obesity. But she and her team also followed trend lines that showed Americans moving toward healthier eating— and surveys that showed customers were more likely to buy from companies acting in socially responsible ways. Nooyi did not, of course, drop the sugary drinks. However, in 2012 the company introduced a mid-calorie Pepsi NEXT, with 60 percent less sugar than normal Pepsi. PepsiCo called it a "game changer." In that year, 49 percent of U.S. beverage volume was in low (or zero) calorie beverages and hydration offerings of juices. The company also added whole grains, fruits, and vegetables to some of its snacks. It even started looking for new acquisitions to expand its healthy offerings: It bought a majority share in what was Russia's leading branded food and beverage company, Wimm-Bill-Dann, to expand its share in yogurt and dairy products. These and other efforts to transform the company are still under way and it's still too soon to declare victory. Have customers changed their stripes at the cash register? Are they forsaking salty and fattening items for healthy ones? These remain open questions.

Nooyi receives kudos from many quarters for her vision to deliver "Performance with a Purpose," PepsiCo's goal of delivering long-term sustainable financial performance while doing what's right for people on the planet. And there has been some recent improvement in the company's performance (e.g., sales growth), but many analysts and shareholders are still waiting to see if the full potential of the long-term strategy can be achieved. Nooyi has responded by making key changes to her management team and rededicating the company to high-margin drinks and snacks, while continuing to expand PepsiCo's "Good for You" and "Better for You" portfolios in an effort to manage for the short term and long term simultaneously. She has not abandoned the strategy, only learned that PepsiCo could not yet maintain the medium- and long-term earnings necessary to make the longer-term transition.

We don't know if Nooyi's vision will eventually match the future. What we do know is that the company has adjusted its strategy to meet the competing demands of short-term and long-term performance and will probably continue to do so in its ever-changing collaborative work required for managing paradoxes in the future.

Review and Reward Systems

Review and reward systems pose a third organizational obstacle to recognizing and managing paradox. Simply put, the systems neither review nor reward paradox management. In our experience, most leaders have earned pay and promotions based on solving puzzle-like problems as they rose up through the ranks. First-line supervisors typically spend 80 percent of their time solving puzzle-like problems— usually technical issues like allocating people and money to a new challenge, fixing a process that is broken or weak, or resolving a customer complaint. To be sure, they may encounter paradoxes more frequently these days—making the quarterly numbers versus maintaining employee engagement, for instance—but that has not significantly changed the negative effect of performance reviews on the skill level of paradoxical problem solving.

In the financial services industry, bankers dealing directly with customers are often encouraged to share leads and clients. Their bonuses and often their promotions are nonetheless based on their individual track records. While leaders are aware they should recognize team achievement, their internal drive sometimes supersedes this awareness. They may not consciously obstruct their people from crossing the line, but they do so nonetheless by keeping the focus on individually based actions—achieving outcomes, generating results, holding others accountable.

Even at the top levels where leaders handle paradoxes most of the time, performance reviews often drive people to stay on the puzzle side of the line. Many such reviews ask for "your top three accomplishments" in the previous year. That's another way of asking you to highlight instances of exercising control, acting consistently, and bringing about closure. Even if you're inclined to wrestle with paradoxes, you will have a hard time later arguing that one of your accomplishments was, "I managed a short-term versus long-term paradox." What matters is that you executed an either/or decision well: You cut factory assembly time by twenty minutes. Or you opened a logistics facility on time and budget. What doesn't matter is that you sacrificed time spent on specific accomplishment to, say, manage the paradox of valuing people (with mentoring) versus performance (with metrics).

The message to would-be leaders is to avoid putting any effort into reconciling the forces of paradox. Although lip service is often paid to being collaborative, people at the top only get rewarded for individual behavior. Award certificates come with the name of just one person on them. Promotions single out one person for credit. In one company where we work, top executives receive pay and bonuses based 80 percent on their division's performance and 20 percent on company performance. The CEO hopes to reverse that ratio, but in the meantime, the system motivates people to put their parochial concerns above company concerns, dissuading executives from working together on paradoxes that cut across the company.

A complicating factor is that many leaders don't have the authority to manage the opposing forces of the paradoxes they face. They are authorized to control only one factor—someone else in the organization is responsible for each of the others. Supervisors might be responsible for client or customer satisfaction, but labor under cost and investment decisions made above. Even if they want to manage the paradox, they lack the control to do so. In addition, although they are charged with making something happen, they have no responsibility for managing rewards and recognition. That key aspect of employee motivation often belongs to the human resource department.

The Obstacles of Stakeholders

Another set of obstacles to managing paradoxes comes from stakeholders, both internal and external: employees, board members, customers, shareholders, regulators, the community, politicians, and others. These constituencies create the same difficulty as internal silos: one special interest vies with others to serve its ends. Each constituency, like each party in an election, presses its leaders to make extreme, either/or decisions. By pressing hard enough, they actually block the collaboration needed to reconcile contradictory forces.

Recall the example of Andrea Jung at Avon (mentioned in Chapter One), the CEO who launched a global strategy required to grow the business. She led the effort to create global brands and achieve cost efficiencies that would fuel innovation and meet the bottom line expectations of investors. As prominent as any other obstacle in reconciling Avon's global-local paradox, however, were the local leaders in key markets around the world who were unwilling or unable to execute the strategy. Ironically, the majority of Avon's six million representatives around the world recognized the need for rationalizing the product portfolios in local markets. Many complained that the brochure, describing the array of products they sold locally, was just too crowded. Most welcomed the idea of global products that would simplify and focus their offer to customers. But resistance came from local leadership, in particular the general management teams in key Avon markets. Many viewed the changes as eroding their power and authority. After all, the shift would mean that many of the decisions they had controlled in the past would now be made at or shared with corporate headquarters. Complicating the challenge for Jung and her executive team, local leaders would often nod their heads and express understanding in meetings. But they didn't follow through with the actions in their local markets to build the brands as anticipated or expected.

Jung discovered that she might have moved too quickly, before local organizations were ready to accept and implement the changes required by the global strategy. She and her team confronted yet another paradox, this one involving the pace of change. If they moved too quickly, the company would not be ready to execute the strategy successfully. If they moved too slowly, Avon would be outmaneuvered by competitors eager to take sales and market share away from them. In retrospect, while the rationale for change was clear to people, Avon may have moved too fast to allow people to gain the new capabilities needed, and too fast to move new people into place to execute the change. This doesn't mean that the vision and strategy were wrong. As we pointed out earlier, they were essential to Avon's ability to grow. The challenge was determining the right pace of change and overcoming inevitable resistance. Some of the resistance to the change came from people who saw themselves as losing coveted authority and control. Others simply did not have the capabilities and experience to do what they knew needed to be done.

Interestingly, the leaders of outside stakeholder groups strive for the same control, consistency, and closure that company leaders pursue. They, too, get caught in solving puzzles, seeking clear and permanent answers. This mentality then drives them to lock horns with company leaders. Neither side is then able to jump over the line to manage paradox. Until both sides get beyond the puzzle mentality, nobody will enjoy the fruits that come from—and only from—bringing people to a consensus over how to manage the paradox.

The Obstacles Within Ourselves

A third set of obstacles to managing paradoxes comes from within each of us. The fact is, paradoxes bring out all kinds of dysfunctional behavior in most people, and that behavior sabotages progress toward reconciliation. The first behavior, covered in Chapter Two, is a desperate striving for control, consistency, and closure. By nature, most people cling to all three, unable to let them go, unable to see another way to approach problem solving.

We observe this in company after company. The behavior becomes self-reinforcing. In one of our engagements, the complaint we heard was simple but hard: *We can get people to understand how the matrix organization works, but people won't let go of control to make the most of it. Anyone even sniffing the possible loss of control gets twitchy.* This is a reality: You can't go far in managing paradox in an organization without people gaining more experience—experience working with each other, meeting multiple expectations, and building trust in their colleagues and stakeholders.

At one large manufacturing company, we spoke with a CEO who longs for a collaborative, vulnerable, open culture where leaders can solve the paradoxes that come up all the time. He tries to make the change, but he and his team regress repeatedly to managing through hierarchy, order, and control. We asked the CEO to think about designing a process that didn't have an outcome in mind, some kind of open-ended way of discovering what leaders need to learn to reconcile contradictory forces.

The CEO had no idea how to construct something so messy and undefined. He wanted openness but also wanted a logical, linear approach. He wanted spontaneity but also predictability. The instinct to control the universe is very strong, especially when performance evaluations affect compensation and rewards. In this case, the CEO began to emphasize qualitative descriptions of accomplishment, asking for "one-page stories" rather than bulleted slide presentations describing goals and accomplishments. He began to describe the transformation of the company as a journey rather than a series of transactional problems to be solved. By changing his rhetoric, he shifted the mindset of his team and much of the organization.

Ambition often reinforces reluctance to let go of the command-and-control approach to problem solving. In the face of a paradox, leaders may ask, "How can I use the confusion to accelerate the course I'm already on?" Or "How do I manipulate paradox to fit my personal objectives?" Or "How do I use paradox to get more of what I want done?" Or "How can I use paradox to look smart, get ahead, and look like the latest kind of leader?" Such questions are symptoms of a leader committed to control—and ironically *not* to bringing people together to reconcile the contradictory forces plaguing them.

One of the aspects of facing up to paradoxes is facing up to ambiguity, and many people don't respond to ambiguity in a productive way. Studies show that people vary widely in tolerance for ambiguity. If you're intolerant, you are someone who "experiences stress, reacts prematurely, and avoids ambiguous stimuli." If you're tolerant, you're a person who "perceives ambiguous situations/stimuli as desirable, challenging, and interesting and neither denies nor distorts their complexity of incongruity."[9] Relatively few leaders naturally tolerate ambiguity, in which a situation can be interpreted in many ways and contains many contradictions and conflicts.

We can confirm from our experience that not knowing how to reconcile paradoxical forces raises the stress level. This is the common situation: You can't get the answer to a problem, and you want one badly. You can't get all the facts because nobody knows them. You can't accept that no long-term solution exists. You can't figure out how to reconcile warring factions, whether inside the company or inside the family. Under the stress of these unanswered questions, you become vulnerable to expressing deeply ingrained negative behaviors. You can default to personality characteristics emerging from your lesser self.

We call this "derailing," and the behaviors that emerge, "derailers." We described these in our earlier book, *Why CEOs Fail*. The derailers differ for every person, but no matter what they are, they undermine the ability to make decisions and lead. The greater the stress, the more prevalent the derailers—and the more destructive their impact.

Maybe you're like some people we know who, when faced with the discomfort of paradox, become arrogant and refuse to consider any viewpoint but their own. Or maybe you're like others, who upon hearing discussion of possible decisions they don't like, become distrustful, immediately questioning other people's motives. Or maybe you're like still others who become volatile under the pressure of a tense discussion. Instead of being open to fresh opposition positions, you react reflexively, which limits your capacity to consider anything outside a narrow range.

One CEO we consulted with was stunned when a client surprised him with news he should have already heard. In response, he exploded in an executive meeting and upbraided the executive who should have passed him the news. The CEO's derailment created an atmosphere of paranoia among his entire team, and the likelihood that it could happen again posed a persistent obstacle in his getting his team to deal with paradox effectively.

Our experience has shown that people exhibit one or more of these eleven derailers:

- Arrogance: You think you're right, and everyone else is wrong.
- Melodrama: You need to be the center of attention.
- Volatility: You're subject to mood swings.
- Excessive caution: You're afraid to make decisions.
- Habitual distrust: You focus on the negatives.
- Aloofness: You're disengaged and disconnected.
- Mischievousness: You believe that rules are made to be broken.
- Eccentricity: You try to be different just for the sake of it.
- Passive resistance: What you say is not what you really believe.
- Perfectionism: You get the little things right and the big things wrong.
- Eagerness to please: You try to win the popularity contest.

Recognizing which derailers apply to you is essential for developing as a person as well as a leader. If they are operating beneath the level of consciousness, they may cause you to crash and burn before you become a good manager of paradox. Derailers may also become a kind of self-defense mechanism when people criticize your actions. Unfortunately, they stop you from being honest with yourself about how you're reacting.

We ran into an extreme form of derailment in an executive who was hoping to land the CEO post when his boss retired. The executive was brilliant and tough, with a stellar career at the company. He had succeeded with an inordinate insistence on control. As long as a problem fell under his command, he delivered results. But he had trouble collaborating, because he would try to exert control even over other executives' responsibilities. He would make a decision and wouldn't back off, even if he couldn't defend his solution. He would not concede a point to anyone.

Under pressure to collaborate in the resolution of paradoxes, he was derailed by arrogance. He was unwilling to consider feedback. He closed himself off from other people's points of view. People accused him of withholding information to control a decision. "I'm not withholding information," he would protest. But he held reports, data, and consumer insights he would not share or would share only belatedly. Although one senior colleague said, "If I had to go to war, this is the guy I would want to follow," others called him a control freak who hoarded data and information. His derailer of arrogance utterly blocked his ability to work with others.

Complete Leaders Over the Line

We all face a long list of obstacles to jumping over the line to action in the face of paradoxical problems. If you're a leader, you have a choice: You can let paradox continue to divide your organization. Or you can mitigate the obstacles and open the gates to developing a more capable, paradox-savvy organization. That is both the risk and the promise for complete leaders today, and we can predict that it will stay so, as the world becomes relentlessly more complex, the nature of problems ever more ambiguous, and the solutions increasingly less permanent.

Some people may continue to think of paradox as an energy sink. But in the hands of a skilled head-heart-and-guts leader, a paradox becomes an energy source. Its potential for sparking breakthrough change inspires people to come together, to think differently, to act earnestly even in the face of ambiguity. That's ultimately what Frank Appel found as leader of Deutsche Post DHL. Once he brought his team together to reconcile their differences in the interests of their stakeholders, the right action for the entire organization was clear to everyone. Instead of responding solely to the expectations of outside or inside groups, they decided their role as "stewards of the enterprise" required them to deliver appropriate earnings to investors while investing the rest of the money for the future.

In the remainder of the book, we describe our advice for how leaders like Appel can quiet the conflicts created by paradox, generate the energy to solve them, and gain consensus on what actions to take.

Taken together, the chapters in the rest of the book are a guide to acquiring the crucial mindsets and skills of a complete leader who can readily jump over the line to manage paradox.

Complete Leader's Checklist for Chapter Three:
Obstacles to Leadership

✓ Beware organizational groups (functions, regions, business units) that splinter the organization by pursuing their own agendas.

✓ Resist planning efforts that assume you can *make* a rational future, when paradox requires you *manage* an unpredictable future.

✓ Beware of incentives that reward people for solving puzzles and ignoring paradoxes.

✓ Know your stakeholder viewpoints and use them to handle paradoxical problems.

✓ Take stock of your personal "derailers"—personality traits that go awry when you're stressed—and don't let them get in the way of collaboration.

PART TWO

MINDSETS FOR LEADING THROUGH PARADOX

4

The Purpose Mindset

It is not enough to be industrious; so are the ants.
What are you industrious about?
—Henry David Thoreau[1]

In 2012, we took thirty executives from GlaxoSmithKline (GSK) to Kenya as part of an eighteen-month, multisegment leadership development program. Among the sites we visited were clinics and hospitals in Nairobi to expose people to the health care system. We also visited a mobile telephone company and microfinance banks to give executives a broad view of the business landscape. We then traveled to Kisumu, on the shores of Lake Victoria across from Uganda. There we witnessed the dire health care conditions at clinics and in homes. We visited a father and HIV-AIDS patient—a man who had suffered from malaria four times, lived in a mud hut, was hungry and abandoned by his family. Without one of the programs that provides antiretroviral drugs for free in Africa, he had no way to pay for GSK's medicines.

One question hit the GSK executives hard: What does it mean to a company like GSK to help play a role in providing access to health care for somebody in such poverty and privation?

The trip to Kenya stemmed from CEO Andrew Witty's passion for finding better ways to serve people in Africa. Witty was determined to figure out how to make a meaningful contribution to health care in the developing world. Witty saw the opportunity for GSK to play a role in helping deliver improved infrastructure in Africa and creating prosperity to lift people out of poverty for good. This would also be beneficial for business in the long term, creating a virtuous cycle.

Witty faced a paradox: How could GSK provide access for people who have little or no money? How do you respond to the health care need while delivering the premium performance expected of a global corporation? How do you raise stock prices for investors while lowering product prices for the African poor?

In London, Witty and his executive team had grappled with the opposing forces of profit and people, disagreeing about the right way to market products in Kenya and other developing countries. Some understood how a company could adapt its business model to help meet the needs of disadvantaged populations. Others felt that charitable or philanthropic measures were most appropriate.

Many drug companies in the 2000s had struggled to respond in Africa in the way many people thought global drug companies should. They had charged top rates for treatments for new drugs, for example, arguing the normal business case that they needed to recoup enough of their investment to reward shareholders and invest in more research. From the business point of view, the pricing was entirely rational.

But at GSK, Witty and others had rethought this approach. Witty's view: "As CEO, I want this company to be a very successful drug company, but not by leaving the population of Africa behind. We need to be a very successful drug company worldwide and be partners with the people of Africa."[2]

Witty changed the discussion to focus more on mission. Mission, not money, after all, gives meaning to the company's work, particularly in the eyes of most employees. Many leaders in business today measure their success in conventional ways: revenue growth, net earnings, margins, and so on. That's what appears on their performance report card, as we noted in the last chapter, so leaders default to this approach. This is true even when executives know full well they are working on a paradox.

But for GSK executives, the trip to Africa was part of treating a paradoxical decision in a different way—by first changing the perception of the decision itself. The perception, as the saying goes, then changes the reality—or more accurately in GSK's case, the shared reality of an entire leadership team. That shared reality, an essential element in collaborating to solve paradoxes, now included the team's memory of seeing a man in a mud hut, dying of AIDS on the shores of Lake Victoria.

It turns out that you can change the reality of a decision-making process with the *purpose* mindset. With this new outlook, you can succeed not just according to conventional business norms but also by fulfilling your aspirations to make the world better. As the GSK executives learned, the purpose mindset spurs a discussion that takes people down pathways of entirely new logic—and discussions that for these executives extended to four sessions over eighteen months. These discussions in turn led to dramatic changes in the way the executives think about solving the paradox of providing care in developing countries. GSK would adopt a policy of flexibility, a purpose-driven solution to an age-old paradox. Specifically, they would be extending the moves they had already made in this direction. In 2009, they had begun selling all patented drugs at no more than 25 percent of the developed-world price in the world's forty-nine poorest nations.

What Is a Mindset?

When we talk about *mindset*, what do we mean? In simple terms, we mean a point of view, a perspective, a lens that narrows the focus to a specific field of concern. The mindset defines the problem's scope—bordered by a frame, constrained by givens, and characterized by assumptions and values. When you change the frame, assumptions, givens, or values, you change the decision—as well as the discussion process behind it.

Flipping the switch on a mindset throws fresh light on the most attractive actions to address a paradox. The advantages of this fresh light are hard to overstate. We all know this from personal experience, of course. Say you are deciding which partner to invite to a summer barbecue. Who would you choose to impress your friends? Who would you favor if you needed to bring someone home to meet Mom? And who would make the best candidate if you were courting a companion to help paint your house? Your mindset creates the tracks for your reasoning. The tracks route you toward a solution.

In business, most leaders fail to clarify their perception of reality. To be sure, they look at decisions from different points of view, but they usually do so in an off-the-cuff, inadvertent, or even unconscious way. They drive down a set of tracks pretty much the same every time: state the business goals, analyze the situation, generate alternatives, articulate criteria for success, research uncertainties, evaluate by trading off pluses and minuses, pinpoint the best solution. This is the script leaders have learned—we all have learned—and we rarely question it.

This form of decision making suits puzzles that have fixed, definitive answers. As we've said before, this is an invaluable start on problem solving. But in today's complex world, filled with paradoxical problems, you need to adapt the process to accommodate irreconcilable tensions and impermanent solutions. You want to methodically—consciously—guide your people with explicit mindsets. If you do so, you help people start to collaborate from common ground in an atmosphere otherwise characterized by utter ambiguity.

How do you construct a mindset? It takes four tactics: posing an essential question, reframing, clarifying assumptions or constraints, and highlighting values. Together, these four approaches steer your mind—and the mind of your collaborators—out of old ruts and onto fresh ground. If you're a leader initiating the mindset, a variation of an old saying is worth heeding: "A healthy mindset is contagious—but don't wait to catch it from others. Be a carrier."

Essential Questions

The notion of an essential question is akin to the concept in education, in which students are asked to explore a question posing basic, deep, and difficult-to-answer queries. An essential question begs for fresh analysis, synthesis, and evaluation of ideas. By nature, it gets at an issue without a right answer, an issue that recurs throughout work or life, that often cuts across fields of thought, that demands advice from new experts. For example, an educator might ask: "Is it acceptable to clone human beings?"

The essential question related to paradox is not something you take off the shelf. You have to invent it, because the paradox at hand simply has no pat or replicable answer. Consider one paradox we all live with: work versus personal life. If you're a young, ambitious leader with loads of career potential, you will naturally lean toward favoring work even as you remain engaged with family. If you're in a later stage of career, you may favor family and challenges outside of work. Many leaders turn down promotions to spend more time with their adolescent children.

As we all know, the idea of balancing work and life can seem like a pipe dream—unless we change the essential question. So we ask: What is the real purpose that motivates most of us to seek balance? And many of us will have a similar answer: *To live a meaningful life.* So we have a new essential question indicative of our new mindset: How do I live a meaningful life?

If we change the essential question in this way, we will then face a related question: "What does success look like?" In the case of GSK, it looks like something much broader than business needs. It prioritizes patient needs in the markets GSK serves. The answer to that question drives any number of actions.

GSK executives responded to the question by resolving to make additional commitments to follow up on earlier ones. Three examples of commitments up to that time:

- Vanquish malaria, particularly in Sub-Saharan Africa, with multiple strategies, including development of a vaccine, now in Phase III trials.
- Increase access to GSK's HIV medicines to help the World Health Organization and UNAIDS achieve their goal of reaching 15 million people globally with antiretroviral treatment by 2015.

- Help eliminate ten neglected tropical diseases by 2020, including lymphatic filariasis (which causes elephantiasis, river blindness, and other maladies).[3]

Framing the Paradox

The essential question kicks off the process of framing, or putting boundaries around, the paradox demanding attention. By framing, you designate some aspects of a problem for a place at center stage, others a place at the wings, still others at back stage or in the alley outside. Or as in Monopoly, you focus all your investments on one street and ignore the rest. Or as in politics, you focus on one slate of issues, like security (energy, food), while setting aside others, like economic stimulus (energy subsidies, price supports). Some concerns stay on the surface to insist on attention; others remain submerged.

In some ways, we have been writing about framing in this book from the start. Our first act of framing was to change our approach to complex problems, reframing puzzles as paradoxes. The paradox frame assumes the problem does not have one best answer, and that any answer will not last forever (or even very long) and will not please everyone. This is a difficult frame to conceptualize. It ranks among the hardest to see and deploy effectively, and so we give it so much attention.

When you customize a paradox frame with a purpose perspective, you highlight some form of "taking the high road." Think about moving your gaze from a narrow, small-world view to a broader, big-world perspective. As with Google Earth, instead of zooming in to focus on your neighborhood, zoom out to focus on the planet. GSK resized its frame to help people confronting its disease specialties in forty-nine developing countries.[4] That's a big frame, and it raises the issue of how big a frame for a purpose mindset should be? The rule is that, when faced with a paradox with any mindset, the frame should accommodate both ends of the opposing forces creating the paradox— in GSK's case, conventional business success on one end and universal health care access on the other.

Executives in other industries face different forces, but they can accommodate the same breadth. Leaders in the financial services industry, after their sometimes embarrassing role in bringing the world to the point of financial breakdown, have done a lot of rethinking about the paradoxes they face. On July 5, 2012, John Taft, CEO of RBC Wealth Management, observed in HBR Blog, "The financial system has become disconnected from its larger social role and purpose, which is to serve as a means to greater ends, helping bridge the gap between the needs of savers (investors) and the needs of users of capital (business, governments, not-for-profit agencies) and efficiently allocating capital and promoting economic growth."[5]

Many leaders in financial services have taken a broader frame. The president of the CFA Institute, John Rogers, writes: "The next generation of leaders in finance will be defined not by the amount of money they amass, but by the stewardship they exercise as fiduciaries and the responsibility they demonstrate to their communities." Interestingly, we have often seen that reframing gives a lot of relief to leaders, who suddenly see out of the darkness of an inscrutable problem to a well-lit avenue for advancing toward a solution. Further, they don't feel so squeezed by other people's expectations that they get control of the issue, get a consistent answer, and get closure.

Clarifying the Assumptions or Constraints

The frame that you choose invariably comes with a lot of baggage. When you decide what's in, what's out, and what's on the edges, you need to make your thinking explicit. What time scale are you considering? How much risk are you taking? How much money are you putting on the line? What kinds of manpower will you need to take action? Above all, what value are you assuming you're adding for customers, employees, shareholders, and the world? And finally, how are you contributing to something beyond yourself—along that high road?

By answering all these questions, you can determine the best frame. The experience of Rogers, like that of Andrew Witty at GSK, suggests that the task for leaders is to reflect on multiple frames and choose the one that best fits.

Larry Fink, CEO of BlackRock, explained that, after 2008, while his company was trying to absorb two major acquisitions, some people in the organization "lost sight of what we're trying to do." The challenge of managing short-term integration of two acquisitions while building a global franchise during unparalleled economic turbulence caused many people to lose focus. Fink said they had to remind themselves why they were in business—to meet the performance expectations of clients. This higher purpose guided the company's decisions about everything—investments, product development, promotions, organizational structure, and governance. Seeing major decisions through the lens of the client helped the company manage the delicate balance of short-term results and longer-term growth.

Part of this process is surfacing assumptions about what aspects within the scope of the paradox are not currently amenable to change. What can leaders control? What can they not control? What decisions have you made already that you cannot change? What decisions will you defer to the future as outside the scope of the present paradox? Many leaders must accept the context in which they are leading: the competitive playing field around them, the history and culture of the organization they lead, the performance expectations of investors, bosses, or peers. GSK, for example, took as a given that it would only pursue profitable business. If the executives had gone to the other extreme, they could easily have said, "We need to fund a charity to give away aid." In the end, they realized you could do both.

Assumptions about how much to loosen control are often those that will give you most trouble. To jump over the line, you will have to loosen your grip on any number of things, and you will want to make these things explicit. For example, you may act more transparently—giving more information out to the public and employees, as did Tony Hsieh, CEO of Zappos. But you cannot share everything willy-nilly. You will have to draw the line, say, on sharing trade secrets, client information, and disclosures as required by regulatory bodies. This requires rethinking "the way things are done around here."

Highlighting the Values

Another part of clarifying a purpose mindset is itemizing values. In some cases, this is just a matter of affirming or reconfirming your company's stated values. In others, you may want to work with others to flesh out the meaning of values. Or you might clarify what the values look like in action, a critical objective of the GSK executives' trip to Kenya. For GSK, the trip provoked a head, heart, and guts leadership experience. The executives' hearts were moved by the firsthand experience of overwhelming suffering; their heads reminded them of the imperative of business performance; and their guts left them resolved to take action.

To be sure, the GSK trip only deepened the inherent paradox—nobody could ignore the demand to respond to each of the many opposing forces. But their common experience allowed them to recognize the rightness of various positions—long term *and* short term, global *and* local, profit *and* people. And that rightness stemmed from viscerally feeling the impact of opposing values. Upon returning from Kenya, the GSK executives found fresh common ground in values of patient access and community responsibility.

When executives go through such exercises, they often experience the "values paradox." The stated values of the organization turn out to drive as many paradoxes as resolve them. Consider Patagonia, the clothing company. Its mission statement implies a range of paradoxes, especially the paradox of increasing sales for economic good while creating consumption that leads to environmental harm: "Build the best product, cause no unnecessary harm, use business to inspire and implement solutions to the environmental crisis." That has prompted Patagonia to take counterintuitive actions. On one Black Friday, when other retailers promoted low prices and high consumption, Patagonia reversed course. It urged customers to "not buy from us what you don't need or can't really use. Everything we make—everything anyone makes—costs the planet more than it gives back."

One of the values many organizations struggle with today is engagement—the commitment to give people room to find meaningful work. Engagement stimulates commitment and generates energy for action. We have worked with one company where senior leaders decided that annual performance reviews were suffocating engagement. When supervisors annually subject people to evaluations, ranking them like grades of beef, people feel someone else has overweening control. The leaders at this company decided to dump the annual performance review and replace it with quarterly checkups that give people feedback and encourage growth. True, the leaders sacrificed the whip of control, but they unleashed the energy arising from intrinsic motivation.

Purpose-Driven Decisions

When you use the purpose mindset, you are not engaging in business problem solving as usual. True, you go through the same steps—analyzing the situation, framing, generating alternatives, and so on—but you have to adapt them. Four factors differentiate problem solving with a purpose mindset from conventional decision making: aligning your personal purpose with the organizational one, elevating the frame for the decision to an unusually high level, engaging in ongoing debate about the frame, and motivating people to debate based on inspiration rather than information.

Your Personal Purpose

Even before starting on the decision-making process, leaders guiding a discussion based on a purpose mindset need to examine their own purpose. Ultimately, your personal and organizational purposes need to line up. Otherwise, you will find your work untenable. We once dealt with an executive we'll call Deborah. She worked for a big company that made food and beverage products, some of which contained high amounts of fat, sugar, and preservatives. As she became more aware of obesity among young boys and girls—and saw the same in her children and friends—she found it hard to reconcile her corporate and parental roles. She simply didn't agree with her company's dismissal of a major health problem.

Deborah at first thought of resigning, but after reflection and coaching, she decided to take a different tack. Although her company wasn't taking a stand for societal health, it did treat employees fairly, helped them develop, and embraced diversity, especially for women. The company allowed her to grow in an environment more open than those at many other socially conscious companies. She decided to stay with the company, and she began to find ways to speak up about obesity, in particular calling on the company to play a role in producing healthy alternative choices for children. Over time, other executives began to agree, and we can speculate that the company will eventually face up to managing the same paradox faced by PepsiCo—healthy food versus a healthy bottom line.

For most people, the story they tell themselves and others about their lives has several parts: work, play, community, and so on. But all the parts have the same themes, represent the same values, go in the same direction. Otherwise, people can't persist with their story— or they have to rewrite it. Defining your purpose is a prerequisite to defining your organization's purpose. You may be unclear how to define your values and beliefs. Or you may think that because of your industry, or the products and services your company produces, you may not have a purpose in the workplace. You may struggle to apply your larger mission to the paradoxes you face daily, as Deborah did. Still, a complete leader makes an effort at alignment so that the problem solving for paradoxes proceeds smoothly.

Richard Leider has written eloquently about the importance of purpose in leading others. He offers questions to clarify why you work and what values you choose:[6]

- What matters most in your life?
- What in life gives you a feeling of satisfaction, inspiration, joy, or openness?

- What do you think the meaning or purpose of your life is?
- Does your life reflect these beliefs and values?
- What keeps you from living your life purpose or being "in the moment"?
- How do you serve or contribute?
- Who are the mentors, teachers, and role models in your life?
- What prevents you from spending your time or high-quality time on the things that matter most to you?

Leider has also developed a Working on Purpose questionnaire to help assess how aligned your life is with a sense of purpose:[7]

- Do I wake up most Monday mornings feeling energized to go to work?
- Do I have deep energy—feel a personal calling—for my work?
- Am I clear about how I measure my success as a person?
- Do I use my gifts to add real value to people's lives?
- Do I work with people who honor the values I value?
- Can I speak my truth in my work?
- Am I experiencing true joy in my work?
- Am I making a living doing what I most love to do?
- Can I speak my purpose in one clear sentence?
- Do I go to sleep most nights feeling "this was a well-lived day"?
- Do I work with others who share my purpose?

Debating the Purpose-Driven Frame

Any purpose-driven personal life is one of struggle. The same goes for purpose-driven organizational life. When you enlarge or elevate the frame of your decisions to include purpose, you cannot expect to close the discussion after a few meetings. You have to leave it open—open not just because you face a paradoxical problem you will have to revisit, but open because wrestling with your personal or organizational purpose evolves with the times and circumstances. No right solution will remain right as you develop into a more mature leader. No closure is possible.

That brings up another factor differentiating purpose-driven problem solving from conventional organizational decision making: the need to spur an ongoing debate. Johnson & Johnson has not shied away from the issue of access to medicine versus the need to maintain profit margins and shareholder returns. CEO Alex Gorsky and his executive committee acknowledge the importance of the paradox. Some observers might think that Johnson & Johnson's storied Credo would resolve the debate by encouraging access. The Credo starts: "We believe our first responsibility is to the doctors, nurses, and patients, to mothers and fathers and all others who use our products and services."[8]

But Johnson & Johnson also takes responsibility for responding to three other stakeholders: employees, communities, and shareholders. Gorsky encourages an ongoing discussion of how the Credo directs company action. The J&J Credo gives leaders the permission and space to talk freely without worrying about being biased in favor of one stakeholder group. The debate in turn develops leaders who think and reason, constantly restoring and refreshing alignment between the Credo and the company's decision making. It also allows the company to recalibrate its approach continuously, adjusting its decision making to fit the needs of a given decision at a given moment in time.

Gorsky often refers to the inherent conflicts embedded in the J&J Credo. He encourages his leaders to acknowledge this inherent paradox and, rather than avoid it, use the Credo to foster discussion, debate, and resolution about what action to take. He believes that having an overarching sense of purpose is critical for leaders attempting to resolve paradox today.

The leaders of today's organizations are not the only ones who have to define and communicate company purpose. The same requirement exists for all of us who hope to lead others during periods of rapid change in business models, markets, and technology. The world may be volatile and business may evolve continuously, but you need to ask: What is my raison d'être? As a manager and as a leader, what do you hope to accomplish? Why does it matter to the people follow-ing you?

Motivate Purpose by Inspiring

In these cynical times, inspiration may seem like an archaic leadership concept. But if any behavior distinguishes the approach of leaders who solve problems with the purpose mindset, it is appealing to people's hunger to have someone raise them to a higher level. You do not have to be a motivational speaker to make this happen. GSK did it with its trip to Kenya. No executive finished that trip without new resolve to make a difference in the developing world.

At Avon, leaders bring representatives from different parts of the world to speak at major management events. Some of these representatives come from humble beginnings, such as the *favelas* of São Paulo, and they speak movingly about how the money they earned through Avon helped them. They used the money to raise their families and achieve security that would have been impossible otherwise. This helps bring Avon's slogan—"a company for women"—to life. It enables leaders in corporate headquarters to see firsthand that they aren't working just to generate profits for the business. They are enabling hundreds of thousands of representatives to make a decent living.

At Johnson & Johnson, the company ended a three-day manage-ment meeting with a visit from a prostate cancer patient. The patient explained how he had received a terminal diagnosis. He had deterio-rated to the point that he began the process of saying good-bye to his family when, for one last attempt at a cure, he entered an experimen-tal trial with Zytiga, a new J&J compound that in his case had the effect of dramatically reducing the prostate cancer tumor. His PSA levels nosedived, his cancer went into remission, and his doctor told him, "You're going to die of something eventually, but it won't be prostate cancer."

As the patient told his story and expressed his gratitude for J&J, its people, and its products, there was not a dry eye among the 150 J&J leaders. They had come to the meeting to discuss strategy and metrics. But the cancer victim's visit elevated the conversation. The internecine debates about functions, business plans, and growth targets felt petty in comparison.

At times, executive teams can struggle in taking a purpose mindset. The purpose seems awfully abstract when considered by a group of affluent executives in a sterile conference room. By nature, people feel removed from its immediacy. To gain the full power of the mindset, you have to animate the room in some way. This is a time when engaging the intellect is inadequate. The head and the heart have to work together to change the conversation.

How do you know if you're succeeding? Complete leaders naturally loosen their attachment to control, consistency, and closure. They naturally set aside the organizational obstacles that have kept them from collaborating. They naturally embrace and seek to realize their own purpose and live the organization's higher values. They see that, although they may be accused of making the wrong decision, they must still act. And they must act today—even if they face ambiguous circumstances, even if the outcome is uncertain—with the knowledge that they must revisit the paradox and consider new actions tomorrow.

Toward Higher Purpose

The purpose mindset has long served as a powerful means to solve paradox. But in recent years, companies have gone further than before in highlighting purpose as a cause for action. The public and employees have demanded it, and if you're a leader you know that when you carefully define corporate purposes, you differentiate yourself from competitors. Complete leaders now heed the power of purpose statements, backed by actions across the company, in solving paradoxes that once seemed inscrutable.

John Mackey, co-founder and co-CEO of Whole Foods, once observed "We have not achieved our tremendous increase in shareholder value by making shareholder value the only purpose of our business."[9] Obviously, companies must remain profit-driven, but making money is no longer enough; it's necessary but not sufficient. Consumers and employees want to connect with a company's commitment to a much broader agenda. Whole Foods' stated mission begins, "We believe that companies, like individuals, must assume their share of responsibility as tenants of Planet Earth."[10]

The legitimization of using a purpose to drive decision making received an extra push, ironically, from the 2008 financial panic. Thereafter, the Harvard Business School Class of 2009 created a new MBA oath, in view of its perception that the panic had partially resulted from leaders with too limited a view of their moral and ethical responsibility. Two hundred and fifty business schools and universities and hundreds of thousands of Millennial MBAs have now signed the oath as an expression of their values in taking positions of leadership in societies throughout the world.

For those signing it, the oath pledges that they will work on behalf of society rather than narrow personal interests, that they will act ethically and responsibly in all they do, and that they will be conscious of the needs of future generations when making present-day decisions. To illustrate, one part of the oath reads, "I will strive to create sustainable economic, social, and environmental prosperity worldwide."[11]

The fact that thousands of next-generation leaders have accepted this mindset as their view of leadership is an important development in reinventing the role of today's corporation in society. It means the generation of new managers will take on a new responsibility: managing the ongoing paradox of achieving business results while acting in accordance with the values of society and the communities in which their companies operate. Leaders like those in the HBS Class of 2009 who believe in something—and who work with a sense of purpose and values—promise to confront today's world of ambiguity and complexity with greater success.

The trend toward higher purpose also received an extra push from the growing discussion in mainstream business circles of what is called "Capitalism 2.0"—or the practicing of capitalism in a way that goes beyond just making a profit. This position has been articulated forcefully by Michael Porter, Harvard Business School guru of business strategy for the last twenty years. In "Creating Shared Value: How to Reinvent Capitalism . . . and Unleash a Wave of Innovation and Growth," Porter and co-author Mark R. Kramer advocate an alternative to traditional corporate capitalism that combines social and community involvement with the pursuit of profit.[12]

Because of this focus on purpose, we found in our interviews that leaders are thinking about the issue a lot more and developing their own organizational and individual definitions of what constitutes meaning. Purpose varies based on factors such as personal values, industry, and country. Here are a few company purposes that we consider noteworthy. They elevate the purpose of the corporation, and in turn allow leaders to readily elevate decision-making discussions about paradoxical problems.

- At BlackRock, the world's premier asset management firm, employees are clear that their purpose is not just to make money, it is also to ensure the financial well-being of those who invest in their portfolio of funds, including teachers, firemen, and labor unions.
- At Starbucks, the purpose is "serving humanity." As founder Howard Schultz says, "We are a performance-driven organization but we have to lead the company through the lens of humanity."[13] When a large institutional shareholder asked Schultz to cut health care benefits, he refused, saying the essence of the brand is humanity, which necessitates providing health care to employees.
- At Unilever, CEO Paul Polman notes: "Our purpose is to have a sustainable business model that is put at the service of the greater good." Unilever is tackling global problems like climate change, disease, and poverty.[14]
- At Dow, the purpose is simple: To constantly improve what is essential to human progress by mastering science and technology.
- At Nike, the company exists to bring inspiration and innovation to every athlete in the world.

- At Colgate-Palmolive, the emphasis is on creating high-quality oral hygiene products for consumers while providing an opportunity for employees and their families to make good incomes and live comfortable lifestyles.
- At PepsiCo, chairman and CEO Indra Nooyi uses the phrase "Performance with Purpose" to describe the company's dedication to great financial results while doing what's right for people on the planet.

What makes a purpose strong and noteworthy? In teaching leaders about how to manage paradox, we frequently begin with the basic question, *What are you trying to achieve and why?* Failure to answer that question at the most basic human level—a level that speaks to the head and heart of every employee—hampers the ability to manage paradox.

We suggest you keep three words in mind that sum up what we've covered so far: clear, conscious, and coordinated. *Clear* because the crisper the purpose, the sharper your picture of where you're going— even if you don't know how to get there. *Conscious* because clarifying a purpose once isn't enough. Put it in a formal document, but create regular reminders to bring it to life through actions, decisions, and behaviors that people remember. *Coordinated* because you want to align your personal and organizational purposes. If you do not, you will encounter conflicts with no-win results, being neither true to your company nor yourself—the situation that Deborah initially faced.

A Final Note

One of the great benefits of a purposeful mindset is that it's energizing. When you know why you're doing what you're doing, you're plugged into a power source. It doesn't make a choice any less difficult, but it provides you with the sense that you're doing the right thing. This adds to the inspiration that comes from visits to customers like the GSK trip to Kenya, from visits to the United States by Avon reps from São Paulo, from visits by customers like the prostate cancer survivor at J&J. The purpose mindset gives you energy to manage a paradox in spite of its difficulty.

In working with senior executives of financial service firms, we often invite an outside speaker who has experienced significant disruption or even public failure to discuss how to learn from difficult experiences and manage hubris. One speaker we invited is Joe Berardino, formerly CEO of the now defunct accounting firm Arthur Andersen. Berardino spoke wisely of his many lessons, but we believe he put his finger on the essence of developing a purpose mindset when he said that as a leader he often relies on three questions the Jesuit fathers taught to help him navigate difficult situations:

- Who are you?
- Whose are you?
- Who are you called to become?

The first question calls for self-awareness and the third question for a vision of your direction as a leader. The second question is the challenging one: who do you work for? Answers range from *the CEO* to *my family* to *a higher power* to *the customer*. It gets to the key issue of purpose: who or what do you really serve?

That question can often open up a broad new discussion about the ways to solve a paradox. And these types of broad discussion are why GSK committed to expanding access to GSK medicines and vaccines for around 800 million people in developing countries. This includes the regions where GSK sells its patented medicines at no more than 25 percent of developed world prices and reinvests 20 percent of profits back into local health care infrastructure projects.

This is the power of changing perception, or shared reality. GSK is now doing things it would never have done before. It practices flexible pricing. It has established a separate business unit responsible for increasing patient access to its drugs in the poorest countries. It has partnered with nonprofit groups like Save the Children and CARE to help ease the shortage of trained frontline health care workers. By jumping over the line to recognize paradox, and by taking a purpose mindset, leaders at GSK have refashioned the model of a leading global drug company.

The purpose mindset, however, offers the complete leader just one avenue to change perception and in turn change reality. Despite its value, it sometimes fails to highlight the relevant issues, especially when those issues relate to conventional business operations. You may then get better results by using or adding the reconciliation mindset, to which we turn in the next chapter. If purpose redirects people to the high road, reconciliation calls attention to fresh solutions along the road we must travel day by day.

Complete Leader's Checklist for Chapter Four:
The Purpose Mindset

✓ Know your organization's higher purpose and let it guide you in resolving paradoxical problems.

✓ Frame the paradoxical problem to answer the question about how you will bring more meaning to work.

✓ Establish decision-making boundaries guided by your overarching goals, aspirations, and values.

✓ Articulate your personal purpose and clarify how it aligns with your organization's.

✓ Stimulate debate of your organization's purpose to keep it fresh and relevant. Remember that purpose appeals to both head and heart.

5

The Reconciliation Mindset

Such welcome and unwelcome things at once /
'Tis hard to reconcile.
—Shakespeare[1]

Bill Weldon, formerly chairman and CEO of Johnson & Johnson, wouldn't give in to critics. People inside and outside the company said he should hire a China chief to juice the 125-year-old company's China business. Three out of four other multinational companies in China had done so. A "Mr. China" could oversee the entire J&J China business, talk with a single voice to the Chinese government, and supervise the development of local products. In the view of critics, the separate maneuverings of J&J's scores of decentralized product divisions were slowing business in China down.

Pressure on Weldon was intense. Not only were his people and partners in China urging him to name a Mr. Accountable, his board also wondered if a new role might clearly define people's responsibilities for the region. A China chief would help J&J act fast and step up the pace of growth.

Weldon called a time-out, however. He relied on what he called a "Chairman's Dialogue." High-potential managers from around the world, including China and the United States, met for a day and a half of unstructured talks. Put your biggest challenges on the table, Weldon requested. Come with a narrative to describe them, and we'll talk the solutions through. No agenda.

When he convened the meeting, he brought his own challenge: How should we act on the China question? Should we reorganize with one chief? Should we stay decentralized, letting all the J&J

product divisions—Cordis, DePuy, Ethicon, Ethicon Endo-Surgery, LifeScan, Ortho Clinical Diagnostics, and others—keep calling their own shots?

Weldon found plenty of his leaders on both sides of the issue. On one side were those who argued that J&J was losing focus on the Chinese customer and Chinese employees. It was too often reselling products developed elsewhere—after reducing the number of features and lowering the price. The lack of a China chief, they said, telegraphed to the Chinese government and Chinese employees that J&J was not serious enough about China.

On the other side were those who argued for the status quo, global decentralization. They complained that, if China were spun off into its own unit, product units would lose control of China product development. They would in turn lose a big slice of business. Worse, they would miss out on the low-cost drugs, devices, and services Chinese inventors would surely develop for their thrifty market—and in the process J&J's separate businesses would lose an edge in markets around the world.

Everyone began to see during the Dialogue what Weldon already knew: Many issues in China impeded business, but the way the business was organized was not one of them. The real issues: China needed homegrown product development to tailor products to the market. It needed a robust training program to develop managers. It needed a better understanding of diseases like diabetes in Chinese society. The "Mr. China" solution was a neat and easy solution, but not the solution that was right.

One manager after another left the Dialogue making similar comments: "Wow, now I see how he thinks. It's really complicated, isn't it?" Indeed, "Mr. China" was a puzzle solution, and what J&J in China needed was a solution to a paradox.

Weldon's efforts illustrate the use of the second mindset for tackling problems loaded with paradox: the reconciliation mindset. Instead of merely arguing over one position versus another, you can lead other people into better understanding the company's interests. You can change the perception of the decision-making reality—

getting people to see the validity of all sides of the story—and so change the preferred actions.

Weldon's dialogue with top-flight managers from around the world showed they could negotiate their way to a smarter "right" action, something in between the extremes. They didn't have to settle for the neat and easy. Interestingly, the biggest obstacle to arriving at that solution was the corporate matrix, as discussed in Chapter Three. When Weldon removed that obstacle as an easy excuse, the right solution emerged more readily. If you are seeking similar results, ready to engage your head, heart, and guts, you can take the path of Weldon and his team.

Outlining the Mindset

You can create a reconciliation mindset in the same way as the purpose mindset: Fashion an essential question, construct the right frame, and clarify assumptions and values. You go about the process in much the same way, but you come up with very different results. Which mindset you choose depends on your sense of what kind of thinking will resolve the paradox most effectively. You might use one, two, or all three mindsets, and in different orders, to bring about the needed change in perception.

Formulating an essential question for the reconciliation mindset will again beg for fresh analysis, synthesis, and evaluation of ideas. It will have no single right answer but instead many answers—as was surely the case at J&J—and the answers will need revisiting, often with the help of new input from new people. Whereas the purpose mindset asks, "How can we resolve this paradox so it serves our ultimate purpose?" the reconciliation mindset asks, "How can we resolve this paradox so it respects the perspectives and supports the interests of multiple stakeholders to create maximum business value?"

The two go hand in hand, of course, but in discussions to stimulate new thinking about paradox, you need to separate them. Or to put it another way, the purpose mindset prompts you to ask why—Why does this organization exist? The reconciliation mindset prompts the question how—How does it create value while fulfilling the purpose? Or, How do you coordinate and align everyone's efforts to deliver premium results?

That's what Weldon was asking. To get the answer, he took the results of the dialogue back to his executive team, which fashioned a series of actions to deal with the global-local, centralized-decentralized, product-geography paradoxes. His team didn't choose an either/or position. To balance the company's global view, they launched a new, local people development center in Shanghai. They also opened a new innovation center in Suzhou.[2] And they started a new diabetes institute tailored to the needs of the Chinese, which worked across all J&J businesses. They encouraged the group of J&J company presidents in China, the heads of J&J's separate companies, to get together and solve problems closer to the Chinese customer.

Framing Reconciliation

The frame for the reconciliation mindset prescribes how much of the organization's decision-making processes to embrace. It should take in less than the how-do-I-help-the-world frame of the purpose mindset, as you will want to limit it to forces within the business. But it should take a holistic view, calling on you to think beyond business and function, as did Weldon. That means broadening the frame so as not to ignore factors—politics, business prospects, the environment, competitors—that can influence later actions. That also means explicitly legitimizing each of the credible polarized positions.

You could easily make the mistake urged upon Weldon: Restricting the frame to one part of the organization, in his case, China operations. But a narrow frame puts you at risk of mistakenly reducing a paradox to a puzzle—"solve the China problem!" And then you would frame yourself out of a good solution. Going simple is tempting: You can then retreat into a comfort zone, using (or misusing) conventional solutions to unconventional challenges. You may gain shelter from the worst critics and conflicts. But conflicts form a crucible for better decisions. The Chairman's Dialogue was Weldon's crucible. In it he built up the heat to create something more nuanced than the neat and easy answer.

Taking an enterprise-wide frame, one that reconciles holistic interests, also figured into decision making in the recent changes at Illinois Tool Works (ITW). Scott Santi, who led the change as vice chairman (he's now CEO), recognized that the company's profitability and growth rate had sagged in a market flush with new low-cost competitors. For years, ITW grew with an acquisition strategy, expanding to eight hundred companies run as individual entrepreneurial enterprises. The strategy fueled growth as the small units responded quickly to customers by offering unique products. By 2012, company sales in polymers, automotive devices, industrial packaging, and many other goods rose to nearly $18 billion.

But to sustain that growth rate, ITW could no longer acquire just a few more small firms. The effect on overall growth would be trifling. Santi saw that the firm had to generate faster and more profitable sales from existing operations. He and former CEO David Speer believed they should change the company's entire business model, affecting all eight hundred units. They would back away from radical decentralization and would form larger business units that could reap economies of scale, which would lead to greater profitability, and in turn, the opportunity to fuel innovation through organic growth. An enterprise-wide frame was necessary to maintain and accelerate the company's business performance.

As with the purpose mindset, you need to clarify assumptions and constraints: the time scale, people and money committed, risks expected, and value added to stakeholders, whether customers and communities or employees and shareholders. You will also have to clarify what decisions remain on and off the table, as well as what you can and cannot control. In China, few companies completely control their corporate structure, for example. They must partner with Chinese firms. Nor can they control their intellectual property—they must share it with Chinese partners. Those considerations deserve a place in discussions of how to operate locally versus globally.

At J&J, senior executives long ago abandoned an assumption held by many multinationals: That J&J units in China would resell lower-priced, stripped-down versions of products produced elsewhere. As Weldon's successor, Alex Gorsky, later noted on a trip to China: "No longer is it sufficient in China to simply take products from other markets and bring them here. That's why more and more we're trying to have experts here in the markets, developing those unique insights around the medical need, developing the products locally. We're investing disproportionately in terms of . . . people as well as capital."[3]

At ITW, Santi committed to maintaining several assumptions about the way the firm had long operated. One was an 80/20 rule. ITW uses a proprietary model to take advantage of its most profitable business. Its business units focus on the 20 percent of its customers who provide 80 percent of their business's value. Another assumption was that the company would continue to operate only where it could deliver differentiated value—in markets where its key customers prized the company's unique products. It further assumed it would recapture its slipping position as provider of best-in-class products in each market. Santi even met with shareholders to stress that, in changing its model, it would not fiddle with such core capabilities. Though Santi sought to change the business, he would not change the core underlying assumptions that had served ITW well for generations.

Values for Reconciliation

The final part of the reconciliation mindset is values. Whereas the purpose mindset focuses on higher-order values, the reconciliation mindset focuses on business-oriented values, translated into measures like profits, margins, cash flow, business growth, customer satisfaction, and employee satisfaction. At ITW, for example, Santi continued to nurture an entrepreneurial culture that focused on speed, quick response to customers, and decentralized decision making. Those values remained strong even as larger business units led by executive vice presidents were created.

The new ITW leadership team has also had to change the way it operates in light of the changes to the business model. Whereas in the past, the team placed a premium on autonomy of the business units, it has moved toward a much greater reliance on collaboration, in view of greater interdependence. Santi's leadership team provides the forum to cement the new behaviors and business practices in place. For example, the company is now placing greater emphasis on moving talent across its businesses in preparation for enterprise roles in the future. This was far less important when the units operated more autonomously. So the company is now focused on reconciling the need to change with the importance of retaining core values. As David Speer told the *Wall Street Journal* at the time of initiating the change, "We are moving to a different strategic view of our business, but not destroying the culture that has made this a strong company. We didn't get to be 100 years old by not changing."[4]

Another company we worked with chose a different path when faced with similar challenges. The CEO and executive team believed they needed a culture of agility, speed, and urgency. Since the company's founding, it had relied on excellence in execution— controlling "110 percent" of everything and making everything perfect. When it held a strategic review, a hundred top managers would gather from a dozen company-wide teams. Each would present 150 slides, in an effort to leave no question the CEO might ask unanswered. They would actually read the text on every slide. That was the ritual. Top executives in the room, meticulous supervisors, checked and questioned every point. This defined the company's form of dialogue.

The company wrestled with the same paradox as ITW, but came from a different position. Its rigorous approach to execution ranked top among company values, but it needed a more radical transformation of its core values. To change things, the CEO made a point to explicitly tell the managers in attendance that the company's values were changing. He surprised his top hundred people when they gathered: *Don't show me your 150 slides*, he said. *I know you've been slaving over them for weeks, but just tell me what you think are the most important things we as the executive team should know.* The top managers gathered were both relieved and flabbergasted at the CEO's expression of trust in them. This was a sign that he had successfully and explicitly conveyed his message that the culture valued a new form of dialogue, an interactive one where everyone agrees and can learn from each other.

Decision Making with the Reconciliation Mindset

When you use the reconciliation mindset to solve a paradoxical problem, your approach to decisions differs from the purpose mindset. True, the basic steps of decision making remain the same, but several factors distinguish them: seeking the sweet spot of reconciliation, using negotiation principles for win-win actions during your collaboration with others, documenting positions to prepare for future change, and motivating people based on their desire for business success.

Shooting for the Sweet Spot

For years, a mindset focusing on balancing two right choices represented the desired state for leaders managing paradox. For those of us who teach paradox management, achieving balance, or not overly investing in one choice or the other, was the benchmark. If you're familiar with this discipline, you know that you then oscillate between opposing positions. Global-local is a classic pair of opposing, paradoxical forces in which you have to keep in mind both global efficiency and responsiveness to the needs of local markets.

In 1992, Barry Johnson published *Polarity Management: Identifying and Solving Unmanageable Problems,* and he argued that to balance a polarity effectively, managers must see both the positive and negative consequences of both sides of any dilemma. To have a balanced mindset, therefore, required not only that leaders keep two opposing forces in mind, but that they also navigate between the two poles, recognizing that a move in any direction elicits both positive and negative reactions. According to Johnson, the ideal is to moderate the impact of both positives and negatives. You don't lock in an unbalanced either/or way of thinking.

This classic approach to paradox management may be overdue for a redefinition in a volatile and complex world. That's because the two opposing positions that characterize the main paradox might shift overnight. That's even more so because most leaders are managing multiple paradoxes at the same time. Today leaders can't simply define the objective as moderating the impact of one side or the other. Nor can they define the objective as oscillating, as if each side gets its day in the sun. In reconciliation, leaders shoot for an optimal position among multiple forces, just as did Bill Weldon, Alex Gorsky, Scott Santi, Frank Appel, and others.

Reconciliation does not require a 50/50 balance of each set of opposing forces. Nor does it prescribe any other quantitative balance, whether 60/40 or even 25/75. As with many questions in life, you need to recognize and acknowledge the extreme positions of opposing forces. But you then search for middle ground as if searching for a golden mean among multiple polarized positions. In geometry, the golden mean sits not halfway between two polar positions but somewhat to one side. In philosophy, the golden mean lies between two extremes as well. When you handle paradoxes today, you need to find a golden mean reflecting a middle ground among multiple axes of polarized thought.

Note that neither in philosophy nor in paradox management does the golden mean fall in the same position in every situation. It varies. For example, the virtue of courage is the golden mean between cowardice and foolhardiness. But the courage you exercise may lean more toward boldness one day, more toward caution another. If your company faces a financial meltdown, courage might mean bold layoffs, even of colleagues, to save the company. If your company simply wants to reverse a mild slip in competitiveness, it may mean a more modest form of courage, allocating money to new product development instead of raising the dividend.

Consider the mean sought by Scott Santi of ITW. The entrepreneurial spirit of his company's business units is paramount to the organization's success, yet the business units must also find a way to unify with the larger enterprise. Santi says, "We love the decentralized entrepreneurial feel, but need to shape that with a cross-enterprise strategy to guide all that energy and entrepreneurial activity. We want to be sure we don't swing too hard to lose the secret sauce. . . . How do you get the best of both and the right balance? It sounds like a compromise but is not an either-or call; it's finding the right mix related to both sides of the paradox." The sweet spot in reconciliation represents neither the excess of one nor a deficiency of the other.

Several years ago, we were asked to resolve a conflict between the two biggest Latin American divisions of a consumer goods company— Mexico and Brazil. The two general managers clashed over the upcoming implementation of an inventory control system for the region. Initially, they argued over the qualities of the proposed system. But conversations made clear that the real issue was cost. Mexico was flush with cash, Brazil the opposite. Brazil didn't want the big new investment to sour its financial results.

Ultimately, the two managers escalated the decision to the head of the Latin America region. He gave Brazil some budget relief and helped fashion a compromise on the system's implementation. He then broadened the conversation to include other general managers and used the conflict at his next regional management conference as a learning case. He went through the rationale for the implementation, conveyed his appreciation for the challenges, and detailed his expectations for a rollout that respected differences across the region.

Though most leaders think about taking a negotiating approach to decision making when working with outside parties, they seem to forget to take the same mindset with internal ones wrestling with a paradoxical problems. John Veihmeyer, CEO of KPMG, notes that teams of people often lose sight of the objective. "If you take time to focus on the central issue versus arguing about solutions, you may get to the answer a lot more easily and effectively. It can be remarkable how much time is spent on questions that are really at the periphery of a problem. Both sides feel that the other is being obstinate but the reality is that they aren't even talking about the same issue." When people talk about the real issues, their positions often change naturally for the good of the enterprise.

This of course is no different from the situation in a community, where neighbor butts head with neighbor. People may argue over the need for new soccer fields, for example, debating issues of noise and trash and traffic. But these are shadow issues. What people really care about is the takeover of sports by the community—versus sticking with private groups. Or about higher taxes from buying and developing new land—versus some pay-as-you-go approach. If people dispense with their positions for or against the fields and instead talk about the contradictions, perhaps they can find a better solution.

Documenting for Change

It may seem counterintuitive to track the upsides and downsides of an option you're not taking. Say you've chosen a Mr. India to direct all South Asia operations, so why bother to consider anything else? But a reconciliation mindset requires that you track the multiple contradictions of paradox continuously and revisit them as they shift. You don't want to swerve from ditch to ditch in your management of paradox, careening, say, from radical centralization to decentralization every couple of years. But what works today may well not work tomorrow, next quarter, or next year.

An infamous example of failure to manage paradox well emerged from the story of Al Dunlap, dubbed "Chainsaw Al" by observers. He won favor as CEO at Scott Paper in Philadelphia in the early 1990s by cutting R&D, people, and investment to boost profitability. Share prices rocketed 225 percent, and Kimberly-Clark bought the company. The board of Sunbeam then hired Dunlap in 1996 to rejuvenate its financial performance. Dunlap took the same approach, but this time it backfired. He believed the main goal of business was to make money for shareholders, and he viewed the solution in unbalanced short-run terms. He cut spending radically, instituted massive layoffs, and used questionable "bill and hold" accounting practices. Sunbeam boasted record short-term success: Earnings in 1997 reached $189 million. But by curbing long-term investments, he spurred Sunbeam's fall. By 1998, Sunbeam's stock fell from $52 per share to pennies in bankruptcy.

Like other CEOs, Dunlap faced a set of paradoxical problems in rejuvenating an ossified firm. But he tried to solve them like a simple mathematical puzzle. He would have done well to document the pluses and minuses of both cutting and investing, so he could revisit his initial draconian moves a year on. Too much of one kind of medicine nearly killed the patient—and he didn't lead his team in reconciling the shifting forces of paradox until it was too late. He showed, in a dysfunctional way, that leaders need to reestablish the golden mean as times change. Even if you believe shareholders rule the stakeholder roost, the company cannot keep creating value if the CEO ignores the paradoxes of long- versus short-term management.

In the financial services industry, even a blip in interest rates can force leaders to reassess decisions recently made. In mid-2013, as long-term interest rates spiked upward from a rock-bottom 1.6 percent, leaders had to take a new look at what products they recommended to clients, how they would develop new products, and how they would talk with both institutional and retail clients.

One executive we spoke with said, "We have great organizational tradition, with a strong connection to roots and values. We have a workforce that has had a lifetime of work with our company. However, we are at an inflection point. . . . It's a tension of [where we've been] and the need to stay relevant. Staying relevant is a challenge to the way we have been."

Reassessing the balance is critical, and if you're armed with current knowledge about upsides and downsides of both positions, you and your collaborators are in a much better position to manage the paradox. In documenting the pluses and minuses of various actions, a note of caution: Most of us unconsciously focus on the positives of the position we're drawn to and the negatives of the position we resist, and we fail to consider the corresponding negatives and positives.

This failing was noted long ago: Psychologists have shown that people naturally process messages to support their previous position, not a new one. In one classic study, two sets of participants, one in favor and one opposed to capital punishment as a deterrent to murder, were given results from two research studies. One study supported the death penalty as a murder deterrent, the other, the reverse. How did participants' opinions change after looking at the new data? The proponents became more "pro," the opponents more "anti." Mixed research consistently polarized people's previous views.[5]

So be careful about selective judgment. The upside of decentralization, for example, is giving business units or individuals more autonomy, increasing accountability and responsiveness to customers and competitors. The downsides are higher costs, duplication, and increased need for coordination across organizational units. The upside of centralization comes from connecting different functions into hubs, resulting in higher efficiencies and reduced costs. The downside is that people at lower levels feel disenfranchised and lose their former sense of control. Like a member of a biased jury, you may find it easy to justify either viewpoint, but you're most likely to go with your initial position.

Many other biases can affect the way you assess both the consequences of various forces and the actions you propose to address them. For example, experiments have long shown that we neglect probability when we face too much uncertainty. And we invariably make different judgments depending on the presentation or framing of information. We tend to do all these things even though we know we are susceptible to them—no matter our education level.

One of many classic experiments shows our susceptibility to framing. Experimenters asked patients in an outpatient clinic, "Suppose you have a serious disease that needs to be treated with medication. Your risk of dying over the next year is 10 percent if you don't receive the treatment." The subjects then learn that only two pills can treat the disease, and that both cost the same and have almost no side effects. The patients then read about medication A: "If you take this medication it will decrease your risk of dying by 80 percent (*four fifths*) over the next year. And for medication B: "If 100 people with the disease, like you, take this medication 8 deaths can be prevented over the next year."[6]

What did people choose? Medication A, by 56.8 percent. Medication B was chosen by only 14.7 percent. This in spite of the medications having identical efficacy. People—including many who had the skill to easily convert either set of data to the other to see their equivalency—favored a presentation of efficacy in relative terms over one in absolute terms. (The rest of the participants didn't care or couldn't decide.) In this and in many other ways, the way we talk about risk and other factors, whether in business or anywhere else, dramatically alters our preference of options.

Motivate for Business Success

Whereas you can use inspiration to motivate people with the purpose mindset, you can rely on people's hunger for traditional success for the reconciliation mindset. People want to be effective, to have an impact, to have the fruit of their labors add to the bottom line. They want to fulfill their desire for competence—succeeding at challenging tasks and achieving desired outcomes.[7] Nobody wants to waste time at work, and everybody wants recognition for being a hotshot.

Consider a division of a $1 billion specialty chemical company. Although the division had 80 percent gross margins, it was only breaking even. Worse, it offered lousy customer service. Product lead times averaged five weeks, half of deliveries ran late, and despite three months of average inventory, it ran out of key stock repeatedly. The division's president received orders: Boost revenues and cut costs or risk shutdown.

The incentives to manage the paradoxes of cost, quality, and customer service gave the president and his executives all the energy they needed to transform their operation. They simplified the product line so that production could focus on key, high-margin products. That markedly boosted capacity utilization and delivery performance—and that was the key to kicking off a turnaround. As a result, orders placed before noon now ship the same day. The division runs with a lean one-month inventory and operates with only two-thirds the original number of workers. The division not only escaped shutdown but also now boasts margins almost double the industry standard.

The same kind of incentives motivated success at J&J, ITW, and the other companies included in this chapter. Conventional incentives dovetail nicely with the reconciliation mindset in solving tough but common paradoxical problems.

A Final Caution

A caution about the reconciliation mindset. Individual personalities can sabotage its usefulness. Driven by traditional incentives, people default to their own interests. Money still ranks at the top—or near the top—of factors motivating people at work. This fact is borne out repeatedly in studies that track how people behave, in contrast to what they say in surveys.[8] When people's bonuses and promotions have long depended on delivering results for their unit alone, whether as part of a function or operating unit, they will stand by their unit. Why would individual executives accept an enterprise-wide frame for a decision if their own division remains the star profit maker? Why would they let their pay get docked by helping other businesses?

John Veihmeyer of KPMG notes that in his experience dealing with paradoxical problems, you have to ask yourself, "What is the self-interest of the person I am dealing with? When you get to the heart of it, most people are motivated by a high level of self-interest. Take the time to understand the motivations of the other individual."

If you are driven by conventional rewards, you are probably loath to loosen control over your kingdom. You will stick with control and consistency to further your own success. Bill Weldon faced that risk in broadening the conversation in the Mr. China decision. Scott Santi faced it in transforming ITW. If you're a CEO, you have to clarify from the start that you expect everyone to take a broad frame, participating in the solution to the paradoxical problems at hand.

Ironically, even many CEOs have trouble loosening control enough to demonstrate leadership that works for the good of the whole. The CEO we spoke of earlier who wanted a culture of agility, speed, and urgency had trouble jumping over the line to manage the contradictions of paradox. When we suggested he instruct his people at the corporate strategic review, "Tell us what your most important problems are and how we can help," he balked. "I can't go there," he said. He was captive of his own culture and processes. He was the general. He gave orders. His soldiers executed. He didn't feel comfortable loosening control, bringing about a new balance between commanding his troops and cultivating participation.

After sleeping on that thought, however, he surprised even himself. The next day he not only stunned his top managers by telling them he trusted them to report on just their most important concerns. He told them: *Let us know how we can help you. We want you to learn from each other. If one team needs help, let's see what it can learn from another team.*

In the past, if people couldn't measure up with their presentations, the CEO and executives would rebuke them. (So much for encouraging collaboration.) But the CEO stepped over the line. Exhibiting the head, heart, and guts of complete leadership, he initiated new behaviors—behaviors that nurture a culture where everybody borrows each other's best practices and people pull the whole enterprise up together.

The temptation not to jump over the line is strong, both for CEOs and for everyone else. When we don't deal with a paradoxical problem, we often hope it will go away. The CEO who overcame his discomfort struggled with his executives over common yet paradoxical questions: Should we have an order-and-inspect hierarchy with perfect execution and predictability? Or should we have a learning meritocracy with imperfect innovation and energy? Reconciling the paradox would enable him to have some of both. He could have a golden mean. And that, in business and life, is the promise of the reconciliation mindset.

That leaves us with one final mindset for solving paradoxical problems. When neither the purpose nor reconciliation mindset changes perceptions to a more helpful reality, you can try the innovation mindset, the subject of the next chapter. If purpose redirects people to the high road, and reconciliation to a fresh middle road, innovation mindset redirects them to a new road altogether. An atmosphere charged with the electricity of creativity may yield just the energy you need to turn the contradictions of paradox into breakthrough solutions.

Complete Leader's Checklist for Chapter Five:
The Reconciliation Mindset

✓ Adopt a mindset to reconcile opposing interests in resolving the contradictions of paradox.

✓ Frame the paradoxical problem in a way that encourages alignment of opposing forces within the organization.

✓ Establish decision-making boundaries by clarifying your business assumptions and operational goals, including performance measures.

✓ Strive for a golden mean between opposing forces, forgoing balanced outcomes for optimal win-wins that serve opposing interests.

✓ Track the upsides and downsides of options not taken, to prepare for fresh, flexible action as times and the environment change.

6

The Innovation Mindset

One is fruitful only at the cost of being rich in contradictions.
—Friedrich Nietzsche[1]

Several years ago, we helped an executive who faced one of the most dreaded tasks in management: Announcing the shutdown of several plants and telling everyone they would lose their jobs. Worse, he had to ask the outgoing employees to help him—not just to close the plants but also to turn them into bigger moneymakers until the scheduled shutdown. And he was in Europe, where he couldn't shutter the plants any sooner than three years after the announcement.

Jack, as we'll refer to this head of sourcing for a U.S.-based maker of consumer products, came into this position after his company bought a much smaller business in Europe. He was charged with cutting manufacturing costs, consolidating operations in cheaper countries, and complying with demands by regulators to reverse quality snafus that had led to several manufacturing recalls.

Workers reacted with anger, of course—and initial indignance at the idea of helping the company do anything. Jack's request seemed irrational. How could he kick employees in the face one day and ask them to boost quality and productivity the next? Jack spoke first with the plant managers. He asked them to visit each other's plants to see how they could work together. After a few weeks, they returned with what they believed would be an acceptable way to proceed.

Appealing to their sense of pride in what they had accomplished, Jack asked plant employees to work "to become world class in their facility before it closed." The company could then meet its needs for improved quality and productivity, and the employees could put themselves in a better position to find new work, their résumés buffed up by having worked in a plant with a world-class reputation for quality and production.

The assumption Jack made was that motivation was complex. Employees would be frustrated and disappointed, but they would also be driven by pride in what they had accomplished. The employees swallowed their anger. Irrational or not on the surface, the solution to the paradox at hand had its own logic. The plants would ramp up production and deliver superior products even as they phased themselves out. Once the employees understood their situation, they decided that customers should not be punished as a result of their anger. They agreed to commit themselves to a range of actions essential to the company: completing production schedules, transferring production lines to other manufacturing sites, ramping down and then closing production lines, and even helping with shuttering the plant.

Innovation is the third mindset for managing paradox, and Jack tapped its potential not only to resolve a dreaded task of factory consolidation but also to find a creative way to act. He could have responded with either/or thinking: Either we keep the plant open and raise quality or we essentially mothball it now. Instead, he chose to work with others to search for a both/and solution. He showed that when you face a powerful contradiction you can come up with an inventive right course of action. Of course, Jack had to make trade-offs, but he showed that in the midst of losses, you can win surprising gains.

This illustrates that at times you will find that the standard equations of business can be turned inside out. You can invent new ones to solve paradoxes with win-win solutions. And you can do this in situations that seem to offer nothing but win-lose outcomes. Unacceptable and irrational approaches morph into acceptable and unorthodox ones.

Jack went beyond the calculus of conventional management in a risky gambit. Ironically, in his case, the paradox posed both the problem and the stimulant for a fresh solution. And the outcome was better than many expected. Because of their association with a highly regarded facility, many employees found work with other companies. All felt they were well treated and took pride in their part of the shutdown, even though they wished the plant could stay open.

Outlining the Mindset

When you believe innovation may be the key to resolving a paradox, you can invoke the innovation mindset just as you did the mindsets for purpose and reconciliation: Investigate essential questions. Test multiple frames. Clarify assumptions and values. More than ever, you have to loosen your grip on control and accept inconsistency. As you jump over the line to a place where you accept that you cannot come up with a single right answer—as clearly Jack could not—the innovation mindset will offer a range of fresh solutions.

Essential Questions

Whereas the purpose mindset asked "why?" and the reconciliation mindset asked "how?" the innovation mindset asks "what else?" With reconciliation, you work inside the box of existing options. With the innovation mindset, you usually work outside. What's a new way to accomplish the purpose? How do you invent new ways to deliver premium results?

Multiple-choice tests list four possible answers often followed by a fifth: none of the above. You may be reluctant to respond with "none of the above." You may feel more comfortable choosing a definitive answer—one that helps you control the future and act consistently. After all, who wants to go into unknown territory for no good reason? But when it comes to managing multiple paradoxes in a complex and ambiguous world, opting for none of the above often produces the right action.

Steve Jobs is the best-known modern leader to have staked his career on the none-of-the-above answer—not just once but many times. His ability to bend reality to reframe his view of the world is now legendary. He made some bold product decisions: moving from the computing to the music business; selling through branded retail stores rather than just existing retailers; changing his profit model from selling only products to products plus applications, music, and service. He showed he was not an either/or decision maker. He was a both leader.

Formulating the essential question with an innovation mindset calls on leaders to focus above all on both—and to do so uncompromisingly. Jobs early on asked, How do you create products that embody a belief in open computing yet are closed to competitors and non-Apple developers? At the time, it must have seemed self-destructive to create products that embraced both open and closed computing philosophies, yet Jobs had the mindset to live and work with such a paradox. Later, he became known for insisting on both for solving a range of paradoxes. Three of them: the rebellious image versus the corporate image, form (design) versus function (engineering), and art versus technology (at Pixar).

Jobs was also famous for espousing the view "never ask the customer for what they want . . . because they don't know what's possible." He said customers could not know they wanted an iPod before it was invented. But once it was created, customers definitely knew they wanted it. In the face of paradox, you often face choices you may not want, but you can use innovation to jump over the line just the same as Jobs—and even go beyond both/and to ask "both—and what else?"

To speak philosophically, when you're using the innovation mindset, you consider not just the thesis, antithesis, and synthesis—not just local, global, and the combined impact of the two—but also something more or entirely different. And what's entirely different can make a significant difference. Or with apologies to Mark Twain, "The difference between the right solution and the almost right solution is the difference between lightning and a lightning bug."

Take again the question of balancing work and life. You can use a reconciliation mindset to ask, Can I equalize the demands of work and the rest of my life? You can use the purpose mindset to ask, How do I find more meaning in life? You can use the innovation mindset to ask, Should I be doing something entirely different with my work and my family? Purpose might suggest a deeper connection with your current course or choices. Reconciliation might provide a saner balance. Innovation might prompt you to take a break from everyday work and life entirely: Move your family for a sabbatical to New Caledonia to learn French, study tropical plants, and live in a colonial culture in the South Pacific.

The related question of "What does success look like?" takes on an unusual form and importance with the innovation mindset. You don't find success in a storefront along the avenue of orthodoxy. You find it in open spaces and wild lands far from the routine and generally accepted. This is not to say that you won't find innovative solutions while using the purpose and reconciliation mindsets, only that the innovation mindset nurtures outliers.

In Jack's case, success looked like a plant shutdown, upgraded employees, and efficient reallocation of company assets to other uses. This was an innovative both/and solution. Could he have gone even further? What if success required a both—and what else solution? What if the employees got together and bought the plant and ran it themselves? Or used their skills and expertise to start a new and different manufacturing plant? Such solutions sound far-fetched, but breakthrough innovations often begin as inconceivable ideas.

Consumers in 1980 didn't know they needed or wanted a mobile tape player until they saw the Walkman. In 2000, they didn't know they needed or wanted a device that could play thousands of songs, fit in a pocket, and not use cassette tapes. They were content with choosing between a portable radio and a Walkman. In 2005, they didn't know they needed or wanted a service to stream music wirelessly, until they found Pandora and Spotify. Paradox is often like that—the choices seem fixed until an innovation appears and changes the game completely.

Needless to say, a problem may not require it, but the innovation mindset pushes you to consider the what else. We think it is fair to say that Steve Jobs was not just a both/and leader, but a both—and what else visionary. Leaps in technology don't come from solving technical puzzles. Nor do they come from asking questions that lead simply to clever syntheses. They come from entering new orbits in an expanding universe.

Framing Innovation

The way to frame a paradoxical problem with the innovation mindset starts with asking, What else? In some ways, we are saying, What's the frame outside the frame offered by reflexive thinking? This is a conceptually elusive question. Decision expert Clint Korver answers it with a story we like:

> A father had two grown sons who were very competitive. He was troubled by their constant competition and wanted them to learn how to cooperate before he died. Since they were great horsemen, he decided to have a race to see which son would get the majority of his inheritance. But, to teach them cooperation, he told his sons that "whichever horse finishes second, that son will get the inheritance." One son promptly jumped on the other son's horse and took off.[2]

As Korver says, the son who took off on the other's horse reframed the situation. Leaving aside whether the solution was fair, the creative son operated from a leap of imagination. That was only possible by seeing the problem in ways most of us would not expect. Putting a frame around the space outside the normal frame is itself a paradox. How do you frame without known borders? This is perhaps why, in new-product-development circles, engineers call the early brainstorming and concept-shaping phases the "fuzzy front end." Fuzzy and messy and hard to control—and yet still essential even in orthodox settings to create new products.

The scope and scale of innovation varies from incremental to breakthrough. At times, a paradox may require only a small, targeted creative approach—in keeping with the Japanese concept of *kaizen* (continuous improvement). In others, it may demand major, organization-wide transformation. We highlight this distinction because developing an innovation mindset doesn't mean every idea comes like a brilliant flash out of nowhere that upends your current reality—although in the case of today's technology companies that often is the case. The nature of the paradox will suggest the scope of innovation required.

Assumptions About Innovation

The innovation mindset is no different from the purpose or reconciliation mindsets: You have to clarify limitations regarding timing, people and money committed, acceptable risks, and expected value delivered to stakeholders. You also need to make clear what related decisions remain firm or malleable depending on the demands of the current paradox.

The assumptions you make are much like constraints in other walks of life. In product design, for example, constraints can stimulate creativity. Charles Eames, ranked as the greatest industrial designer of the last century, had this to say: "The sum of all constraints . . . is one of the few effective keys to the design problem—the ability of the designer to recognize as many of the constraints as possible; his willingness and enthusiasm for working within these constraints. . . . I don't remember ever being forced to accept compromises, but I have willingly accepted constraints."[3] Eames produced legendary designs in architecture and furniture by solving design paradoxes.

Whole Foods faces the traditional paradox most companies encounter. On one hand, like all businesses, the company is driven by profit; on the other, it wants employees to be committed, engaged, and actively representing the Whole Foods brand. If the company gives employees overly generous pay and benefits, profits will go down. If it pays people at or below the industry average, it risks high turnover and low morale. As Whole Foods has grown, its practices have gotten scrutiny—its customers and workers have entered the debate about how to address the paradox of profit and people.

Whole Foods co-founder and co-CEO John Mackey, author of *Conscious Capitalism*, recognizes the paradox of profits versus employee compensation. He sees a third approach. Whole Foods compensation policies make clear that Mackey assumed from the start that he would share the profit pie broadly with employees, instead of lavishing extra money on executives. Here are three elements of the company's policy:[4]

- Employees can earn additional compensation based on group performance incentives and receive benefits far beyond the industry norm.
- The CEO's pay and bonus are capped at fourteen times the average employee's pay.
- The company distributes stock options to the majority of employees rather than just the top tier. The top 16 percent of executives receive 7 percent of all options with the remaining 93 percent distributed to employees at all levels after reaching a certain point in tenure.

The apparent assumption in this system? Short-term gains for shareholders may be sacrificed for long-term goals for the company—and profits may shrink owing to a bigger payroll. But the actual assumption is different: The company will make up any deficit through superior customer service, higher morale, and lower turnover. In other words, Mackey is not trying to balance profits versus payroll as a trade-off. He is shooting to achieve *both*, and the way to do so is to redistribute the rewards pie in an unconventional manner.

Some people might argue that Whole Foods is taking a risk of failing to attract top leadership talent by capping the CEO's compensation and limiting stock options. But you can also argue that this risk is offset by performance-based compensation that gives leaders opportunities to earn additional rewards. It is also offset by operating principles that attract leaders who value socially responsible capitalism.

Values for Innovation .

The last part of the innovation mindset is values. Here again the values can help you define the frame. On one hand, you may want to stress one or several values. On the other, you may leave the decision on what to stress wide open, giving yourself and collaborators a broader frame yet one still bounded by the company's basic values. Whereas the purpose mindset stressed higher-order values, and the reconciliation mindset stressed business-oriented values, the innovation mindset stresses values chosen as stimuli for creative thinking.

At Colgate, several years ago, the executive leadership team chose the company's commitment to discipline and focus for rethinking. For nearly two decades, the company had run a disciplined business-planning process. The leaders and teams running each major business would spend weeks generating information on financial and operational performance to share with the senior management of the company in New York. A team of senior leaders would visit the field (that is, the divisions and major markets) to go over every detail in the business review process. This would happen a couple of times a year. The process was demanding and time-consuming. The detail required was endless, the discipline unrelenting.

This process served Colgate exceptionally well for many years. It underpinned its success and contributed to its standing as one of the most outstanding companies in the industry. But as the world became more complex and the future more and more uncertain, top executives began to question whether this approach needed to be changed. They asked: Are we so submerged in the quantitative analytics that we are in danger of missing some of the signals in the external environment that the world is changing in ways that can affect the business? Is the process becoming a sclerotic routine and wasting too many hours that could be devoted to other important business issues? In big-picture terms, the executives wondered if they were managing the paradox of control versus autonomy effectively. Or were they, in effect, acting like inspectors checking compliance with factory specs when they should be acting like leaders checking future business scenarios?

Senior managers decided they needed to change the planning process to make it more responsive to the contemporary needs of the business. They revamped it to create more opportunity for open dialogue between senior management and local leadership. They didn't want to lose the discipline and focus that were hallmarks of their success, but they did want to provide more opportunity to identify (and respond to) big, critical business issues in each of their global markets. So today, senior management asks local leaders to identify what they believe are the most important issues in their markets in addition to providing a high-level view of the most important metrics associated with business performance. They seek dialogue along with presentations. The local teams now have more opportunity to work collectively with senior management to solve issues and to diagnose complex situations and plan effective strategy.

One of the values stressed by many companies today is sustainability. This sets up strong opposing forces—profit versus planet—that often multiply the complexity of paradoxical problem solving. A good example comes from Nike. The company recently grappled with a paradox over a popular line of black athletic pants. Nike has long opted for green-first manufacturing, and it resolved the paradox of planet versus profit by using recycled polyester to manufacture these pants.

In the marketplace, however, Nike found that many customers preferred the black athletic pants sold by a competitor, Lululemon. Lululemon pants were blacker and tighter, in large part because they were made of virgin polyester. This raised the thorny issue of the temporary nature of solutions for paradoxical problems. When you revisit and rethink them, you may come up with a different right solution.

In revisiting its decision, Nike faced a tough choice: stick with its environmental commitment or substitute a virgin material for the pants. Nike leaders knew that taking a step back from its commitment to green-first materials was not only wrong for the environment, it would disappoint many Nike employees and other stakeholders. At the same time, losing market share to an up-and-coming brand like Lululemon was unacceptable to other employees and shareholders. The Nike brand president was asked to make the decision.

No resolution looked possible. The brand president looked toward Nike's purpose. He reminded the team working on the product of Nike's mission: to "unleash potential through sport" for individuals. When a stark choice emerges between sustainable materials and performance materials, he reasoned, the latter should win because it stays truer to Nike's mission and values. Nike's mission also includes "creating a better world," which ensures that the company will revisit the decision again as times change. Without values to guide this decision, the brand president would have been adrift.

To extend our earlier product-development analogy, once a concept moves beyond the fuzzy front end, it goes into commercialization. In new product development, the fuzzy front end does not always deliver a concept that succeeds, so developers remain nervous as it moves into the market. They refer to the transition between concept and commercialization as the "valley of death." Will the concept get to the valley's opposite side? So goes the uncertainty with concepts you develop with the innovation mindset. They may die en route to implementation. You have to be ready to restart work with collaborators to come up with solution 2.0.

Decision Making with the Innovation Mindset

When you use the innovation mindset to solve paradoxical problems, you end up recasting your decision-making discussions in a new form. You don't try to transcend the issues, as with the purpose mindset, or to negotiate a golden mean, as with the reconciliation mindset. You seek novel approaches. Your decision process resembles the steps in new product development: Identify and listen to customers (stakeholders) who are making claims on the decision. Explore their unmet needs, clarifying the opposing forces represented. Generate concepts for solutions that capitalize on the either/or tensions between the opposing forces, and then screen alternatives, assess risk, build a business case, and take action.

Of course, that's not the way things really unfold, because nobody has found a way to run new product development with the predictability of trains on a railroad. The process is less sequential and more roundabout, more iterative, less definitive. It involves people who brainstorm, float hypothetical actions, and suffer the setbacks of trial and error. They plan, test, back up and plan again, brainstorm more, float an idea, gather more data, plan again, and so on. The solution evolves to something more and better, just as in agile product development.

In other words, instead of running trains on a railroad, you're driving bumper cars in an experimental laboratory. Several factors distinguish decision making with an innovation mindset from the purpose and reconciliation mindsets: considering multiple frames, inventing more and divergent options, and motivating people to create.

Reframe and Reframe Again

From the start, the innovation mindset stresses multiple frames. Interestingly, the limits are not actually known in advance. In some ways, the innovation frame is not a frame at all. It is the unframe. You and your collaborators have to struggle with that old problem: You don't know what you don't know. And that means your route to success comes with experimenting. You've committed to finding what else can work, so how do you come up with the frames to foster that innovation?

We are reminded of poet William Blake's metaphor about "mind-forged manacles." In framing a problem, your mind's manacles hold you back from taking new points of view. We suggest first fully understanding the complexity of the paradox. Make sure you have really jumped over the line, perceiving and accepting the situation's full range of contradictions. You will want to identify all of the different factors that are under tension—and will always stay that way—almost like the poles of a magnet.

Sometimes the opposing forces are hard to see. As an example, in many industries today, leaders have come belatedly to appreciate the contradictory forces of confidentiality versus transparency. For years, they took for granted that secrecy and proprietary knowledge, know-how, processes, and plans provided value. The greater the secrecy the better. Steve Jobs believed in this principle until his death—and perhaps that was appropriate for Apple. But today those two forces work in opposition in a way unlike the past. To come up with unique solutions, you may want to frame a problem to encompass those forces instead of separating them.

Take for example Procter & Gamble's open platform for research and development. Traditionally, R&D at big corporations was a bastion of proprietary and secretive behavior. P&G's leaders, though, recognized they were dealing with a series of paradoxes: internal versus external, short term versus long term, big ideas versus incremental improvement, security and protection of ideas versus boundaryless exploration. The explosion of research and the advent of crowdsourcing convinced them not only that many good ideas existed outside P&G but that they would enjoy many benefits from opening up thorny problems to a wider group of thinkers and scientists.

P&G began posting some research and business challenges on the Internet and inviting others to help solve them. Over time, "open source" has become a standard in R&D across large companies. P&G leaders in effect reframed the question of R&D effectiveness to include a new set of paradoxical forces. They then could more clearly arrive at the notion that by making their R&D approach transparent— unthinkable a decade ago—they opened themselves to big gains. They now disclose what they are researching and what they are discovering they need. They also encourage organizations throughout the world to compete to solve the problems they are focusing on. Note how they redefined their own value contribution from originating and controlling ideas to sourcing, sifting, and executing multiple ideas.

Another way you can multiply frames is to broaden the conversation—as we mentioned for the reconciliation mindset—as well as broadening your gathering of information. As Bassem Bitar, the chief strategy officer of Solidere, says, "The less you communicate the more problems you have. The more you communicate, the fewer problems you have. In complex organizations, you have to leverage multidisciplinary teams rather than working in silos." As with the case of Solidere in Chapter One, an innovative solution to developing Beirut came from embracing the concerns of a broad cross-section of community leaders and groups.

A third way you can multiply frames is to embrace reflection and incubation. In our work, we usually find that reframing comes after travel, either within or outside the company. In fact, travel experiences make up some of the biggest sources of reframing. Consider the experience of one health care CEO who traveled to India and China. For years, his company had run a business making disposable instruments. The CEO saw in his travels that companies in other countries took his firm's instruments, resterilized them, and sold them again. Some instruments turned over fifty times before disposal—without compromising patient care. The restore-and-resell companies were thriving by offering low prices and easy access, just the right approach to win the business of customers who can ill afford high-priced single-use instruments. The CEO's visits to this vibrant reuse marketplace spurred a reframing.

In the United States, low cost and high sophistication are opposing poles in the health care paradox. You can't have both. But firms in China and India showed that businesses *can* reconcile these forces. The reframing spurred the CEO to seriously consider new questions: Should the firm cannibalize that market by going into the reuse market? Could it make money on both? He saw in the end that he had no choice. The entrepreneurs in developing countries made the decision for him. The company entered the reuse market, building a new operation for collecting, sterilizing, and reselling used instruments.

Inventing New Options

The innovation mindset stresses divergent thinking, a foundation of creativity. That's not to say that the other mindsets don't encourage the same. But with the innovation mindset, you should champion the creation of dissimilar options, using creative thought to integrate multiple opposing forces for action into a range of rational and right solutions.

We worked with one big retailer that faced a common problem nowadays: How to run both a bricks-and-mortar and a digital store. How can a company that has thrived on big-box retailing thrive on virtual retailing as well? That is, how can both operations win, in such a way that the executives running the digital operation don't profit at the expense of the executives running the traditional one? In retailing, this is the paradox of the decade.

The CEO's team looked at a range of options. One was to split off the digital store and run it as a separate business. Another was to have the digital store report to and serve the bricks-and-mortar operation. A third was to have the bricks-and-mortar operation report to and serve the digital operation. The choices are among those many retailers have looked at, and each forces executives to invent entirely new ways to work together, without allowing one person's operation to cannibalize and shut down the other.

In the end, the CEO left it to his three top people, two from the stores and one from the online operation: Figure out how to work together, he said. Neither operation will report to the other. Neither will go it alone. You will solve the contradiction of turning competing operations into collaborating ones. The outcome remains in the works, but the example shows that success comes from invention, not reconciliation to find a middle way (which has not worked for big-box stores), nor from purpose (which does not directly address the prime operational issues).

In this vein, note that for addressing complex problems, unconscious thought may work more effectively than conscious thought. That is, when you want to do a math problem, choose conscious thought, because the conscious mind is good at following rules. When you face a complex issue, choose unconscious thought—thinking in the shower—because the unconscious is much better at associative, intuitive, and nonlinear thinking. This all assumes you have studied the data first consciously, of course.

In research on this subject, Ap Dijksterhuis and Loran Nordgren cite their "best of both worlds" hypothesis: "Complex decisions are best when the information is encoded thoroughly and consciously, and the later thought process is delegated to the unconscious."[5] The two researchers define conscious thought simply as thought with attention. Unconscious thought is thought without attention or with attention directed elsewhere.

Examples of how the unconscious spurs greater creativity appear in Dijksterhuis and Nordgren's extensive experiments, in which they induce unconscious problem solving in a variety of situations. In one of the simplest, when people were asked to come up with new names for pasta, those distracted with another task for several minutes before answering—thus forced to use unconscious thought—came up with much more variety (although the same total number of names).[6]

A separate set of experiments showed that the unconscious appears more effective at solving problems with many variables. When people were asked to choose between four apartments described by twelve traits, the conscious thinkers most often couldn't decide which was the best, even though one was rigged to be clearly better, and one worse, than two middle-of-the-roaders. The unconscious thinkers accurately chose the most desirable apartment.[7] The data suggest you should engage your unconscious to improve your conclusions on all sorts of paradoxical problems, which typically bristle with variables.

One focus of the innovation mindset by companies today is the concept we talked about earlier, "shared value," coined by Michael Porter. This remains a big challenge, as indicated in a survey by MIT and Deloitte LLP in 2013. Fifty-two percent of firms around the world gave themselves a 3 on a 1–10 scale for "social business maturity," a measure of essentially running a socially responsible business. Only 17 percent ranked their company as a 7 or above.[8] Porter and Kramer recognize the complexity by calling into question the traditional capitalist approach of organizations, saying it is no longer viable because it fails to address crucial economic, environmental, and social issues.

Porter and Kramer say the failure of companies to address sustainability has made firms a target of social activists and regulators. It has also alienated various stakeholders. Attacking what they refer to as an overly narrow definition of value creation, the authors integrate the paradox of "making good" and "doing good." In their view, every major corporate decision that affects profitability should factor in everything from social to customer concerns. Similarly, every significant social, economic, environmental, and stakeholder decision should factor in profitability. They propose a radical redefinition of capitalism in which social policies and moneymaking strategies are integrated continuously and broadly.

Chipotle has done this thinking, maintaining a dual focus on profitability and "Food With Integrity." According to Chipotle, "Through our vision of Food With Integrity, Chipotle is seeking better food from using ingredients that are not only fresh, but that where possible are sustainably grown and raised responsibly with respect for the animals, the land and the farmers who produce the food. A similarly focused people culture, with an emphasis on identifying and empowering top performing employees, enables us to develop future leaders from within." Chipotle's innovative "making good" and "doing good" model has paid off. Since first trading publicly, the share price has risen from $22 in 2006 to more than $400 as of late 2013; this is a gain of 1,800 percent in just over six years.

Motivate Through Creativity

How do you motivate people to act on the innovation mindset? Mainly through the power of the creative act to excite people. If the purpose mindset harnesses people's desire to find meaning at work, and the reconciliation mindset channels their desire to earn success and rewards, the innovation mindset capitalizes on the way creativity makes people feel more alive and vital.

Research over the years by Mihalyi Csikszentmihalyi on creativity shows that many people who are acting creatively experience greater well-being or happiness—in his terms, "flow."[9] Though the research on creativity reveals a complex relationship between how people feel and how creative they are, leaders can play on the allure of the process of discovery and invention to motivate people to solve paradoxes in a fresh way.

But we offer one major caveat: Turning people's creative juices on demands deft management to remove the typical obstacles that make people cling to the status quo: Performance appraisal systems that reward winning results, not entrepreneurial efforts. Recognition systems that praise short-term results and ignore long-term work on innovation. Promotion practices that raise up people who execute like good soldiers as opposed to people who innovate like entrepreneurs. To succeed with innovation, you have to remove people's fear of failing, fear of looking dumb, and fear of retribution.

A study by Capgemini Consulting and IESE Business School found that, when it comes to innovation, executives respond most to extrinsic motivation—the promise of achieving better results. Employees respond most to intrinsic motivation—the excitement of creating.[10] This poses a challenge if you're leading an executive team in the creation of the innovation mindset: You have to get your colleagues to curb their hunger for results long enough to appeal to their drive to be creative. The innovative thinking that can then take place can lead to rich innovative rewards.

One study of top management teams shows the principal predictor of innovation among executive teams is support for it—in the form of expectations, approval, rewards, and practical assistance. Among a number of factors influencing innovation at this level, such basic support accounted for 46 percent of the variation in overall innovation. This suggests how much leaders can control the establishment of the innovation mindset, even though it may not normally rank as a high priority for people at the top level.[11]

We were sitting in a top-management meeting several years ago that made this point particularly clear. The CEO and executives were debating how to come up with a better offering of services to complement their offering of products. Like many executive teams, this one was trying to engineer a compensation system to motivate the creation of the right kind of product-development mix. The executives remained divided despite an endless swirl of suggestions. If people follow the money, what's the right way to pay them?

Out of the blue, the CEO announced that, from that point onward, all the executives in the room would be earning the same salary and bonuses. Gone were tailored pay plans. This was unheard of. But the CEO quickly showed what he was about. As if he just turned an ignition switch, his announcement triggered the innovation mindset. The executives, to that point in heated debate, dropped their disagreements. *At that moment*, the climate of the room changed: The executives worked like a congenial sports team all shooting for the same goal, dedicating to winning together with a new product-service mix. We marveled at the transformation.

Final Thoughts

As our stories show, the head, heart, and guts are all critical to make the most of the innovation mindset. Not just the head as often happens with the reconciliation mindset. And not just heart as often happens with the purpose mindset. But all three—how else can you act boldly to hit the reset button with a bunch of strong-willed executives? How else can you deal with challenges like the "fuzzy front end" and the "valley of death"?

Our client Jack certainly demonstrated he could rise to the occasion. He had the head to provide the intelligence to clarify purpose and strategy. He had the heart to provide the emotional intelligence to lead a diverse, global workforce and to focus relentlessly on talent development. And he had the guts to provide the courage to do the right thing in an uncertain world. Jack gave people a three-year time line, limited funds, and the expectation of defect-free production to meet regulatory requirements and customer demands. He came up with a solution in which people won three years' worth of professional development, even though they lost their jobs.

Of course, a leader cannot rely on mindset alone to solve paradoxical problems. Given the number of facets to paradoxical problems, the number of people with a stake in them, the ambiguity of the future, the wealth of data that bears on them, the conflict they create, and the volatility of events—a mindset is necessary but insufficient. And that brings us to the next part of the book: our shortlist of the most effective tools for solving paradoxical problems. These tools, used along with the mindsets, provide the essentials for the complete leader.

Complete Leader's Checklist for Chapter Six:
The Innovation Mindset

✓ Adopt a mindset that fosters the invention of unorthodox solutions, using both/and thinking.

✓ Frame the paradoxical problem to serve opposing forces, resolving contradictions by asking how else can we win?

✓ Put boundaries around decision making by clarifying constraints on risk, spending, effort, and values.

✓ Reframe and reframe again as if conducting a new product development exercise.

✓ Rely on divergent thinking, as opposed to convergent, to develop a diverse set of dissimilar options.

PART THREE

TOOLS FOR LEADERSHIP

7

Scanning for the Right Paradox

Read not to contradict and confute, nor to believe and take
for granted . . . but to weigh and consider.
—Francis Bacon[1]

Working as consultants around the world, we encounter a persistent concern among company CEOs: Leaders from the executive team on down have become prisoners of their experience. The CEOs say: *We need people to diversify their thinking, exercise imagination, loosen up their control, get out of their comfort zones. Only by doing so will we come up with the right solutions to today's paradoxical problems.*

We hear this concern so many times that we sometimes think of ourselves as coaches in open-mindedness. Leaders today recognize they spend too much time talking with their peers—and too much time in familiar, comfortable office and plant settings. They too often don't respond to the obvious need to get out of their offices. They almost seem to think they can think their way to diversity. But of course that isn't true. They have to step out and immerse themselves in it.

We recently heard an anecdote from western Kenya, not far from where we worked with the team of GSK executives. An expatriate worker observed that outside organizations, concerned about the shortage of fuel for cooking, had brought in efficient charcoal-burning stoves. But few local people used them regularly. Why? Because they liked gathering around the "hearth" of the fires just outside their back doors. Moreover, the only way to stir their favorite staple—a cornmeal mash called *ugali*—is in a big kettle. And you can't cook the thick *ugali* mixture on a lightweight stove. You can only stir it on a perch of three solid campfire rocks.[2]

The point is that leaders, like the perches for stoves in Kenya, need to balance their thinking on more than one point of experience. They need several points—or many—or they won't have the mental material to best solve paradoxical problems. Too often, the global executive relies on insight from within the organization, trying to cook up something new and nourishing without insights from partners and stakeholders throughout the world.

If you're a leader, you probably recognize you spend too much time talking with your peers and company insiders. That's why, in part, leaders at GSK took a trip to Kenya to explore local conditions. They were heeding an old yet newly relevant message: If you're someone with insular and elitist views, you block the resolution of complex problems.

But that's not all. If you have a limited base of experience, you will have trouble determining which paradoxes to attack in the first place. What is the priority? We often ask executives when we first meet them: What's your leadership agenda? What are you trying to accomplish? Can you identify the paradoxes you really want to focus on? We often discover they haven't thought about their priorities in that way. They don't know which of a dozen significant problems they should devote their time and energy to.

The Value of an External Focus

Over the past thirty years, leaders have shifted their focus from hierarchical structures to business units to teams to networking. Today they stress acquiring knowledge, learning skills quickly, and adapting to a volatile, ambiguous, and complex environment. Most futurists predict that we will move along a trajectory that makes the world harder to understand and navigate through an increasingly tangled web of contradictory forces. To be effective in this new world, no matter what level you're on, you need to develop an "other" focus: What *other* things should I and my colleagues read?

What *other* people should we meet? What *other* experiences should we have?

Companies like Plantronics, AT&T, Ericsson, Twitter, PwC, and Google help their people use outside networks and talent to inspire creativity, solve problems, and get products to market faster. But this is not the norm. In the United States, rugged individualism remains the cultural model. Global leadership expert Stephen Rhinesmith has shown the United States and Australia as the most individualistic countries in the world. Individualistic leaders try to control the flow of information and maintain a fortress of confidentiality. Connecting rather than creating—becoming a networker, alliance maker, and relationship manager—remains awkward.

We can't blame many leaders for remaining insular. They are responding in ways that reflect traditional incentives: You have to receive credit for achievements to get promoted. You have to get control of your work to please the boss—"For goodness sake," the boss says, "No surprises!" And you get paid for this year in and year out. You often don't get paid at all for the big-picture thinking that comes with a diversity of thought and experience. If you've been in this system, you know you get paid mostly for puzzle solving.

But if you want to be a complete leader, this sort of caution will block your development. Embracing best practices from others, admitting to not having the solution, and absorbing the variety of the world prepare you to identify paradoxes and select right actions.

In a study of hospital top-management teams, researchers found a strong correlation between cognitive diversity and decision quality. The researchers surveyed eighty-five CEOs and team members and found that when leaders held diverse beliefs and preferences, they elicited more conflict with each other during decision making. But the conflict led to greater understanding, commitment, and higher decision quality. The authors concluded that even when top executives clashed personally, the increased debate stemming from differences in the way people thought improved decisions, as long as the executives trusted the competence of other members of their teams.[3] This is further evidence that, as crucial as analytical thinking and problem solving are, securing ideas and information from the other has risen immeasurably as prerequisite to prioritizing, originating, and reshaping action.

The Practices of Scanning

As a leader, you will need to collaborate with others to poke, prod, and partake of every opportunity to expand your group's knowledge, deepen your experience, connect with people, and in short get everyone out of their comfort zones to see what really matters. This is of course as true in life outside as inside the corporation. We recommend four practices:

- Questioning assumptions
- Seeking new knowledge
- Connecting with others
- Seeking new experiences

Practice 1: Questioning Assumptions

The first act by leaders is to admit they don't know everything. This comes hard to most top bosses, because saying "I don't know" feels weak and indecisive. In our consulting, we rarely work with top leaders who openly reveal honest confusion or ignorance. The confidence required to climb the company ladder is incompatible with the willingness to express uncertainty. But leaders, like the rest of us, are often wrong, so we recommend that those having a hard time opening up take an interim step, namely, questioning assumptions. You can do this as part of setting the tone with one of the three mindsets. Once you see that your assumptions have foundations of sand, you have a much bigger appetite for fresh ideas.

Research on cognitive biases clearly shows that presenting people with facts or statistics that demonstrate social, economic, or industry changes doesn't get them to challenge their assumptions. We all tend to ignore facts that don't agree with our perceptions. Our experience has taught us that one thing causes another, and even when data show that the causal story we have developed no longer explains reality (if it ever did), we hold tightly to it. That's one reason why, as Nobelist Daniel Kahneman says in *Thinking, Fast and Slow*, "Intuitive predictions are almost completely insensitive to the actual predictive quality of the evidence."[4] How often have you projected with confidence how your life will unfold in the next couple of years—only to find the future refusing to cooperate?

We see examples time and again of bias when leaders face game-changing paradoxes. The best-known example comes from the auto sector. For years, everyone in American manufacturing felt the way to improve quality was to inspect finished products. Moreover, you couldn't produce higher quality and lower costs at the same time. The paradox of cost and quality, people widely believed, was irreconcilable. It took seasoned managers more than a decade to shake that story, and they did so only when they could no longer ignore the Japanese model. Japanese car companies steadily eroded U.S. market share by building quality in rather than inspecting afterwards. Ironically, managers in many industries still have not grasped that principle and its accompanying practices, even as Toyota has grown into a global colossus by elaborating it.

As an exercise, you might want to systematically examine the assumptions that hold you prisoner. Many managers have recently benefited from questioning the formerly irreconcilable notions of environmental performance and low cost. They have in turn profited handsomely by giving customers both. Other managers have benefited from questioning the mutual exclusiveness of high pay and high profits in retailing. We cited John Mackey and his pay practices as turning this notion on its head. Still other managers, such as those at GSK, have benefited from questioning the contradictory notions of making profit and serving the poor, perhaps influenced by C. K. Prahalad's groundbreaking book, *Fortune at the Bottom of the Pyramid*, which argues that the poor need goods and services, and they have money for the right thing delivered in the right way.

This calls out the big question for all of us: What assumptions do we hold that, a decade hence, we will realize are nonsense? Are we ready to lead others in questioning those assumptions? This brings to mind the old saying: "The mind is like a parachute. It works better when it's open."

Practice 2: Seeking New Knowledge

After you learn to enter the don't-know world, you can more readily see the paradoxes most important to the company's future. With the help of the three mindsets, you can also see paradox-solving insights all around you. Those insights come from scanning a wide range of print and digital media. A report by Forbes.com/Insight revealed that competitor analysis, customer trends, corporate developments, and technology trends rank far and away as the prime focuses of executives scanning their environment. Societal and political trends ranked far below.[5] This suggests that, in a paradoxical world, executives are scanning too narrowly.

Your scanning should always include deepening knowledge in macro trends, including effects of globalization, demographics, and technology. Here are six top issues to watch:

- *Dramatic growth in Asia and Africa.* Tens of millions of people will soon join the middle class in Asia, and this will pose many paradoxical questions. The question for Western companies today is whether to wait or invest. Asia will explode with new growth—one of our clients forecasts a 500 percent growth in its business in the next few years. Africa is also emerging as a contender for rapid growth of a middle class, as China invests heavily on the continent and oil and mineral development provide an ongoing influx of cash. At the same time, the earth has shrinking capacity to absorb even a new Chinese middle class—soon to exceed that of the United States. How should companies trade off the demand for growth and planetary sustainability?

- *Robotics changing the way we live.* Robotics and cloud computing will transform our lives as machines replace routine tasks in work and life, and as a result, eliminate many jobs, especially managerial, intermediary, and relationship roles. While innovations like 3D printing will increase our productivity and enhance welfare, we face the prospect of reinventing concepts of work, livelihood, leisure, and personal fulfillment. One paradox: Should an organization make big investments in untested concepts to transform its business, or should it hold off to milk current technology, risking falling behind?

- *Major diseases cured or controlled.* A world-renowned cancer researcher recently shared with us his belief that many chronic, lethal diseases won't kill people ten years from now. Doctors will have the ability to retard disease progress and extend life even more than today. What will this mean, and not just for health care? One paradox: Do we push for faster, better, deeper innovations in the quality and length of life regardless of the costs associated with them, the inability of societies to provide the services, or the potential to increase the gap between the haves and have-nots?

- *Ever more transparency.* We see no end in sight for public and political demands that companies measure and report performance. As concerns over specific issues such as climate change or social consciousness grow, more firms will rate companies publicly and rank them numerically. Poor performers can expect to receive bad publicity, sanctions from government, downgrades from analysts, witch hunts from politicians, and consumer boycotts. What new paradoxes will arrive? One will be the intensification of the need to decide between profitability and sustainability.

- *More sophisticated network influences.* Networks will continue to evolve beyond the control of leaders, presenting the paradox between the inner circle and the periphery. Meanwhile, people alternately want more surface connections and deeper and more meaningful ones. How do you achieve the right blend of external networking and attention to internal factors associated with business performance? How will you assess the quality, and not just the scope, of information and ideas that emerge from networks? The proliferation of information demands that we decide which sources we should listen to and which to ignore.

- *Changing needs of the workforce.* Expectations in needs and work style vary with each generation—Baby Boomers, Generation X,

Millennials, and so on. You need to recognize the importance of leading increasingly diverse talent. How do your people use their own experience to understand others without making the wrong assumptions about what others are looking for?

Practice 3: Connecting with Others

We have observed in many industries a similar pattern: People who have been promoted to top jobs exhibited competitiveness by personally delivering outstanding results, besting others to shine and take credit, and exerting control to deliver predictable outcomes. But these people now face a new world, where they can solve paradoxes more effectively through coordinated interplay, achieving shared objectives, and looking beyond one another's prescribed boundaries. These leaders have to fight a reliance on a select group of colleagues and advisers to get things done. If you are like these leaders, you have, consciously or not, probably divided the world into us and them. In your mind, the us group is the only one that counts. You will now have a hard time making the most of contacts in the them group, even though that group is much larger and more diverse than the us group.

We once ran a program for two merging banks, and we encouraged leaders to reach out and invite members from the other bank to join their teams. Not surprisingly, those leaders who were the most inclusionary, measured by a psychological test, formed better teams and received critical pieces of new information. The control-focused executives lagged on both counts. We have used the same test on executive teams and CEOs for twenty years, and we have noticed a distinct shift. Historically, more control-oriented leaders became CEOs or senior executives. In the last ten years, this has abruptly changed. More inclusion-oriented leaders emerge as CEO because of the need in large companies to bring people together rather than attempt to control people and events.

The control-focused dysfunction is just what leaders need to avoid when they face a range of paradoxical problems today. You instead need to embrace a broad network so that you position yourself on the information pathway. Success stems not just from connecting the dots but from connecting the people.

Ultimately, you will need to cultivate a sort of collective leadership, building a more complete picture of the environment by sharing knowledge across the network, whether that network operates at the foot of the water cooler or in the virtual world of social networks and online forums. You might think that chief executives network naturally outside their immediate work groups, but that depends on the CEO. Researchers in one study found that only CEOs with board appointments outside their industry tended to "focus more on broader sectors of the environment such as the economic, political/legal, socio-cultural and technological factors that could affect their firm's operation." Other CEOs tended to keep more in touch with developments in their own industry, leading to a homogenization of attention by the CEOs in the same industry.[6]

Although the study looked just at manufacturing companies, it points to the narrow focus leaders today need to avoid. Leaders need to expand their networking to other sources of intelligence that go beyond competing CEOs and peers. They also need to encourage their people to do so, asking them to take a risk by going outside their function or team to elicit the views of opposing functions. Or ask them to invite in an expert with a controversial viewpoint. Or insist they study the moves of a formidable competitor.

Practice 4: Seeking New Experiences

As so amply illustrated by the GSK executives' trip to Kenya, broader experiences form the basis for a clearer view of paradoxes and how to prioritize solving them. As consultants, we help executive teams use short-term trips and events that thrust them into unfamiliar environments that challenge their opinions. Leaders usually react with less certainty about what they know. They become more willing to look at situations with an open mind. And they have a better idea of where to place their energy.

As for foreign experience, across five studies, researchers showed that people who have lived abroad (rather than simply traveling abroad) are more creative. That creativity is expressed as insight, association of ideas, and idea generation—in short, bringing to the table something novel and useful. In one study, the more time a sample of MBA students studied and lived abroad, the more quickly they solved two problems: one of them required finding an inventive but necessary solution to negotiating the sale of a gas station. The most creative solution promised the seller a bonus of a job at the station at a future date—enough of a bonus to get him to accept an offer lower than his reservation price.

Another study showed that it was the time spent adapting to unfamiliar local conditions that explained the higher levels of creativity. Interestingly, experimental studies showed that priming students with memories of their expatriate experience could also raise creativity.[7] Although it is unclear whether this effect leads to enduring changes, it at least goes some way toward showing that experience leads to creativity.

Most executives draw from a narrow range of experience. Because of their socioeconomic status, many live protected lives, shielded from interactions with others who may be from a different economic situation, cultural context, or political or economic philosophy. They have never wrestled with the ambiguity of working in different systems with different people. They have succeeded precisely because they have deep experience in their industry and jobs, as well as because they have learned lessons from that experience they can apply in similar situations. But that school-of-hard-knocks experience also encourages them to repeat actions with metronomic regularity, depriving them of an openness to see alternative strategies. They stick with the tried and true. They act reflexively and not reflectively.

Experience is a great teacher, of course. But if you are going to solve paradoxes today, you need to be on guard against ossified thinking. You can counter the hardening of opinion through personal retreats, acting counterintuitively, seeking feedback from others, and stopping to learn from teachable moments during new experiences.

You will want to encourage the same in people you work with, whether on or off the job.

Developing a Point of View

All of us come to view the slate of paradoxical problems in work and life with a different worldview. The components of that view run the gamut. Do the people you associate with believe in cooperation or competition when it comes to interacting with others? In independence or interdependence when it comes to connections? In individualism or collectivism when it comes to groups? In tolerance or intolerance when it comes to judging outlying behaviors? In universal or relative truths about ethical action? In achievement or self-actualization when it comes to aspirations? What are people's beliefs and assumptions and objectives? How do they acquire knowledge and learn? Set goals? Organize priorities and relationships?[8]

Worldviews can be specific and abstract, tangible and intangible, conscious and unconscious. We often assume our worldview stems from variables such as gender, ethnicity, nationality, education, functional expertise, and so on. But a person's worldview is far more complex, a rich fabric woven with individual fibers reflecting the range and nuance of personal and work experiences. Many leaders have an execution mentality, for example, which works well for getting work done when times remain stable and circumstances fixed. But what about during unstable times—when paradoxes with evolving contradictory forces dominate? This mentality, though just one fiber in the bigger fabric, blocks them from nimbly jumping over the line.

The more experiences you have as a leader, the better able you will be to handle paradoxical questions. Your worldview will become increasingly nuanced with each step outside your comfort zone. It will allow you to more easily exhibit a continuous reinvention mentality. You will see different ways to get things done—ways that can only stem from scanning and immersion in the broader work and societal world.

To achieve quantum leaps in productivity or to reconcile the irreconcilable, we advise every senior leader today to think every day about how the six issues we mentioned affect the company's business model. Where do the paradoxes lie? Which deserve the leaders' attention? Some of them may require willingness to engage in creative destruction, or reshaping as one executive calls it. Can you get rid of products, processes, and policies that soon may become a drag on the organization? What is worth preserving and what is worth destroying? Sometimes resolving the paradox of stability and change is the hardest of all—and only constant scanning of the horizon will tell the complete leader which action to take.

Complete Leader's Checklist for Chapter Seven:
Scanning for Paradox

✓ Clarify your assumptions about how things work, questioning ill-founded biases and outmoded rules of thumb.

✓ Scan broadly in print and digital media for micro- and macro-trends, going beyond a study of competitors, customers, and technology, and ask yourself what trends could disrupt your business.

✓ Strive to connect to people outside your inner circle, bucking the habit of talking to—and thinking like—people just like you.

✓ Seek new personal and work experiences to broaden your perspective, clarify your priorities, foster creativity, and help you reject ossified thinking.

8

Scenario Thinking

What we agree with leaves us inactive, but contradiction
makes us productive.
—Johann Wolfgang von Goethe[1]

In Chapter Three, we described how Deutsche Post DHL CEO Frank
Appel and members of his executive team debated a tough issue over
balancing short- versus long-term demands. The question: Should
they use year-end cash to show good financial results today or invest
for tomorrow? Executives from finance and the company's divisions
each represented their stakeholders—shareholders versus customers.
They each took a stand to advocate for the silo of their interest. They
believed it important to forcefully represent their point of view.

As it turned out, we simplified the story. The executive team
members at Deutsche Post DHL faced much more than one paradoxical problem. They faced many of the contradictions that bedevil
global corporations today: continuity versus disruption, globalization
versus localization, sustainability versus profitability. They wrestled
especially over the issue of sustainability. As far-sighted and skilled
executives, they asked some interesting questions: What would
happen to their company or any company with mass migrations of
people, the boom of megacities, changes in disease patterns and sever-
ity, the development of new power sources, and other climate-related
changes?

We have learned in such situations to use a key tool called
scenario thinking. Scenario thinking is a formal method for questioning
assumptions, exploring alternatives, and analyzing the upsides and

downsides of multiple possibilities. It is a disciplined way of looking at current and future factors shaping your world, your industry, and your markets, and then analyzing how your organization can plan for and react to future possibilities. Scenario thinking forces you to loosen control enough to rise above conventional wisdom and your own biases.

Deutsche Post DHL executives wanted to explore what the world could be like in five or ten years. They wanted to know what would affect their current organization and their investments in businesses for the future. Hiring an outside consultant to help them assess technological, demographic, and social change, they came up with five scenarios:

- An out-of-control global economy with countries exploiting natural resources and competing with each other for these resources.
- Megacities growing at astonishing rates.
- Lifestyles becoming more customizable.
- Paralyzing protectionism creating barriers to competition around the world.
- Climate change creating global resilience and local adaption.

These scenarios helped Deutsche Post DHL shape a larger discussion about the strategy of the company and which strategic options to pursue—options for both individual businesses and the collective whole. The discussion included people's judgment as to the likelihood that various scenarios would materialize and how well equipped the company was to handle them if they did.

In many paradoxical situations, data don't reveal what's right—in spite of impassioned arguments by finance staffers, operations professionals, and others marshaling dozens of slides and spreadsheets. Numbers alone simply can't point to the right outcomes, because they don't show the entire picture, and they are often based on a set of assumptions that may or may not be correct. Debates over data thus lead to arguments that go nowhere. Who's to say what all the dots of data mean? What's in the black and gray space in between? Nobody can say.

Scenario thinking can help teams pull back from such disagreements, or at least have a more informed and constructive dialogue about differing points of view. It calms the discussion and creates a mechanism for alignment as everyone works together to connect the dots. As people explore situations and develop assumptions together, shared insights emerge. As they test the ideas within a group dynamic, individuals with different views can line up because they are operating outside their usual space—free of baggage and many biases. They don't have to insist on consistency.

Chapter Seven discusses the first way complete leaders can use their heads to resolve paradoxes. This chapter takes up a second. If you want to expand your team's creativity, anticipate possibilities, and assign probabilities, bring people together with scenario thinking. This would be no different from a family reimagining its future by constructing scenarios of moving to three different towns. In one, a university provides a solid economic foundation and cultural environment. In another, an attractive climate and abundant water provides lush agricultural opportunities for self-sustenance. In the third, a burgeoning tech sector provides an economic base for product development, exports, and innovation. The scenarios get everyone thinking more deeply.

The Value of Scenario Thinking

Because of scenario thinking's mind-expanding effect, we encourage leaders to use it regularly. By playing out a story—instead of following a strategic trend line to seek a solution to a supposed puzzle—you can go in fruitful new directions. Cross-cultural research on decision-making styles reveals that 75 percent of people in Western societies are fact-based while only 25 percent are intuitive. If you're an engineer or other linear thinker by training, you require a 90 percent probability of success before making a decision—and if the probability dips below that percentage, you delay your decision to gather more data. However, scenario thinking can free fact-based people from their normal mental constraints.

This effect was confirmed by a novel study of 129 executives and workers from ten organizations in which researchers tracked people's commitment to various mental models of their organizations. Employees with political models of their organization—autocratic, bureaucratic, technocratic, or democratic—reduced their reliance on that model after a session of scenario planning. People with financial mental models—believing company control resided in the accounting department—reduced their reliance on their model as well. "From a practical perspective," wrote the investigators, "this research provides support for the use of scenario planning in organizations as an effective tool for helping employees think differently."[2]

Other researchers have shown that scenario planning helps firms capture a range of value, including a better ability to perceive, interpret, and respond to change and improve organizational learning. A 2013 study examined seventy-seven big European firms across various industries that engaged in scenario planning activities. The researchers defined the companies as top-, medium-, and low-performing (according to sales growth) to gauge any differences in value contribution. The data showed that all companies benefited from scenario planning activities, especially in their increased perception: "gaining insights into changes in the environment" and "reducing uncertainty." But the high-performing firms, the ones that reported the best results, also cited benefits ranging from identifying "opportunities and threats for our product and technology portfolio" to "fostering conversation about the overall strategy of the company."[3]

Our experience is that scenario thinking stretches people's perspective. The stories embedded in scenarios extend plot lines in a way that facts cannot. Many younger, more creative companies such as SmarterComics, SynLabs, and BeachMint, which extol creative thinking as their source of growth, engage naturally in scenario thinking. Older, more established companies, where people are asked to push the boundaries of logical, rational, defensible positions backed by multiple PowerPoint slides, normally don't do as well and can benefit the most by exploring it.

The Practices of Scenario Thinking

Over the years, we have developed four scenario-thinking steps to help you push the boundaries of what many people think is possible or logical:

1. Take someone else's perspective.
2. Define future possibilities.
3. Filter scenarios with facts and intuition.
4. Diverge and converge.

These steps constitute a coaching method that can guide you in thinking imaginatively about paradox, triggering new thoughts and encouraging people to devise a range of provocative future possibilities, as well as estimating the risk associated with them. As in Chapter Seven, the steps require tapping a diverse set of people to engage in the process. Who has the best feel for the future environment? These people should be on the team.

Practice 1: Take Someone Else's Perspective

The first step in scenario thinking is to make a conscious effort to adopt another person's point of view. This simple practice of empathy often opens participants up to understanding, if not accepting, what is important to others. To be emotionally intelligent, you need to get inside another person's head in a way that you can feel what they feel and understand what they are experiencing. This is necessary advance work for scenario thinking.

Most people in top positions are locked into one perspective and consider that perspective vital to being a strong leader. Such certainty in the face of ambiguity, however, blocks their grasp of the motivations and viewpoints of others. The practice of perspective taking sounds simple, but in our experience, a shift of viewpoint is one of the hardest challenges for people in a fast-moving, global, connected world. Ironically, with so much choice, when you select the data, media sources, and even friends to reinforce your own reality and view of others, you become less in touch with what's going on around you. The Internet, though rich in many ways, can actually make us poor in seeing the other side of things.

We often encounter executives who complain about the changing workforce, and we find older leaders in particular cite the lack of commitment and motivation of younger people. These complaints often come from top executives, the best paid, invariably from another generation. They don't believe younger generations want to work hard or make a difference. We have found just the reverse is true, so in such cases, we put together a focus group of young people and convene a meeting behind a barrier that allows top executives to hear but not see the younger workers.

In a facilitated discussion, the younger workers quickly open up about their work lives, in spite of knowing top executives are listening. The flow of the conversation? We ask workers what it's like to work at the company, and they often say it's frustrating, that it's hard to get things done, that they are unclear about the strategy or direction of the company. The executives are surprised; in their experience, at their level, it's easy to get things done and the strategy is clear. We ask workers what it's like to work with their supervisors, and they say it's difficult, that it's hard to get their supervisors' attention because they are so busy, that they don't get a lot of feedback on how they're doing. The top executives easily get other people's attention and mostly know where they stand.

The conversation continues in like vein, the workers becoming more candid as time goes on, and the executives becoming more surprised with each comment. The top brass begins to see that the workers take company values seriously—even more seriously than the executives in some cases. They work hard at advancing their careers, in spite of volunteering in their communities and taking care of families. They are committed and motivated—but they hit roadblocks the top executives never experience.

We then bring the workers to the other side of the barrier to meet the executives, and the conversation takes a congenial turn. The executives ask the questions. They want to learn about the workers' jobs, community work, recreation on weekends, difficulties in balancing work and family, and so on. The executives develop genuine empathy as they realize they are talking to idealistic, committed, hardworking people. They drop jaded stereotypes and invariably leave the session making essentially the same comment: "I had no idea!" They didn't realize they had people of that caliber, who faced so many challenges. In the session, they were touched by a different world.

Short of such a facilitated event, you can develop your perspective taking with the following exercise: Think of a business situation in which you're trying to influence someone you work with—a direct report, a boss, a customer, an outside partner that you know is resisting your leadership agenda. Ask yourself: How am I trying to move this individual? What are my most important purposes, concerns, and values? What are the other person's purposes, concerns, and values? The key is to articulate the other person's wants credibly and convincingly while at the same time clarifying your own objectives.

Now begin to look for the intersection of your own purposes and concerns with those of the other person. What is that person attempting to accomplish or achieve through the behavior in question? Can you see it objectively and compassionately? Refrain from judging that behavior—but try to describe it. What does the person really require? How might this requirement be different from what you had previously assumed? What specific thing might you do or say to fill this need? These questions will help you flex your empathy muscle, which puts you in the right frame of mind to proceed with scenario thinking.

Practice 2: Define Future Possibilities

The next step in scenario thinking is to define some future possibilities that stem from the contradictory forces of paradox. For instance, the paradox that vexes most managers is control versus delegation. On one hand, you may recognize the need to give your direct reports more responsibility and autonomy so you can do more and they can better respond to the issues they face—issues that increasingly require more creative approaches. On the other hand, you feel confident that your insight will speed the decision-making tempo, and you are tempted to intervene, offer guidance, and check up on progress.

Now craft three future scenarios that might affect this situation. For example:

- Two years from now, your boss is promoted, you are in your boss's job, and you now require a flatter structure, a competent individual in your role, and you need to stretch your own capacity because you have been asked to do more and perform at a higher level.
- Three years from now, you're remarried, your blended family has three adolescents, you need to spend more time at home and less at the office or traveling. At the same time, you have a different boss with whom you are not aligned and who expects you to work longer hours and travel more.
- Four years from now, you're managing almost all of your team virtually—some work from home, some are located in other parts of the world, and your company has moved to a hoteling space model and eliminated your office completely. Not only do you lack the ability to monitor anyone's work, the culture of the company now requires trust over supervision.

Think about how your control-versus-delegation decisions could be changed by each of these scenarios. What are the negatives and positives? How will you experience them as the future unfolds? If you in turn apply different mindsets to your scenarios, what actions might you take? Does a purpose perspective give you new insight? A reconciliation perspective? An innovation perspective?

Now consider instead a situation at the corporate level. For instance, at PwC, the global accounting and advisory firm, a team sought to understand the future of talent. What would the future workforce be like? How would it operate? What picture of that future should an executive team consider?

When PwC tackled this issue, it focused on eight opposing forces that it felt would most influence the way people will work in 2020:

business fragmentation versus integration, collectivism versus individualism, technology controlling people versus technology giving way to the human touch, and globalization versus protectionism. The PwC team winnowed the forces to the four most important: fragmentation versus integration and collectivism versus individualism. Those forces then governed the creation of four scenarios, which in the process of refinement were reduced to three.[4] (See Figure 8.1.) These gave PwC a way to understand how talent shortages, technology advances, sustainability efforts, and demographic and cultural shifts will affect the nature of work in the future.

In describing these three scenarios, PwC issued a report, "Managing Tomorrow's People: The Future of Work to 2020." The report describes different cultural, talent, managerial, and individual implications for tomorrow's workforce. (See Figure 8.2.) This of course will help PwC prepare for managing people tomorrow, and it can also help other companies.

The future states PwC described are relevant not because they predict the future but because they suggest implications executives must consider to prepare for tomorrow. The future will probably not be green, blue, or orange. It will be a world with a combination of factors represented in the three scenarios. As a leader, your task is not to select which world your company will operate in but rather to understand the options and in turn the skills you want to develop in your people today. At the same time, you want to be looking for signals that suggest the actual emergence of certain scenario components. For leaders used to producing strategic plans with single visions of the future, scenario thinking frees up creative thought, allowing you to lay out alternatives and get the company ready to respond.

Practice 3: Filter Scenarios with Facts and Intuition

The third step in scenario thinking is to assimilate each scenario with the help of added data, statistics, metrics, reports, studies, and research. That is, look ahead to dealing with the implications of these future worlds. What will you do? What will your company do? Who can help you? For example, in the hoteling scenario, what specific

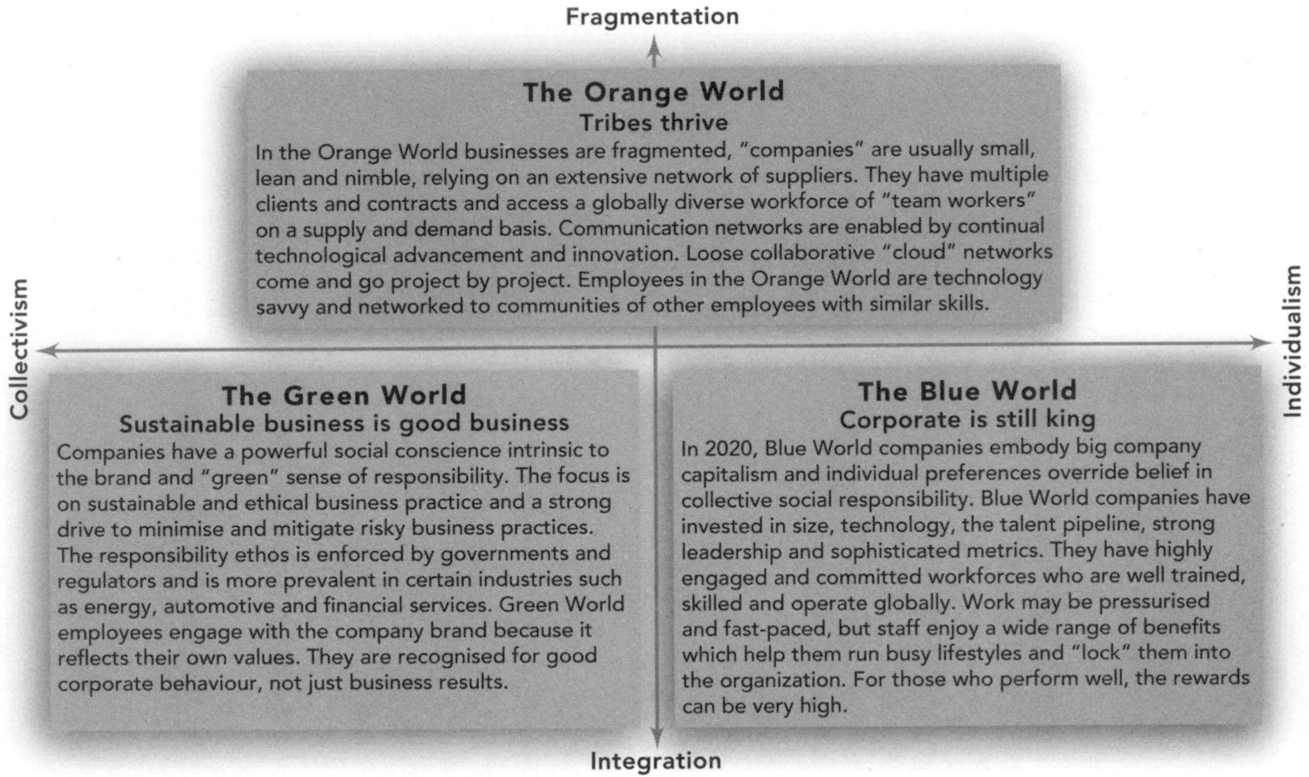
Fragmentation
The Orange World
Tribes thrive
In the Orange World businesses are fragmented, "companies" are usually small, lean and nimble, relying on an extensive network of suppliers. They have multiple clients and contracts and access a globally diverse workforce of "team workers" on a supply and demand basis. Communication networks are enabled by continual technological advancement and innovation. Loose collaborative "cloud" networks come and go project by project. Employees in the Orange World are technology savvy and networked to communities of other employees with similar skills.
Collectivism
Individualism
The Green World
Sustainable business is good business
Companies have a powerful social conscience intrinsic to the brand and "green" sense of responsibility. The focus is on sustainable and ethical business practice and a strong drive to minimise and mitigate risky business practices. The responsibility ethos is enforced by governments and regulators and is more prevalent in certain industries such as energy, automotive and financial services. Green World employees engage with the company brand because it reflects their own values. They are recognised for good corporate behaviour, not just business results.
The Blue World
Corporate is still king
In 2020, Blue World companies embody big company capitalism and individual preferences override belief in collective social responsibility. Blue World companies have invested in size, technology, the talent pipeline, strong leadership and sophisticated metrics. They have highly engaged and committed workforces who are well trained, skilled and operate globally. Work may be pressurised and fast-paced, but staff enjoy a wide range of benefits which help them run busy lifestyles and "lock" them into the organization. For those who perform well, the rewards can be very high.
Integration

Figure 8.1. Three Worlds of 2020

Source: "Managing Tomorrow's People: The Future of Work to 2020" (PricewaterhouseCoopers, 2007).

	Green World	Blue World	Orange World
Workplace culture	Focus on socially and environmentally responsible business practices	Fast-paced, global operator, with high performance culture	Flexible and highly networked with a focus on the short term
Employee profile	"Your corporate values match mine — I belong here."	"Only the best work here — I am the best."	"I will work with you because it suits me right now."
People management style	Coaching and nurturing to promote the right behaviours	HR is a hard discipline, very metrics focused with rigorous recruitment processes	Emphasis on global talent sourcing, global guilds replace the HR function
Key themes	CS and transparency underpin everything to drive moderate but steady growth	Controlling talent is key, the line between home and work is blurred	Small means agile, innovative and able to adapt to change quickly
Corporate ethos	Sustainable business for a better society	Perform well all of the time and everybody wins	Networks make the world go round

Figure 8.2. Implications for Three Worlds

Source: "Managing Tomorrow's People: The Future of Work to 2020" (PricewaterhouseCoopers, 2007).

capabilities would you require to lead in this increasingly likely world? What companies are doing this successfully now? What techniques do role models use who lead others virtually?

PwC offers a good example of adding facts to deepen scenario thinking. On top of drafting scenarios, the company interviewed more than 2,700 graduates who had been offered jobs with PwC. Some results confirmed conventional thinking about the future; some defied received wisdom. For example, most soon-to-be-hired Millennials (73 percent) surprisingly expected to work regular (rather than flexible) hours, no matter their country of origin. The vast majority (over 80 percent) deliberately sought work where the firm's approach to corporate responsibility reflected their values—a figure that was nearly the same in the United States and China, at roughly 90 percent.[5]

As important as the facts are, add intuition to the mix. What do your instincts tell you about the various scenarios? Do you think you would be more controlling or less when working in a more technology-rich environment? How do the facts you've collected inform your hunch about the future and how it will change or evolve? Your intuition, albeit influenced by biases, stems from a rich library of implicit knowledge—unarticulated wisdom that allows you to weigh in on the validity and risk of different scenarios. You can only infer the future from current facts, but by using intuition you have a valuable source of added insight.

In a *Harvard Business Review* article, Pierre Wack elaborated on merging facts and intuition for better scenario thinking. Wack, a pioneer in the field, believes that intuition is not just a tool to help leaders face difficult choices, it actually helps leaders creatively expand their view of the world. Writes Wack: "Scenarios deal with two worlds: the world of facts and the world of perceptions. They explore for facts but they aim at perceptions inside the heads of decision makers. Their purpose is to gather and transform information of strategic significance into fresh perceptions. This transformation process is not trivial—more often than not it does not happen. When it works, it is a creative experience that generates a heartfelt 'Aha!'

from your managers and leads to strategic insights beyond the mind's previous reach."[6]

One technique we use to get leaders to employ their intuition is to ask team members to suggest how they see a particular paradox-related story about the future unfolding. Then we put key words from each person's story on a chart and use that device to discuss what is likely and unlikely to take place in this future scenario. Is the current obsession with growth likely to be relevant five years from now? How important will sustainability be in this scenario? We can also ask practical questions about what leaders can do now. For example: What type of cost approach do we need to begin building today?

Practice 4: Diverge and Converge

The final step in scenario thinking is to diverge your thinking and then converge it. To do so, share strategic or personal scenarios with a diverse range of people, both within and outside your circle: direct reports, peers, consultants, partners, and students. The more people involved in building scenarios, the more accurate the scenarios are likely to be. With a diverse group, you can churn out possibilities and take conversations in wide-ranging, unexpected directions—just as at Deutsche Post DHL and PwC.

We are suggesting a form of crowdsourcing, involving a wide range of people and perspectives, to increase the amount of creativity and knowledge integrated into each scenario. In bringing together diverse viewpoints to inform scenario thinking, you challenge the assumptions embedded in each scenario. Of all the things we've considered and discussed, what assumptions do we think are most valid about the future? What degree of likelihood (and risk) would we associate with each scenario? What plan of action seems feasible given each scenario? How well would we respond to each scenario if it were to occur?

When Deutsche Post DHL wanted to test various scenarios and strategies, it brought together groups of younger high-potential leaders around the world and asked them to critique, challenge, or reinforce different assumptions and scenarios. The company assumed that technology would play a larger role in logistics and that younger employees, being more wired and technology savvy, could provide the best input. The executives were right—the young leaders challenged, revised, and ultimately produced a much better product that took into account the future role of tools the younger managers knew intimately—social media, mobile computing, location tracking, massive analytics, and so on.

The younger workers understood better than their older counterparts the impact of social media, online shopping, and the impact of one's network on buying decisions. In the unfolding Deutsche Post DHL strategy, many strategic choices about how to serve customers in the future were shaped by the input of these younger colleagues, who played an important role in the strategic planning process by offering a different perspective on the impact of technology.

Following diverging and converging, leaders will find the scenarios that best suggest ways of managing paradoxes. For most companies, managing the paradox of preserving the core traditional business versus investing in adjacencies to develop future businesses bedevils management teams and leaders. Scenario thinking is particularly helpful in dealing with this paradox, as the tendency is often to go with the known core when money becomes tight. Should Deutsche Post DHL consider new businesses suggested by scenarios or stick to its knitting? As noted in Chapter Three, an effective CEO Frank Appel voted to invest in the future of his businesses. But the right action depends on the circumstances, and Appel will naturally reconsider the actions as circumstances change.

Follow Up by Acting

If you're a senior leader, consider the question posed by Marcel Cobuz, senior vice president for innovation at Lafarge: "Do you have a breed of managers who see paradoxes everywhere, or are people simplifying the world?" If you think strictly in terms of implementing a single strategic plan, you may be simplifying the world into a puzzle. With so many contradictory forces acting, no single plan can get the future right. Understanding the implications of paradox calls on complete leaders to rein in their urge for control, consistency, and closure. Instead, they want to play out the different possibilities for resolving the tensions of multiple contradictions. Scenario thinking is the tool for doing so.

Once you have gone through these four steps, you should have advanced your skill in comparing and contrasting alternatives, a tremendously valuable capability in jumping over the line to deal with problems in a complex, volatile world. But beware a common mistake: Failing to do anything in response to your scenario thinking. This is the point where scenario thinking most often breaks down as a tool to deal with an organization's contradictory forces. You may go through the exercise pro forma rather than as an engaged participant. You fail to ask yourself: What core insights have emerged from this process? You don't ask the critical question: What can I actually do with this wisdom? You generate ideas, but you don't turn these ideas into usable plans and actions.

We return to this challenge in Chapter Twelve. In the meantime, note that the costs associated with *not* acting grow exponentially as you become a more senior leader. The intensity of choice and intensity of consequences both mount. That very intensity should be an incentive for redoubling your efforts to find common ground in scenario thinking, and in turn, uniting with your collaborators in common action.

Complete Leader's Checklist for Chapter Eight:
Scenario Thinking

✓ Adopt the point of view of others to develop empathy for and understanding of what the world looks like through their eyes.
✓ Explore visions of the future with scenario thinking, stretching your mind beyond your current worldview to imagine future possibilities and risks.

✓ Construct future scenarios that anticipate the contradictory forces you face today and ask yourself how prepared you are for each scenario.

✓ Elaborate each scenario with research, dialogue with colleagues, and your intuition about the future to test the likelihood of each.

✓ As in the innovation mindset, use divergent thinking for diverse scenarios—but refine the scenarios with convergent thinking.

9

Stakeholder Mapping

As for me, all I know is that I know nothing.
—Socrates[1]

Why do some managers perceive relationships with stakeholders as involving risk, conflict, and trade-offs, while others perceive them as rich in opportunity, interdependence, and mutual benefit? That was a question that Donal Crilly of London Business School and Pamela Sloan of HEC in Montreal set out to answer.[2] Their findings help explain how managers can position themselves to better handle paradoxical problems.

Crilly and Sloan discovered that company leaders view the role of stakeholders in one of three ways. Some leaders treat stakeholders at arm's length. They see interactions with stakeholders as transactions and govern them with contracts. Other leaders work with stakeholders arm in arm. They see interactions as partnerships and govern them through team-like relationships. Still others work with stakeholders as if joined at the hip. They see interactions as collaborations and govern them through an especially high level of trust and interdependency.

Not surprisingly, Crilly and Sloan found that the leaders of arm's-length firms are the ones that see decisions involving stakeholders as full of risk, conflict, and trade-offs. Leaders of the other firms tend to see them as full of opportunity and mutual benefit. We might translate these findings to say that leaders of the arm's-length firms tend to say "Distrust and verify" when it comes to stakeholders. Leaders of the arm-in-arm firms say "Trust and verify." And leaders of the joined-at-the-hip firms say "Trust and value."

Which kind of leader are you? The ramifications of your answer are huge. If you're in a firm with warm and comfortable stakeholder relations, you naturally bring more people into decisions related to paradoxical problems, and in turn develop options with more knowledge, know-how, and a broader perspective. If you're in a firm with standoffish stakeholder relations, you probably cherish working the levers of control, and in turn put yourself at a disadvantage in coming up with solutions to the toughest problems facing organizations today.

Crilly and Sloan's findings, although just one study, confirm our experience in coaching leaders across industry. Those who come from firms that naturally reach out to stakeholders quickly move beyond either/or choices to both/and choices when faced with paradoxes. They accept fewer trade-offs and obtain more win-wins. They more naturally adopt purpose, reconciliation, and innovation mindsets, and they drive more swiftly toward paradox-resolving actions.

In Chapters Seven and Eight, we began to show how complete leaders use their head, heart, and guts in decisions. We showed how to engage your head in scanning the environment and shaping options with scenario thinking. In this chapter, we show how you can engage your heart—your emotional intelligence—in understanding and accommodating the needs of stakeholders. We call this *stakeholder mapping*.

We devote a chapter to this topic because stakeholders figure into almost all paradoxical problems. When you debate how to solve paradoxes, you are actually debating the gains and losses for various vested interests. On the surface, you may debate the issues. But underneath you are really arguing over the future and fortunes of various constituencies.

Recall PepsiCo chairman and CEO Indra Nooyi's struggle to deal with the issue of sugary and salty foods. One of the major persons involved was former Mayor Bloomberg of New York, who sought to tackle obesity by regulating products sold to New Yorkers. PepsiCo agreed that there was a problem, but they did not think that the former mayor's solution adequately addressed the complexity of the issue. Yet PepsiCo couldn't ignore the needs of this stakeholder because of the size of the market and the visibility the nationally known Bloomberg gave to the issue.

The Value of Stakeholder Mapping

For many years, leaders who concerned themselves with stakeholder management ranked stakeholders in order of priority. In turn, they found ways to meet stakeholder demands to keep everyone satisfied (more or less). This approach stemmed from the thinking of a pioneer in the field of stakeholder thinking, R. Edward Freeman, a professor at the Darden School at the University of Virginia. But Freeman, with whom we work today, will tell you his thinking has evolved, and we agree with his new outlook. The interests of stakeholders today, he says, are jointly held. The only way to create value for the long term is to integrate the interests of multiple stakeholders in a single strategy.

To leaders who see only risk, conflicts, and trade-offs in stakeholder relationships, Freeman offers this observation: Your critics are always going to be there, but behind every critic is a new business opportunity. "How else are you going to get better if you don't have critics?" he asks. "Ultimately you need someone to give you detailed advice on what's wrong with what you're doing and how you could get better."

When executives ask for Freeman's advice, he has this to say: Put yourself at the center. Figure out who affects you and whom you can affect. Think about the stakeholders around you in a new way, not as constraints but as resources. When you encounter the opposing forces of a paradoxical problem, tap this extended set of resources to create fresh value.[3] You often get back more than you give away.

One of the most vibrant examples of a joined-at-the-hip firm creating value with stakeholders is Whole Foods Market. Whole Foods Co-CEO John Mackey has long championed a stakeholder philosophy. He says stakeholders are like spokes on a wheel. How do the self-managing teams at Whole Foods and their variety of stakeholders create the operating apparatus for the company? "We co-create it," says Mackey in an interview with Freeman. "The stakeholder is involved in that creation."[4]

In other words, the structures, processes, and strategies used in running Whole Foods stem from work by people in the stakeholder network. As a recent example, Whole Foods gathered a number of internal and external stakeholders to figure out standards for farmed mollusks (shellfish such as clams, mussels, and oysters). Whole Foods seafood buyers, people from the company's quality standards and food safety teams, oceanographers, and twenty East Coast farmers met in spring 2012 to go over draft standards. They talked about production-system aquaculture (versus wild capture), disease prevention, preventing impacts to sediments under farms, harvesting, predator control, traceability, and other topics. Out of that meeting came refined standards.[5]

How do companies keep focused on business when involving stakeholders in this way? By having a clear answer to the following: For what reason is the company creating value? Why is it doing what it's doing? At Whole Foods, Mackey and his people have decided, at least in part, that their purpose is to create healthy communities through healthy eating. Note that this approach does not raise the question of stakeholder ranking. It calls instead for putting a priority on asking stakeholders to act as resources to solve paradoxical problems. Company experts, scientists, environmentalists, and farmers all have a role.

In a separate development at Whole Foods, stores often sponsor farmers markets in their parking lots. The company actually invites local competitors (farmers) to sell produce at its doorstep. It even organizes the markets. This in turn helps Whole Foods fulfill its goal of creating healthy customer and supplier communities. The payback presumably shows up in the long term: Goodwill and shopping traffic contribute to healthy store sales and to an overall upward trend in demand for the products Whole Foods specializes in—healthy and locally grown food. Whole Foods, by organizing stakeholders around a purpose, has created a virtuous, value-creating cycle with stakeholders adding value all along the way.

The Process of Stakeholder Mapping

Every company is different, and so are the paradoxes leaders face. That means that every leader has to figure out the right process for stakeholder mapping, which will vary with the decision, the level or location in the company, and whether it involves only internal stakeholders or external. Here are practices we have found useful:[6]

- Identifying stakeholders and their positions
- Analyzing needs and behaviors
- Developing new strategies for stakeholders
- Devising new ways to interact
- Devising integrative strategies to manage paradox

Practice 1: Identifying Stakeholders and Their Positions

The first key practice is singling out the constituencies your company regularly influences or is influenced by—or more generally the constituencies the company affects or is affected by. Where do your company's interests intersect those of your stakeholders? In what fields of work or play do you and your stakeholders help or hurt each other? A complete stakeholder map makes explicit both the broad groupings and the particularly relevant subgroups—not just customers, for instance, but urban professionals in India, not just employees but finance staffers in regional offices.

Once you've listed your stakeholders, identify their interests and concerns. For example, at Colgate, CEO Ian Cook might include the concerns of a number of high-level stakeholders: Investors focused on financial performance, stock prices, and consistency in meeting growth objectives. Regulators responsible for product quality and maintaining ethical practices. Consumers wanting products to meet their standards, expectations, and needs. Employees seeking stable and fulfilling jobs. Customers—in Colgate's case, store buyers—who need to stock products that sell and perform. Professionals—dentists, veterinarians, and others—who use and recommend products for their patients. Each of these stakeholder groups has different needs and different expectations of Colgate. One of Cook's challenges is to ensure that all stakeholders' needs are met simultaneously.

That's the top level. The particularly relevant subgroups depend on decisions related to investment or marketing or product development. The professionals might include veterinarians concerned with specific pets. Colgate's pet food unit—Hill's Pet Nutrition—produces foods for prescription pet diets. Consider that some pet owners have cats troubled by hairballs that can cause choking, gagging, and vomiting. Colgate prescribes a diet and line of food that addresses that directly, and although Cook probably doesn't detail constituencies and concerns at that level, paradoxical problems may require just that kind of depth of stakeholder segmentation.

The result of the initial mapping of stakeholders is simple: A visual map and an analysis of how important each facet of a paradoxical issue is to each stakeholder. This is essentially an audit of stakeholder interests.

In the same way that managing paradox has become more complex, so has stakeholder mapping. Consider the medical device industry, in which we often consult. The most basic stakeholder question is a difficult one: Who is the customer? In the past, the answer was easy: patients and doctors. But now many players act like customers: hospitals, which have become centralized buyers; regulators, who weigh in on what can or can't be sold; courts and litigators, who decide risks of product liability; insurance companies, which decide what services deserve reimbursement. That makes mapping constituencies and analyzing the intersections of interest more difficult—and revealing.

Practice 2: Analyzing Needs and Behaviors

A second practice is gaining a deep understanding of stakeholder needs and behaviors. Most leaders go short on learning enough about their stakeholders to empathize with their point of view. You need to ask: How are people affected by my decisions on paradoxical problems? Am I sensitive enough to know what delights or dismays people about my actions? Do I have insight into their point of view so that I can reconcile differences? What are they willing to give up and what are their root desires? How could they change their behavior so they become more competitive or more cooperative?

Ed Freeman suggests an intriguing exercise. Describe your current stakeholders' behavior at the intersection of your interests. Write down a few bullet points. Then ask: How could that behavior change to help us fulfill our purpose? And how could it change to hurt us? The exercise yields four kinds of stakeholders: Those who can change their behavior to help you a lot or hurt you a lot. Those who can help you a lot but not hurt you (or hurt you more). Those who can hurt you a lot but not help you. And those who can do neither.

Freeman notes that you have to pay attention to the opportunities and risks in each case. As for risks, the people who are your strongest supporters are those who can often change the rules in a way to hurt you a lot but not help you much more. For example, if you drop your pension plan and reduce health care coverage, you could alienate loyal employees, badly hurting your ability to perform and attract talent. As for opportunities, counterintuitively, the people who are your critics are those who can often change in a way that helps you a lot but can't hurt you much (or hurt you much more than they already do). For example, long-time environmental activists can shift from antagonists to partners in changing your processes and products to give you marked competitive advantage in serving customers. Ironically, critics can help you most to co-create fresh actions to deal with paradoxical problems.

A deep analysis allows you to rationally reconcile differences. At one of our consumer-products clients, we consult with a top manager, Allison, who is in charge of global branding. She is responsible for strengthening, protecting, and evolving the global brand. She also has responsibility for marketing efforts to boost local sales from Hong Kong to Melbourne to Mexico City. She lives a paradox, a work life pulled in two directions, one for the good of the company and one for the good of local units. The pull is especially strong between the needs of unit heads in the developed and developing world.

The only way Allison can resolve the paradox is to understand the local stakeholders in the company—the marketing directors, general managers, and division presidents of country units. They do understand the importance of maintaining and strengthening the performance of global brands. Nevertheless, their primary objective is to focus on local needs and sales. Should they add sugar to make their product appeal more in India? Should they change the packaging? What type of product portfolio will work best in their markets?

Allison has to know what they can and can't do while protecting the brand and brand promise and while also meeting the needs of the local market and helping leaders meet their performance objectives. This means she has to help local units do two things: Create the marketing capability to sell products that meet the tastes of local consumers in the next three to five months—and stay firm on protecting global brand equity over three to five years. This juggling act is ongoing because the local markets are constantly changing—new competitors emerge, commodity prices change, regulatory hurdles appear. So she must be ever vigilant about the local versus global tensions.

Practice 3: Developing New Strategies for Stakeholders

A third practice is to develop strategies for creating more value with the help of stakeholders. We opened Chapter One with a story about Ron, the new chief operating officer of a media and technology company. Ron maneuvered himself into a battle with multiple internal stakeholders, to the point that he accomplished little—either for the company or for burnishing his reputation for results. Ron knew who his stakeholders were, but he failed to listen to or analyze their needs and behaviors. To him, the regional sales chiefs were simply a roadblock to his superior plans and stratagems for building market share with a smarter brand, new website, new loyalty programs, and new customer amenities.

Ron faced stakeholders whose support he initially took for granted—but when he angered them they hurt him badly. Ron finally succeeded by analyzing the needs and behaviors of these stakeholders and coming up with a new personal strategy to succeed—a strategy to communicate humility through listening and negotiating.

He had to come down from his perch of superior intellect and accept that others in his matrix organization had power and ideas of their own. He had believed that when he rose to a position at the top, he could control people by fiat. But in fact the reverse was true: The higher he went, the more dependent on others he became. His need for stakeholder mapping was intense.

Interestingly, one of the paradoxical elements embedded in the problem Ron faced was the contradiction between trust and change. The more Ron pushed his change program without buy-in from others, the more he damaged the organization's trust in his actions. Ron didn't initially grasp that he had to balance the quality of his ideas with the need for ownership of the ideas by his stakeholders. Had he practiced stakeholder mapping more explicitly, he could have pinpointed from the start the stakeholders whose support he had to maintain—and the strategies for doing so. Instead, he swiftly under-cut that support, and his efforts to repair the damage took six months of hard work.

The need for effective, thoughtful strategies is just as important when it comes to external stakeholders, whether they are in a position to help or hurt your company. Among the strategies effective with outsiders are changing the rules of the relationships, changing beliefs about the firm, trying to change the stakeholders' objectives, adopting the stakeholders' positions, and changing the forum and subjects of discussion.[7] As Ed Freeman points out, after the landmark settlement against the tobacco industry, the company leaders faced stakeholders who could hardly hurt them anymore. The companies changed the rules in different ways: Some took their critics' position that they had to reduce the harm done by their product. Others argued for more federal regulation and control.[8]

Practice 4: Devising New Ways to Interact

A fourth practice is to devise new ways to interact. Many of us assume we know other parties' viewpoints. But in decisions that affect people both inside and outside the firm, this is rarely the case. You need new ways for understanding needs, and this requires creating new opportunities, forums, and rules of interaction. How can you design a new process for interaction that brings out the most new material and perspectives for decision making? If business operates in an ecosystem, how do you involve the members of the ecosystem in the discussion? What is the right venue and process for co-creating new value for the whole system?

In one development, NGOs have taken the lead in bringing companies together from across industry to wrestle with the tough issues of climate change. CERES, the nonprofit founded after the Exxon Valdez oil spill, convenes eighty member companies to improve the firms' social and environmental performance. CERES members today come from many industry sectors, with companies ranging from GM and Starbucks to Bank of America and Exelon. CERES brings together leaders from the business, investor, and advocacy communities to exchange perspectives and enhance competitive advantage with sustainable strategies. This kind of venue, in which CERES will facilitate meetings between companies and institutional investors, did not formerly exist.[9]

In our consulting work, we help company leaders create new venues. We helped one large insurer, for example, meet directly with potential customers. From groups of people who signed up for focus groups, we identified those individuals who did *not* buy from the company but who bore no grudges against it. We then solicited their participation in deeper research, in which we asked them if researchers could talk to them individually in their homes. The researchers then spent the morning with customers, observing the customer's habits and asking about preferences. The researchers also happened to be top executives, who remained incognito. That allowed them to listen to consumers' concerns directly. They could hear firsthand why people spent money the way they did and why they chose not to buy from the insurer.

The giant brain of a company is only as smart as its capacity to collaborate. The brain comes from everyone reaching out and using each other's expertise in these different ways. In the past, leaders often communicated in a one-way fashion both within and outside the company. By jumping over the line to paradox management, leaders transcend this puzzle mentality, engaging more stakeholders and in turn enlarging the joint brain for greater achievements. The Internet and social media today provide added channels for conversation, allowing leaders to learn at Twitter speed.

As we mentioned in Chapter Six, Procter & Gamble pioneered the use of social media by putting some of its most vexing R&D challenges on the Internet for all to see and provide input. Nowadays, inventors and artists with a new idea rely on crowd-funding websites that encourage feedback and investments. Many large companies such as Nike use employee websites to seek input on human resource issues and even product development—asking employees for opinions and ideas about how to deal with new inventions, product ideas, or even policy issues. The Internet today allows the brain of a company to expand by incorporating many nodes of input from around the world.

Practice 5: Devising Integrative Strategies to Manage Paradox

A final practice is to devise new strategies that accommodate the behaviors, interests, and strategies of all stakeholder groups. For that, we circle back to our three mindsets: How can our joint purposes and values guide us to mutual value-creating actions? How can we reconcile our interests, as we might in a negotiation, allowing our principles to create win-win actions? Or how can we innovate to accomplish both of our objectives in new ways? This approach works just as well with people inside as outside the organization.

Consider the challenge facing large consumer goods companies. Although their products are ultimately used by the people who purchase them off the shelf, their customers are large retailers who resell the products to the public—companies such as Walmart, Target, Tesco, and Walgreens. Complicating their challenge is that these customers will also be offering competing products—Walmart sells both Coca-Cola and Pepsi, Colgate and Crest, Panasonic and Samsung. Competitive advantage will go to the consumer products companies that devise the best strategy for ensuring that both their needs and Walmart's are met. This is one reason why companies form dedicated teams of people to work directly with major retailers. PepsiCo has a team of people located in Bentonville, Arkansas, whose job it is to work full time with Walmart. Companies like PepsiCo want to be sure they develop strategies that are good for them and good for their customers.

A Basis in Trust

Senior leaders will always face contradictions, and they may believe they will always face the knotty task of trading off the interests of one stakeholder with those of another. Somebody will get short-changed. This presumption is the antithesis of mapping and managing for stakeholders. In the short term, leaders may indeed trade off one stakeholder's interests with another's—employee salary raises for continued investment in innovation, for example. This may stem from a reconciliation mindset at a time of pinched resources. But in the long term, the knottier task is to find the intersection of interests where the stakeholders together create more value than the company could on its own.

This requires ongoing stakeholder mapping—not just episodic or ad hoc. It also requires something else: a high level of trust by stakeholders in their leaders. In this respect, we cite an equation: Trust equals stakeholder orientation divided by self-orientation. Benefiting from stakeholder mapping requires subsuming your own agenda—an agenda encompassing both your ambitions for yourself and your ambitions for the company—within the agenda of all combined. Stakeholder trust grows in proportion with the numerator (the whole) and inversely with the denominator (the self).[10]

Johnson & Johnson is one firm that has long sought to practice this approach. Its Credo specifies that the company will serve not just customers but employees, communities, and shareholders. This gives J&J leaders the permission and space to talk freely about stakeholder issues without worrying about being biased in favor of one stakeholder group. The debate over access to care versus profits proceeds under this presumption. Do you give inexpensive access to a compound in some countries or maintain global pricing and hence profits? As at Johnson & Johnson, it is an ongoing debate. The company and its leaders know it will have to constantly recalibrate. But the discussion is valuable in developing leaders who can think and reason, which ultimately leads to alignment between the J&J Credo and decision making.

You have to have a lot of emotional intelligence to let go of the headstrong intellect that thinks of all actions in terms of profits and instead plays to the good of the entire ecosystem of stakeholders. This is where we come back to the importance of moving from an arm's-length mentality to an arm-in-arm or joined-at-the-hip mentality. If you're a leader of a firm like the former, you manage with all head, like the latter, with head and heart. In the end, if you're one of the latter leaders, you will better master the challenge of managing paradox.

Complete Leader's Checklist for Chapter Nine: Stakeholder Mapping

✓ Map the external constituencies your organization affects or is affected by. What are your intersecting interests?
✓ Determine how each stakeholder could change behavior to either help or hurt you. What are the opportunities and risks?
✓ Develop strategies for creating more value with the help of stakeholders. How can you use them as resources to change the rules of competition?
✓ Devise new ways to interact with stakeholders, including new venues and processes to encourage co-creating value.
✓ Use the three paradox mindsets to devise strategies to manage paradoxical forces of all stakeholders together.

10

Dialogue for Alignment

*The way of paradoxes is the way of truth. To test reality we
must see it on the tight rope. When the verities become
acrobats, we can judge them.*
—Oscar Wilde[1]

How do you get a team of top leaders to fully understand each other's
point of view? And to aim for the same targets and outcomes? You
often can't, at least not easily, especially if you're talking about a big
company. Even the best executives can't fully detach themselves from
their biases and personal motivations. The truth is, you can bring a
group of leaders to the trough of engagement with each other, but
you can't be sure they will drink.

That was the problem faced by Cameron Clyne, CEO of National
Australia Bank (NAB), a company we mentioned in Chapter Two.
Clyne sought to have his top leaders gain an enterprise-wide perspective, a viewpoint that would help them improve their management
of the company as a whole, as opposed to just championing its parts.
He had already tried changing everyone's goals and rewards to motivate them to align around a holistic view, but he was dissatisfied. Now
he was trying another tactic instead: dialogue.

By *dialogue* we don't mean crowded conference calls and e-mail
correspondence copying thirty people. We don't mean one-way communication of vision and goals from the boss to the troops. And we
don't mean horse-trading intelligence over the Internet. We mean
face-to-face, give-and-take conversation in which people have the
time to appreciate how the other participants think *and* feel.

Clyne was particularly interested in having his top executives align their views on resolving the tension between long-standing contradictory goals: investing to grow market share and saving to bolster the bank's balance sheet (capital ratio, funding ratio, loan-loss provision, and so on). When Clyne tried to gain agreement, his executives debated the issue, some arguing for cutting costs while others for investing in new products or capabilities. But they couldn't gain consensus, and Clyne had to make the decision himself.

The executives were trapped by their own perspectives, so Clyne took a chance. He paired executives who disagreed with each other. He asked them to retreat to a place away from the company office and develop a point of view that represented a third colleague's perspective—whether the colleague led personal banking, business banking, wholesale banking, wealth management, risk, finance, human relations, technology, or whatever. These were people who knew each other mostly from meetings. They didn't regularly walk into each other's offices or go to each other's staff meetings.

Not surprisingly, the paired executives returned with brand-new proposals—fresh, spontaneous ideas for tapping new market opportunities, new efficiencies in technology use, and new savings from sharing resources. Clyne had never heard these ideas before. Instead of the executives pressing him to make either/or decisions, they were proposing both/and ideas, in particular a more integrated banking operation. That's just what Clyne was looking for. And today, the bank's strategy prescribes a transformation from five operating units to a single integrated architecture with common services, common product platforms, single customer files, and a single back-end across the enterprise.

This came from executives' abandoning the habit of passionately advocating only their point of view—a first for the group. It also came from understanding underlying motivations—for example, that however much executives wanted the bank to succeed, they unconsciously had sought first to expand their own unit's control. And with better understanding of themselves and others, they could work together to come up with options they'd never considered before.

The first option is to teach others. This may begin with simply helping others see they are dealing with a paradox, and they can go beyond the either/or thinking that has driven their dead-end conversations. An executive at a leading technology company says, "What makes up a culture in technology are technologists. And they are binary thinkers. We have five thousand binary thinkers in situations that aren't binary. It's a challenge for me. How do you get them to think about the 'and'?" Awareness through dialogue that you're not dealing with just a puzzle is the first step.

A second objective is to solicit opinions and ideas. Many people today persist in thinking dialogue is a way to convey *their* message. But dialogue is a way to understand others' interests—and the reasons why they act as they do. We all have limited perspectives, and our ability to learn from others determines our ability to handle paradox successfully. Dialogue helps you elicit views in ways that make others feel safe, valued, and heard. One executive we know put together a cross-functional team to have a heart-to-heart discussion about the company's portfolio strategy. Although the executive didn't normally convene a team for this purpose, he decided to solicit views on synergies, pitfalls, paradoxes, and history. The dialogue allowed him to work out disagreements and create alignment. That in turn ended the problematical pattern of flip-flopping every month, which had been a reflection of lack of strategy.

A third objective is to challenge assumptions. Susan Scott, author of *Fierce Leadership*, writes, "The truth will set you free—but first it may thoroughly irritate you." You must be willing to examine your own assumptions, which may happen through challenges from others. You may find it hard to recognize the beliefs you're clinging to—"bigger is better," "inspect what you expect," "the boss decides," "take care of number one first," "facts trump feelings." Such unconscious assumptions often lead us to ignore a paradox or defend one resolution of the paradox and discount another. Jaap Jonkman, formerly vice president of talent at NAB, notes, "Under every argument there is an underlying assumption. [We need to] look at the subtext that [makes us think] we should be doing something one way or the other."

A fourth objective is cultivating and demonstrating empathy for others. We work with one global company in which the finance staff views the business unit leaders as spendthrifts who can't be trusted. The business unit leaders naturally see finance people as micromanaging control freaks. The CEO sees himself as the arbiter of constant conflict. We encouraged uncensored and open-ended conversation to help people grasp why other individuals defend their positions so passionately. Even if people don't agree, they can gain more tolerance and appreciation for alternative positions—and in turn integrate elements of them into their thinking. In many jobs, people limit conversations to their inner circle, which only entrenches a single viewpoint.

The final and overriding objective is to align interests based on a higher mission. You want this alignment whether you take a purpose, reconciliation, or innovation mindset. Bringing the conversation around to a larger aspiration can mitigate conflicts and break deadlocks. That's what helped Cameron Clyne jar his top leaders into recognizing that they had been too narrowly focused on partisan views. They could instead co-create something better.

Dialogue today has become a skill in decline. A number of factors seem to come into play. First among them is the speed of business and the distances that separate colleagues. Many people schedule their workday in fifteen-minute segments and interact with virtual team members around the world. They don't give priority to dialogue that helps the whole company. We worked with one bank executive who, in meetings of the top team, viewed his role as representing and defending his function, always subtly looking for an advantage. He described his role as similar to being a member of the U.S. Congress, defending states' rights against the encroachment of the federal government. He was thus unable to engage in conversation that didn't end up in debate, conflict, or superficial agreement to be undone by later actions.

Other factors that make dialogue hard relate to your skill. Some people don't or can't deal with the ambiguity and confusion a paradoxical problem poses. They fail entirely in jumping over the line when the conversation heads into gray areas. One executive says, "Some people are more intuitive and can act [on paradox] with incomplete information, but we aren't wired the same." Others remain so relentlessly logical and rational that they cannot get their minds around the notion of paradox. Still others simply tense up, and the tension triggers the derailing behaviors covered in Chapter Three—such as becoming distrustful or arrogant or volatile.

The Practices of Dialogue

Many books have been written on dialogue and conversations, but we highlight five techniques we use regularly to help clients resolve paradoxical problems through meaningful dialogue:

- Pose transcendent questions
- Facilitate role-playing
- Structure and monitor the conversation
- Provide 360-degree feedback
- Follow a framework

These practices are much more useful than unmanaged, free-wheeling discussions or brainstorming. We discourage those activities, as they often lead to recurrent debates with each side digging deeper into the ruts of bias.

Practice 1: Pose Transcendent Questions

You've probably heard the old joke: "What did the monk say to the hot-dog vendor? 'Make me one with everything!'" Keep that in mind when conducting dialogue. The vendor may be focused on the elements of dressing the dog. The monk (or leader) needs to stay focused on a more transcendent end point. Here are a few questions to that end:

What will our industry look like in five years, or twenty years; how must our organization change given the future state; what is our long-term strategy?

What is the bigger issue than the paradox we're experiencing?

What's important to our customer (patient, consumer, user), and what's crucial for other stakeholders?

What are competitors doing that we can learn from?

How would we like things to look in the short term, say, three years; what do we need to do to achieve that three-year picture?

Practice 2: Facilitate Role-Playing

As in the case of Cameron Clyne, a common way to deepen dialogue is to have people play different functional roles—finance chief plays marketing boss, say. Another form of role-play is illustrated by an exercise in a recent executive program we ran at one of the world's largest banks. The CEO asked us to write a case depicting a recent acquisition, a transaction that triggered a clash of opinions over the risk versus return of the joined banks. In discussing the case, the executives each took on the role of a different colleague.

The resulting role-play was illuminating. The same debate from a couple of years earlier replayed itself, when the CEO had to simply overrule people with strong opposing views. This time, however, people couldn't summon the same certainty of argument or passion of conviction, because they could see more sides of the debate. The CEO concluded the exercise by saying, "Why can't we do this in our regular executive meetings?"

Practice 3: Structure and Monitor the Conversation

In free-form dialogues, people's emotions get in the way of thinking in purpose-driven, balanced, or innovative ways. If you're the leader, you need to separate emotions from issues by structuring conversations: Acknowledge up front that everyone has a different personal purpose and values. Make sure the participants all have a chance to talk about their own hot-button issues. Allow people to express their self-interest, reasoning, and motivations. Clarify how different people are fierce proponents of clashing views. Recognize your own emotional attachment to a position. Then seek alignment.

Note that *alignment* does not mean unanimity. People will disagree to the end on some issues. But you can bring about consensus in spite of disagreement. You need to show you want to hear people's views and demonstrate that you are willing to vet the views and put them in context of a purpose, reconciliation, or innovation mindset. With alignment in hand, even people who agree to disagree can then look for actions that strike everyone as acceptable.

Think of monitoring as a separate task in a structured dialogue. Keep track of the emotions attached to arguments. Breakthroughs tend to come on the wings of rising emotions. We have found that the first sign of conversational progress may be an expression of gratitude, shared laughter, or empathy. One executive we interviewed noted that when her team began to make progress, people would distance themselves from the talking points they carried to the meeting. "It's as if they lean back from the table or push their notes away, and then I know they're moving to a higher level of discussion." Whatever outward gesture you observe, seize the moment and seek alignment.

Practice 4: Provide 360-Degree Feedback

Many times people honestly don't know what roadblocks they have thrown in the way of the dialogue. We worked with one investment banker who regularly assembled first-rate, multimillion-dollar private-equity deals. We first performed a 360-degree feedback exercise for him, polling colleagues, reports, and clients to understand his work habits and behaviors. We found he considered his most productive time as that spent building ties with CEOs, studying financial statements, and nurturing outside relationships. He didn't spend much time with staff, gaining alignment in conversation. As a result, his staff ran in different directions, developed conflicting views, and spent time on the wrong things. The simple unveiling of this managerial blind spot allowed him to discover what should be his most productive time: dialogue with staff, deepening understanding and aligning their efforts.

Practice 5: Follow a Framework

Conversations to manage paradox can be tricky to orchestrate. People get embroiled in heated, circular debates, and they end up talking about a wicked paradox as if it were a tame problem they could solve like a math equation. To improve the dialogue in the face of paradoxical problems, we find it helpful to work with frameworks to clarify concepts and get everyone to understand the dynamics at play.

We often team up with colleagues Mickey Connolly and Richard Rianoshek, coauthors of *The Communication Catalyst*.[2] Connolly and Rianoshek cite three axioms of human communication:

- All humans have purposes (things they're for), concerns (things they're against), and circumstances (constraints within which they have to work).
- When people perceive you are unaware of or opposed to their purposes, concerns, and circumstances, they will resist, producing waste.
- When people perceive you are aware of and sensitive to their purposes, concerns, and circumstances, they will communicate and collaborate, producing value.

Connolly and Rianoshek advise leaders to "look for the intersections" (Figure 10.1). Alignment comes from the intersection of *your* view, composed of your purposes, concerns, and circumstances; *my* view, composed of the same for me; and the facts or circumstances that will guide our actions. As the leader, shape the conversation so that people all express their own views and identify common ground. With a shared view of interconnections, you can then turn to ideas for managing the paradoxical problem at hand.

Another framework we like to use addresses the fact that no action to resolve paradox lasts for long, so as circumstances change, and as you learn from experience, you have to adjust. That brings into play what Connolly and Rianoshek refer to as the Cycle of Value (Figure 10.2). The Cycle of Value shows how learning occurs, and it

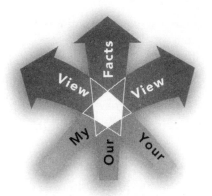

Figure 10.1.   Find Intersections for Alignment
Source: Mickey Connolly and Richard Rianoshek.

Figure 10.2.   The Cycle of Value
Source: Mickey Connolly and Richard Rianoshek, *The Communication Catalyst* (Chicago: Dearborn Trade, 2002), 19.

is readily applicable to the cyclical nature of managing paradox in an ongoing, iterative way. Creating cycles of value is the goal of any leader using conversation to address paradox. Ideally, the rate of learning is equal to or greater than the rate of change, which today means revisiting paradoxes and revising action multiple times a year.

Figure 10.3.   The Cycle of Waste
Source: Mickey Connolly and Richard Rianoshek.

Connolly and Rianoshek note that leaders require vigilance in detecting signs of the Cycle of Value's evil twin, the Cycle of Waste (Figure 10.3). Whereas the Cycle of Value has at its core alignment of purposes, concerns, and circumstances, the Cycle of Waste begins with disagreement. This disagreement stems from the either/or position—an entrenchment inside of *my* view and the unwillingness to explore *yours*. Disagreement yields defensiveness, and the accompanying emotions spur participants to destroy the validity of the opposing point of view. This happens all the time in companies that face paradoxical problems but cannot acknowledge them. It is especially common in matrix organizations, where the opposing forces of paradoxes enter almost every key decision, and leaders have to work hard to keep the Cycle of Value turning, one round of alignment after another.

We recently worked with one client that was attempting to install a major human resources system throughout the world. Up until the launch of the system, the finance and human resources directors did not agree on who should have responsibility for payroll and did not fully trust each other. Much of the planning for the "go live" day was accompanied by either/or disagreement. Predictably, the system launch did not go well. Many employees did not receive their paychecks, the database was not sufficient to make accurate decisions, and multiple system glitches compounded the problems. People started pointing fingers at each other, and the company spiraled into the Cycle of Waste. A fact-finding study was launched, key people lost their jobs, and the lessons of the cycle of waste were costly for everyone.

Patience, the Virtue in Dialogue

One of the biggest challenges for leaders conducting dialogue is that it requires patience, which takes time, and in the interim you risk having people accuse you of indecisiveness. This is a hazard you should brace yourself for. Rest assured, though, that most such criticism is premature. Time after time, we have orchestrated conversations that evolve to entirely new places after six or nine months. That comes from multiple conversations, feedback, reflection, and growing engagement in managing paradoxes the right way.

We worked with leaders of a large pharmaceutical company who faced the need to cut costs by $4 billion while boosting revenue 10 percent. Predictably, finance people talked only about cost cutting, commercial leaders about hiring more sales reps, and R&D leaders about investing more in research and development. The leadership team deadlocked on an overall plan early on, but six months later, after much rumination about possible options, they agreed on a balanced approach—combining multiple sales channels, eliminating select sales reps, using social media to connect with doctors and patients, and eliminating some work tasks while redesigning others.

What often takes time is overcoming the natural human belief that other people know most of the things we do. All of us accumulate knowledge or experience that causes us to assume others have accumulated the same. It's a human weakness. In what has become known as the "tapping experiment," conducted at Stanford University by Elizabeth Newton, subjects were designated as either "tappers" or "listeners." The tappers were asked to list twenty-five songs they believed the listener would likely know. They were then told to tap out the rhythm of the songs so the listeners could identify them. Before starting, the tappers predicted what percentage of songs the listeners would get correct. As it turned out, the tappers wildly over-estimated at 50 percent. Listeners could identify only 2.5 percent of the songs.[3] The lesson: When you know something, it's hard to believe other people you work with don't know it as well.

Put another way: When the music is so loud in your own head, it's hard to imagine that others can't hear the same tune. That's why patience matters. Dialogue over time helps people hear each other's music.

One final tip for helping this process along. It comes from John Gottman, a marriage counselor who wrote *The Seven Principles of Making Marriage Work*. Gottman coined the "the 5 to 1 ratio," arguing that in successful relationships, people have five times as many posi-tive interactions as negative ones. Moments of agreement, expres-sions of gratitude, asking questions, being nice, showing empathy and kindness—these all occur five times as often as the moments of criti-cism, anger, and hurt feelings.

Gottman's findings can be extrapolated to the workplace. Interviewed by *Harvard Business Review*, Gottman noted: "You could capture all of my research findings with the metaphor of a saltshaker. Instead of filling it with salt, fill it with all the ways you can say yes . . . 'Yes,' you say, 'that is a good idea.' 'Yes, that's a great point, I never thought of that.' 'Yes, let's do that if you think it's important.' You sprinkle yeses throughout your interactions—that's what a good relationship is." What Gottman is describing is the importance of affirmation—an essential tool in finding the intersection between people's values, concerns, and points of view.

And this furthers alignment more than many other techniques, bringing people to the point of understanding what they're all *for*. But this won't happen unless you, as a leader, set the emotional tone for it, allowing people to air what they're against but seeking align-ment for larger, shared objectives and actions. Sometimes this is the reason people believe dialogue is only a soft, feel-good, time-eating procedure to buy peace among adversaries. But affirmation helps surface the best options and leads to better decisions, execution, and results even in pressure-cooker situations.

We wish the world at large would value dialogue more, and not downplay the value of person-to-person conversation in resolving contradiction. Too many of us retreat into social cocoons with people of similar minds and passions. We fail to look out the window to take in diverse or adversarial opinions and instead keep our gaze facing into a mirror reflecting only people like us. In work, in politics, in international relations, this only adds to partisanship. Consider the deadlock in your workplace, in your community, among your elected officials. Dialogue in search of alignment could unlock the solutions needed to solve the paradoxical problems of our time.

You have to wonder: What if everyone jumped over the line together? But of course that doesn't often happen. People don't have the training, or the inclination. People may start with "yes, that's a good idea," but they soon sense a battle and say, "no, that's a non-starter." Peace turns to poison. And that brings us to the next and last of our tools for managing paradoxes: dealing with conflict.

Complete Leader's Checklist for Chapter Ten: Dialogue for Alignment

✓ Initiate dialogue to explore personal biases, assumptions, perceptions, and ideas, using empathy to understand polarized positions.

✓ Align viewpoints by posing questions that transcend everyday differences, for example, asking for a view of the industry ten years hence.

✓ Ask people to play the roles of their antagonists to help them internalize other sides of the debate.

✓ Structure and monitor the dialogue, to prevent emotions from creating conflict and derailing alignment. Try 360-degree feedback.

✓ Use a dialogue framework to find intersections of views; create a "Cycle of Value" (constructive) and avoid a "Cycle of Waste" (destructive).

11

Quelling Conflict

Resilience is based on the ability to embrace the
extremes—while not becoming an extremist.
—Gary Hamel[1]

Among our clients are leaders of the most elite businesses in the world, but they sometimes call us in over the most elemental of problems: People fighting over a decision. Often a top-executive team has begun a dialogue to solve a divisive and paradoxical problem—only to regress to shouting at each other. Insults fly, trust drops. We can often guess the root cause when we get the phone call: They have unwittingly let the contradictions of paradox spark a personal feud.

An example: We received a phone call from a CEO who had hired an executive as a change agent. The new man was charged with guiding a hidebound culture that valued control, consistency, and closure toward one that championed innovation, agility, and responsiveness. The CEO complained, however, that the change agent had run amok, shaking people's trust with uncomfortably fast, reflexive, and creative behavior. The change agent, in turn, complained that the CEO was trying to pressure him into getting in line behind the cultural behaviors he had hoped to transform. We ended up in the middle of an emotional spat.

Another example: We received a phone call from a CEO who had launched a new business to replace an old one. The old business produced a flood of cash, the new one not a trickle. The old-business leaders raved about their sales and loyal customer relationships, while the new-business leaders raved about their new technology, new industry, and their role as leaders of the future. The new-business leaders unfortunately couldn't resist: They floated jibes that made people in the old business feel put down, second class, and producers of products on the road to obsolescence. We again ended up in the middle of a fight—along with the CEO.

The truth is, people who are fighting in organizations—however professional they profess to be—don't restrict themselves to the issues. In many cases, they begin thinking and acting as if their rivals and nemeses are deluded and wrongheaded. They may seethe at their adversaries' barbs and misdirection. In no time they begin telling themselves things like "Don't let the idiots get you down." They believe they are fighting the fight their job requires. They are good soldiers. They fully intend to win out over the idiots, as they have many times before. They are not losers.

However much leaders talk about win-wins, when caught off balance in the ambiguity and contradictions of paradoxes, they often default to behavior that suggests they think of business as a zero-sum game. Although they may engage in dialogue to gain alignment, they let emotional issues hijack the conversation. Indeed, although dialogue should help everyone figure out what the group is *for*, personal conflicts drive people into focusing only on what they're *against*—and they're usually against each other.

This is a time when you need another tool for advancing the decision process—conflict management. On skilled executive teams, the contradictions of paradox don't necessarily lead to conflict. Leaders recognize paradoxes and the related contradictions early on. But on many executive teams—like the ones we've just introduced—people either don't recognize paradoxes or ignore them as they focus on perceived personal slights. Leaders can prepare to deal with this barrier to decision making with conflict management. Even if you cannot see the sparks of conflict in time to snuff out the fire, you can help people move to the real paradoxical issue fast enough to ensure a timely decision.

The Value of Conflict Management

Personal conflicts that stall decision making in the face of paradoxical problems are more common than many leaders would like to let on. The reason is simple: In the vast majority of organizations, leaders lack one critical characteristic of a high-performance team: putting difficult issues on the table. Organizations today stress team play and consensus. Conflict is seen as a weakness. So leaders pretend to get along, even when they seethe inside. They bury conflict, which smolders slowly and persistently. That is why complete leaders prize the skill of conflict management.

When conflict flares up, you may not even know the root cause at first. You may think you have to sort out a set of opposing values, differences in long- versus short-term thinking, divergent views of priorities, a mismatch of loyalty to stakeholders, or some other personal belief or behavior. But the truth is that contradictions give rise to the conflict, as people cling to a preferred solution to paradoxical problems with no right and permanent answers. This was true of the CEO who brought in the change agent. It was also true of the CEO trying to launch a new business.

At such times, you need to draw on the third of the three elements of a complete leader: guts. Chapters Six through Ten discuss how leaders need the head and heart to devise ways to solve paradoxical problems. This chapter turns to the courage to use conflict management to defuse disputes and break the paralysis that stalls decisions. The contradictions of a difficult paradox may have sparked disputes, but personal differences fuel them. You have to have the courage to put issues on the table and then manage the conflict that inevitably arises.

Ironically, the most common spark for conflict, obvious as it may seem at this point, is failing to recognize paradoxes in the first place. Oblivious to paradox, people let self-interest and preferred loyalties deflect their attention away from wrestling with key contradictions. They get caught up in interpersonal frictions that escalate the conflict. Nobody distinguishes between resolving the contradiction and resolving the conflict. But this is like getting caught up in a food fight—arguing over who threw the first drumstick—and leaving underlying tensions unaddressed. You have to have the wisdom to see through the noise of the conflict and call a paradox a paradox, essentially our message in Chapter One. You have to separate personal issues and business contradictions.

The way you perceive the clash you're facing isn't just an issue of semantics. It governs your advance toward a final decision. If you perceive a debate as a personal, verbal war, you and your adversary react like hostile parties, committed to winning and walking off with the spoils. If you perceive the debate as a dialogue to find an appropriate resolution to a paradox, you and your adversary mutually see an opening to put down your weapons and smoke the peace pipe, finding a reasoned, equitable way to gain alignment. You see that the conflict is a sideline skirmish—albeit a skirmish you may have to play to some denouement.

As we've found repeatedly in our consulting work, when leaders grasp this point, you can practically hear a huge sigh of relief from all involved. To repeat in a different way, when you're talking about contradiction, you're talking rationally about difficult core issues, without personal emotions. When you're talking about conflict, you're talking about personal issues in which people have personal stakes and get personally emotional. Note another difference: You can resolve personal conflicts permanently. You can never permanently resolve any contradiction, as the opposing forces remain and require permanent management.

So contradictions by themselves are not—and do not create—conflict. It is the people facing contradictions who manufacture the conflict, whether intentionally or not. Conflict is disagreement that seems as if it can only be resolved by one faction or person winning. Paradox, on the other hand, involves two or more opposing positions that must be managed without losers and winners. This isn't to say that conflict won't come up when contradiction has to be managed. It almost always does. And it's not a sign of failure. It's inevitable when people work together, especially in matrix structures, which almost by design force people to walk on each other's toes. But you can then use conflict management as a tool to prevent interpersonal quarreling from swamping a rational decision process.

As we mentioned in Chapter Three, if you're rewarded by your organization or driven by your constituency to advocate for one position and fight the opposing one, the step to seeing the paradox behind your conflict may not come easily. In professional service firms, for instance, there's always an ongoing fight for who owns and serves the client. It may be well and good for a firm to encourage client sharing, but if managers are rewarded based on how many billable hours they can charge a client, they will probably find themselves in conflict with other managers who are eager to bring some of that billing into their group. Leaders need to read such situations to discern the paradox beneath. They can then use the energy attached to spirited disagreement to fuel a higher-level discussion on resolving the contradictions.

A variety of side issues trigger conflicts when the real issue at hand is resolving a paradox. One is that a proposed solution may threaten to make some people feel rewarded and others punished. Another is that the solution may threaten to undermine people's ability to perform their role (as finance person or business-unit leader). A third is that an attractive alternative may lead to one person controlling the outcome, leaving a colleague feeling powerless. Still another is that a resolution may seem to reaffirm one person's set of values and violate another's.

The change agent we mentioned earlier seemed to violate the CEO's values. The old-business leaders we mentioned believed their roles were threatened and demeaned. The executive we called Ron in Chapter One tried to control the way regional salespeople managed a new marketing campaign. People on the receiving end in such situations can become indignant and vengeful—and cease to collaborate on efforts to manage the paradox at hand.

Consider the example of two leaders we will call Tim and John, two banking client representatives in the same district, focused on high-net-worth clients. John and Tim argue over how much information they will share about their sales districts. As a private banker, John believes he leads a team with deep client expertise and that the client focus his team brings requires them to build relationships encompassing confidential financial planning. As a commercial banker, Tim feels that everyone in the district banking team should provide the maximum amount of information about their clients and their needs, and that many of John's private clients who own businesses would benefit from what the commercial bank offers. John doesn't see the point of sharing information unless the private-bank team identifies a client need—at which point he will make a referral to Tim.

On the surface, it may appear as if they just don't like each other or they are fighting over functional turf. However, at the heart of the conflict are the opposing goals of transparency versus privacy and enterprise versus business unit. Tim believes that greater transparency improves a team's functioning. John, on the other hand, has his own way of dealing with his clients and feels it would be a violation of trust for him to spell out the details of what his clients disclose to him in confidence. Tim believes that the bank owns all clients, and that key leaders should have access to relevant information about all bank clients.

Who's right? They both are. What they are trying to resolve is a conflict stemming from the contradictions of a paradox, two equally valid principles regarding information sharing. How they resolve this conflict—this interpersonal tension—will determine the degree to which they are able to establish a collaborative working relationship. Neither realizes that their relatively straightforward disagreement is more complex than it appears—that even though they are taking opposing positions, both are right because transparency and privacy both are valid and reasonable stances.

To rise above such partisan positions requires consciousness and will. Whether to help yourself or help others, you need to be aware of the negatives of becoming mired in conflict and the positives of identifying the contradictions of true paradoxes that have no single, long-term answer. And you need to have the guts to raise the question, even when forces in the organization may encourage a conflict. Every competitive leader likes a good battle, but inside an organization, complete leaders keep their eyes on the long-term, productive work of resolving contradictions, even as they do the emergency work of putting out the fires of personal conflict.

The Practices of Conflict Management

Many authors have written about conflict management, but in our experience, we have found six practices especially useful in helping leaders resolve conflict stemming from paradoxical problems:

- Recognize roles
- Acknowledge others' views
- Bring people into the same room
- Invoke the customer
- Start at the point of agreement
- Use a system of conflict management

Just to be clear, we are not talking about conflict as it refers to disagreement over how to handle the tasks required in managing a well-understood paradox—tasks like interpreting facts, debating alternatives, devising policy, and so on. This task-based conflict is a good thing. Research shows it often leads to deeper and more deliberate decision making. One study even found what might be called the "Goldilocks effect": A moderate level of task conflict on work teams stimulates the most innovation—more than too little conflict (which causes inactivity) or too much (which causes a slowdown in processing and evaluation).[2]

We are referring instead to conflict in relationships, or personal clashes stemming from differences in style, values, preferences, and loyalties. These conflicts are the skirmishes on the sidelines of the main event, not the main event itself. No doubt, you've witnessed or been part of a conflict that escalated in ways that hurt your relationships and the ability of your team to get things done. You were so confused, angry, or resentful—or two people who reported to you reacted in one of these ways—that it was impossible to see beyond the conflict and manage the underlying paradox. When you focus on how another person is treating you, you fail to break through to the real work of paradox management.

Practice 1: Recognize Roles

The first practice for defusing a conflict is to recognize the roles people are playing. Ron Heifetz, co-founder of the Harvard-Kennedy Center for Public Leadership, advocates depersonalizing conflict by understanding how people often respond to roles rather than personalities. In such instances, leaders can remind people that roles are the primary catalyst for their negative feelings. This sometimes helps them step away from the personal response to an unpleasant exchange and view it with greater objectivity. The disagreement on an issue may persist, but considering the dispute in larger terms can provide the emotional distance to glimpse the paradox behind the dispute.

Consider the conflict between Sally, the head of finance for one of the largest companies in the world, and Josh, a business unit head. Sally, who sees herself as responsible for creating a world-class global finance organization, wants to upgrade the finance person who works in Josh's group. She suggests one of her global finance staff—someone she likes and thinks would do well working with Josh's team. Josh resists her suggestion, preferring to name his own finance person, someone he knows well and who has experience working within his business unit. (Complicating matters, Sally and Josh see themselves as competitors for the CEO slot a few years down the road.)

Though the decision seems straightforward, Sally and Josh have a number of heated exchanges. They can't resolve their different views on the subject and finally appeal to the CEO to make a decision. This is the point where we were called in to help resolve the conflict, and we could see that each was most concerned with fulfilling the responsibilities of the roles assigned to them. In other words, they were arguing from the point of view of their corporate positions. Josh felt the business unit had the right to make the decision, and he needed someone who understood the business unit's needs and financial planning system. He also needed an individual with an aggressive, short-term focus on the numbers required to deliver the results for his business unit.

Sally felt the corporation had the right to make the decision, and she needed a finance person who would fit with her mandate to build a world-class global finance function that would be more strategic and better serve the long-term interests of the organization. She thought Josh's candidate lacked the broader organization perspective and the ability to understand the type of finance talent needed in the future for a changing organization in a challenging industry.

A tug-of-war based entirely on one power center vying with another ensued. Beneath this conflict, however, both executives were missing the basic paradox: how to serve the opposing interests of the enterprise and the business unit. While they were arguing about who owns the talent in the company and who gets to manage it—very common conflicts in companies today—the paradox was a more complex right-versus-right issue. The upshot? With our pointing out the role conflict, and asking Sally and Josh to take a step back and consider what the finance requirements for the organization were for the next five years, the two executives found common ground.

The question was really this: What type of CFO would the company need in the future? What kind of finance person would help Josh's business unit achieve the results he (and the company) wanted as well as help the enterprise grow in the way the CEO intended? Josh and Sally both realized neither of their candidates fit, and instead they should look for someone who could do both—help Josh achieve his short-term business results and have the potential to provide the company with the financial acumen it needed in the future. With the conflict over roles defused, they agreed they needed to search outside the company to find the right person for the job.

Practice 2: Acknowledge Others' Views

This second practice is the simple tactic of acknowledging other people's views. When people feel their point of view is being ignored, they become entrenched in their positions. As basic as this problem may seem, people get surprisingly angry when they believe nobody cares enough to hear them out. When leaders spend enough time listening to show someone they do care, they can quickly defuse situations and allow both sides to be more thoughtful and adaptive.

This doesn't mean we suggest you help people collaborate by just listening. Allowing people to air their views, as in noncritical brainstorming, works poorly. Give-and-take is necessary. We believe some groups miss this fact. In a study that asked three groups of participants to suggest ways to alleviate traffic congestion in the San Francisco area, the group that brainstormed with strict instructions not to criticize one another's ideas offered fewer innovative ideas than the group with instructions to debate ideas as they came up. The brainstorm group fared little better than a control group, which received no instructions at all on how to conduct its discussion. In total production of solutions, the debate group produced significantly more ideas than the brainstorming group. The conclusion? "The basic finding . . . is that the encouragement of debate—and even criticism if warranted—appears to stimulate more creative ideas."[3]

So acknowledging people's views in a discriminating forum remains imperative for moving swiftly toward innovative decisions. Shweta Kurvey, an executive we work with, encourages her employees to consider both sides of the equation by asking questions. "It validates and acknowledges what they [the team members] feel," she says. "Can you help me understand the pros and cons of the approach?" By expanding her teams' views through the use of questioning, Kurvey can better manage paradox by both recognizing people's ideas and allowing her teams to consider differing viewpoints.

Practice 3: Bring People into the Same Room

The third practice is to bring people face to face to build trust. This may again seem awfully simple, but many leaders don't use it often enough for a number of reasons: the fear that putting feuding parties together will make matters worse; the scientific-management mentality that eschews messy conversation for analytic decision making; the logistics of getting people in different divisions, offices, or countries into one room; and the trend toward virtual meetings. Although face-to-face encounters can be challenging to manage when heated conflict has already erupted, you should consider them absolutely necessary to build trust between feuding parties.

Once you get people in conflict into a room, you can facilitate the building of trust by asking the following questions: What's right about each of your positions? What are we both trying to accomplish? What is our overarching purpose? Ask questions that help people find mutual interest and alignment. The majority of people are capable of gaining alignment if they are face to face and a paradox-savvy leader grounded in establishing trust facilitates the session.

One leader we know at a professional services firm routinely fired off e-mail notes criticizing the work of his people and colleagues. He would sit at his computer late at night and create these brilliantly crafted analyses of what others were doing wrong. The missives became legendary in the firm, referred to as Sandergrams (fictitious name). Though he was a high-level leader, he relied on giving feedback this way for several reasons, but mainly because he was an introvert, intimidated by interpersonal conflict, unable to confront people face-to-face. He found e-mail correspondence safe.

The problem for a leader handling conflict this way is obvious. First, he created a culture of fear in which people dreaded receiving a Sandergram. Second, one-way e-mail communication is the worst way to resolve complicated differences of opinion because in most cases it exacerbates conflict. We worked with him to eliminate the Sandergrams and get people with whom he had a conflict into the same room with him. They then talked through their differences, relying on the give-and-take normally required to achieve understanding and ultimately a resolution. He became anxious and fearful before every conflict-resolution session. But in the end, he was able to resolve differences in a much healthier way.

Practice 4: Invoke the Customer

The fourth practice to help break an angry deadlock is to bring in or bring up the customer. Given that everyone's purpose is to create value for customers, invoking customers and their unmet needs can put everyone's gripes and grudges in a new light. While this can be done in a variety of ways, the most effective is often meeting with customers—getting customers and people from outside marketing or sales functions in the same room. In most companies, many insiders have never met a customer face to face. With customers in the picture, people feuding within the corporate family can then better see their joint goals, set partisan issues aside, and see the contradictory forces of the paradox they need to manage.

Think back to the GlaxoSmithKline executive trip to Kenya discussed in Chapter Four. Though all executives differed in their viewpoints upon departing from London, they found common ground as they talked with prospective customers in the challenging health care environment in East Africa. The experience helped executives who were battling over various decisions talk about their disagreement in new ways that reflected their observations of serving people too poor to pay developed-world drug prices.

Practice 5: Start at the Point of Agreement

The fifth practice is to start the discussion among warring parties at the point of agreement. Instead of having the same old argument a hundred different ways, seek confirmation where you can find it. Agreement might be over team purpose or a particular organizational goal. Finding congruence or alignment—what Mickey Connolly, mentioned in Chapter Ten, called "areas of intersection"—gives people confidence they can work out other differences. Connolly notes that people typically look for intersection in their view of results. But many times this is where conflict is fiercest, and people need to back up and look for more basic areas of agreement—typically, related to larger purpose. If the team can agree on "where we're headed," it can then have a more effective discussion on "how we'll get there."

At BlackRock, the world's premiere asset management firm, the chief investment officer in one of the businesses has nine portfolio managers reporting to him. Each has a different set of funds with a different set of issues. Invariably, their businesses have different needs that can often bring them into conflict, or at least drive them to run their businesses independently. The CIO believes, however, that the funds have enough in common that they create more value as a community than alone. So he brought the team together for a conversation about what they shared and how to achieve similar goals without sacrificing the autonomy that all needed to run their businesses. They all then recognized the value of bringing in the best talent through a strong recruiting program. They also recognized they had more power if they went to the talent market together rather than separately. So they agreed to beef up their recruitment efforts, coordinate their plans, and combine forces—an initial bridge to iron out additional differences.

Practice 6: Use a System of Conflict Management

The sixth practice is to understand people's personal preferences and behaviors when faced with disputes. The Center for Conflict Dynamics has developed a model for identifying constructive and destructive responses to conflict that can be useful in the hand-to-hand combat that sometimes accompanies efforts to resolve a paradox. The center divides responses into active and passive, both of which are required when managing paradox (Table 11.1). Its assessment tools and developmental suggestions are beyond the scope of this book. But the classification of responses shows that people all come at conflicts differently. It also shows we can equip ourselves with a range of techniques to reduce the probability of differences devolving into interpersonal conflicts. Or if they do, to taking the wasted emotions linked with differences out of the dialogue and staying focused on the task.

Managing paradox requires the use of both active and passive techniques depending on the situation. The key is that leaders must understand and favor constructive instead of destructive factors. For example, leaders need to be sure to keep people in the game who might otherwise avoid conflict by retreating to their offices. They also

Table 11.1. Responses to Conflict

	Constructive	Destructive
Active	• Perspective taking • Creating solutions • Expressing emotion • Reaching out	• Winning at all cost • Displaying anger • Demeaning others • Retaliating
Passive	• Reflective thinking • Delay responding • Adapting	• Avoiding • Yielding • Hiding emotions • Self-criticizing

Source: Adapted from Mark H. Davis, Sal Capobianco, and Linda A. Kraus, "Measuring Conflict-Related Behaviors: Reliability and Validity Evidence Regarding the Conflict Dynamics Profile," *Educational and Psychological Measurement* 64 (2004): *Version 4*, Table 1, page 711.

need to help people maintain their focus until they get at the underlying paradox rather than constantly capitulating in hopes that the conflict will go away.

We know one leader who went overboard in his efforts to placate his boss, and as a result, lost the respect of his people for not dealing with the contradictions of the larger paradox. Another executive we worked with couldn't understand why people were afraid to give her bad news, even though every time they did she flew into a rage. The conflicts she created by her behavior prevented progress in collaboratively managing paradox.

The creators of the CCD model encourage people to understand their "hot buttons," the types of people and behaviors that can upset or irritate them like no others. Some of us get our buttons pushed when an individual is untrustworthy, unappreciative, self-centered, or aloof. Being aware that these traits can spark a fire and developing strategies for managing them can help defuse a situation and move the conflict from the personal focus to the real issues of the paradoxical problem.

In one of our engagements with a big accounting firm, we brought people from tax, audit, and consulting practices together using the CCD model. We were trying to find a common purpose, look at ways to resolve differences, and increase everyone's revenue. The model helped everyone understand the many ways to resolve conflicts and view their hot buttons. When someone acts in an unpredictable way, or abrasively, what impact does this have on you? It can elevate emotions so that you don't even see facts to resolve the conflict at hand. The model helps reveal how business issues can become personal issues. In turn, it helps leaders nip the turn toward the personal in the bud.

Leading Beyond Conflict

Conflict won't go away; it will always be a barrier to decisions on paradoxical problems. People simply don't instinctively look for ways to reconcile two valid but opposing positions. Instead, they look for rival leaders who block their ambitions. That's human nature. Even if people do dimly understand they're walking into a personal-conflict trap, they walk anyway, fearful of losing if they go backwards. They are unwilling to sacrifice their personal position. This happens even if they sense the larger, long-term upside of compromising and yielding to another point of view. Of course, this same pattern appears in homes and communities. Consider the furor that arises in community after community about what food will be served in school cafeterias.

Unfortunately, the sequence of events often runs this way: The paradox presents contradiction, the contradiction is interpreted through the lens of human self-interest as a clash of personal interests, the clash enflames emotions. If you're the one to intervene, you try to keep combatants from beating each other up, and you focus on cooling things down. But beset by an atmosphere of wrath, stress, and confusion, you are expected to resolve the conflicts with biblical acumen. Are you ready with the wisdom of Solomon, the patience of Job?

In companies, the hostile atmosphere, the need to satisfy vocal constituencies, the expected speed of decision making, the stress— they all act to drive leaders' focus away from the opportunity. You then have to get all parties to step back and see the conflict from a utilitarian perspective. And that poses the challenge: To advance the decision process, you have to transcend the conflict. That's what we helped the CEO and the change agent do. That's also what we helped the leaders of the new business do. Without the added tool of conflict management, collaborating to solve paradoxical problems would not be possible.

With this chapter, we end our discussion of the five tools for managing paradoxes. By using scanning, scenario thinking, stakeholder mapping, dialogue, and conflict management, you will be well equipped to engage your head, heart, and guts to serve as a complete leader. In the next chapter, we cover one element that remains to help you jump over the line: self-development. If you want to manage paradoxes adroitly, you need to look inside yourself to spot weaknesses that block your full transformation to complete leadership.

Complete Leader's Checklist for Chapter Eleven:
Quelling Conflict

✓ Defuse conflict by seeing your antagonists as diligently playing their roles with benign intent, as opposed to vexing you with their personalities.

✓ Acknowledge other people's points of view, lest you worsen the conflict by signaling that you neither listen nor care.

✓ Bring people face-to-face in the same room to build trust. Don't let fear of feuds, historical antipathies, or heightened emotions deter you.

✓ Invoke the customer and start a conversation by identifying what everyone agrees with.

✓ Use a conflict-management system to identify and mitigate destructive behavior, especially when hot buttons inflame emotions.

PART FOUR

YOUR PERSONAL CHALLENGE

12

Developing Yourself

The curious paradox is that when I accept myself just
as I am, then I can change.
—Carl R. Rogers[1]

Chapter One started with the story of Ron, the COO of one of
the world's best-known brand-name companies. He mistook paradoxical problems for puzzle-like ones, attempting to exercise complete control to the exclusion of regional managers. In the process,
he missed the value of using collaborative tools, in particular stakeholder mapping. In this chapter, we highlight another lesson: To
manage paradox in collaboration with others, you have to be able
to manage yourself.

It's worth taking another look at Ron's story, emphasizing this
personal-management angle. Ron was acerbic, highly intelligent,
quick, and had a great track record. He routinely came up with a
string of knockout marketing ideas. What he wasn't so good at was
getting others to align with his ideas and buy in to them. People were
intimidated by his genius and unable or unwilling to rally behind his
initiatives. In fact, they called him the "brilliant asshole."

He was not aware of how others saw him. He believed that, while
his style was sometimes abrupt, others could see that the ends he
accomplished more than justified his aggressive means. A 360-degree
feedback exercise, however, revealed that people were so intimidated
they refused to challenge him or offer ideas that they believed would
be shot down. They believed he wouldn't listen to other points of

view and was operating on false assumptions, riding roughshod over their positions. People said they'd like to tell Ron: "You're not as good as you think you are, and no one is signing up for what you want them to do."

Ron's failure to manage himself is all too common among senior leaders. Too often, people do not adequately develop the interpersonal skills for collaboration, do not get beyond the thirst for control, consistency, and closure, do not work to mitigate their personal derailers, and do not overcome the human reluctance to act in the face of ambiguous, paradoxical problems. If you're a leader, you may be outstanding at accomplishing tasks, but you may have neglected your ongoing development as a paradox manager.

Upon getting feedback, Ron realized that it didn't matter if his ideas were great if nobody wanted to pitch in to make them succeed. He resolved to change. In the weeks following, he made a conscious effort to ask people for their opinions; to listen seriously and respond to what they had to say; to back away from his impulse to believe he was right when he doubted others; and to change his mind in front of other people. His colleagues began to respond to him in a new way. Many people were surprised that beneath that haughty exterior beat the heart of a genuinely nice guy.

Getting Fit as a Paradox Leader

Despite being elevated to jobs where problems are full of contradictions, many leaders initially lack the mental and social muscle to function as paradox leaders. When they worked their way up through lower levels in their organizations, they did not deal with the daunting challenge of complex paradoxes. How about you? Are you fit to work with a team collaboratively to solve paradoxical problems? Have you personally developed yourself to manage in a world where paradoxes make up most of your difficult decisions? And if not, what do you need to do to become fit?

A picture of what's required emerges from a study of twelve top management teams across nine diverse business sectors. Researchers

Wendy Smith, Andy Binns, and Michael Tushman sought to identify the behaviors of teams that managed paradoxes successfully. They found four characteristics that led to success: First, the teams experimented with new behavior they believed would be needed to lead and manage their organization in the future, and not just today. Second, they built an overarching vision that encompassed both traditional and new ways of operating. Third, they learned and debated how to operate in a more complex environment—they held seminars with outside experts, scanned the environment for signs of changes that would affect their businesses, debated the relevance of new ideas, and stretched themselves to think paradoxically. Fourth, they deliberately sought conflicting perspectives and engaged in conflicting dialogue.

These findings corroborate our experience, and we believe the four characteristics stem first from the ability of individual leaders on the team to release their firm grip on control, consistency, and closure. Team members cannot fruitfully collaborate if someone always insists on controlling the outcome while excluding others. Nor can they do so if someone insists on acting consistently with old mental models even as times change. Nor can they act effectively if everyone demands closure on problems that need frequent revisiting. They can succeed only when they work among others who know that control, consistency, and closure work well for straightforward, puzzle-like problems, but are wholly inappropriate for the paradoxes of work and life.

Another essential factor in managing paradoxes is trust. John Veihmeyer, CEO of KPMG, notes, "It is not always the speed and ability to make a decision [that matters], but how much . . . the people you need to be involved in the decision trust and respect each other." You can think of trust as the glue that holds people together. Its absence makes it virtually impossible to explore unknown or untested ideas, or to collaborate when tension ramps up in dealing with complex challenges.

In practice, we believe the most visible factor that sets apart developing from developed paradox leaders is the learning that comes with dialogue, debate, and experimenting, as the Smith, Binns, and Tushman research suggests. John F. Kennedy said it best: "Leadership and learning are indispensable to each other." Developed leaders are eager to acquire knowledge, even if it contradicts their beliefs. They don't retain control of the conversation; they extend control to others. They try to stretch themselves in new ways. We suggest asking yourself the following questions to get better at dealing with paradoxical problems:

- How comfortable are you with uncertainty? Do you rush too quickly to find a solution to complex problems? Do you exhibit the patience required to find the right approach?
- Can you take action in the face of ambiguity and avoid paralysis when the solutions to your problems are not obvious?
- Do you frequently solicit ideas and opinions from individuals outside your function? Your organizational level? Your organization? Your industry?
- When heated arguments take place on your team, do you take a step back to help people find areas of alignment? Or do you wind up taking sides and trying to win the argument?
- When was the last time you changed your mind after hearing someone voicing a position that you hadn't considered before?
- How fast do you form opinions and make decisions? Do you jump to conclusions early or after a period of discussion, thought, and questioning?
- Do you spend enough time requesting feedback and reflecting on what you hear?
- Do you try to cut through the clutter of complexity and ambiguity by finding the simple, straightforward course of action?
- Are you aware of your weaknesses and how they they're related to your strengths?
- When you take a position on an issue, do you consider the downside of the position and the upside of the opposing points of view?

- Do you ever admit you're wrong? Are you able to veer from a stance you've taken for months or even years when you see a better option?
- How often do you encourage people to come up with fresh alternatives to the conventional wisdom or the standard answers? Do you have tolerance for taking the less-traveled path?
- How often do you use contrarian thinking? Do you ever consider doing the opposite of what's expected? How many times have you actually done the opposite?

These questions help you assess your vulnerability, openness, consciousness, and willingness to move outside your comfort zone for fresh thinking and approaches. It's easy to fool yourself into believing you're a learner. Most people would never acknowledge that they don't learn from their experiences. In most companies, few people see themselves as rigid, closed off to fresh thinking, or unable to take risks and embrace the unknown.

We once worked with a company where the biggest problem was often people's need to be right. After going through the strategic planning process, leaders ignored challenges, refused to look at new data, and were unwilling to say they might have made some mistakes. They became stuck on the puzzle side of the line, shoes glued to the pavement.

People can unwittingly close themselves off to new ideas, the opinions of others, and feedback that doesn't conform to their own views. This stems from their listening only to their own inner circle. Or it results from failing to cultivate a network of people who can provide the insights and perspectives necessary to understand how paradoxes can be managed. All of us operate out of at least some allegiance to our existing positions. Many of us aren't even aware how we reflexively shut down people who beg to differ.

Becoming a complete leader who is skilled at managing paradox takes time. The following points summarize what we've suggested so far—behaviors to practice over an extended period. These will expand your capacity for leading groups in managing paradox. Note how straightforward they are—and yet endlessly difficult to execute:

- *Practice control selectively:* When you take control, ask yourself: Would I get better results by giving it away?
- *Recognize foolish consistency:* Be consistent in your words and actions, but understand when it's time to change your mind based on new information or changed circumstances.
- *Tolerate a lack of closure:* When you encounter a paradox, tell people at the start that closure is not the goal. Instead, the goal is to understand what action to take now, while expecting to revisit the challenge over time.
- *Invite honest feedback:* Becoming aware of how your approach to paradoxes is seen by others can give you insight on how to manage them more effectively.
- *Solicit the greatest diversity of input possible:* Too many leaders rely on a tight-knit coterie of trusted voices. As David Jensen, a research and educator on leadership, says, "A closed mind is a wonderful thing to lose."
- *Reflect on what you hear:* Give yourself time and space to absorb what you learn. Ask yourself: "What if the people I disagree with were right? How would things play out? What do they know that I don't?"
- *Change small behaviors:* Start small and build up to a more developed leader one habit at a time. Use a "test and learn" process.
- *Focus on building and maintaining trust:* Hugh McColl, the former CEO of Bank of America, often pointed to the "paradox of trust" for senior leaders: "When you are the top, you must earn the trust of people while you, on the other hand, must extend trust to others."[2]
- *Become comfortable with impossible organizational goals:* The appearance of unachievability often stems from paradox. For instance: Reduce expenses by 25 percent and grow revenue by

25 percent. To prepare for this, move to a continuous reinvention mentality.

- *Reconcile fact-based and intuitive judgment:* With today's time pressures, leaders must combine analytics with intuition. You will never have all the data to decide analytically. Invoke the 80/20 rule.

The litmus test of leaders who have developed a full set of paradox management skills is how they manage the contradiction of valuing people versus valuing performance. Most organizations give both top priority. But if you always value one, how do you always value the other? In particular, when do you remain loyal to people and when do you let them go or decide you can give them the promotion they want? How do you resolve the case of a person who no longer fits or performs?

Here are two stories to illustrate the difficulty:

- Danielle is an executive with a large corporation, and people love to work for her. She sticks by and sticks up for her people under almost every circumstance. Everyone knows that she is fair, goes out of her way to help her people learn and grow, and has empathy to spare. Yet Danielle also is incapable of getting rid of the deadwood on her team, of which she has accumulated plenty over the years. She accepts every excuse in the book for failing to complete an assignment on time or on budget. Consequently, she is a poor implementer—she isn't trusted with getting things done. Her inability to manage the paradox of people and results makes her what we call a Beloved Loser.

- Jack is a senior leader who is loyal to his people to a fault—a major fault. He promotes individuals he is closest to, regardless of whether their abilities and achievements make them right for positions of increased responsibility. At the same time, he champions meritocracy. He lobbies HR for a better system that rewards talent rather than seniority, yet he fails to see how he doesn't walk the talk. The paradox of loyalty versus fairness escapes him. For this reason, he is what we call a Hypocrite; even the people to whom he is loyal and promotes see him that way.

Leaders who fall into the category of Beloved Loser and Hypocrite have not learned how to manage paradoxes. They must understand the forces they are trying to reconcile and make decisions that show they are able to work through these types of contradictions.

Overcoming Derailers

Among the most personally sensitive aspects of self-development as a paradox leader is learning to overcome derailers, the obstacles mentioned in Chapter Three. Under stress, we all can express destructive behaviors that undermine our effectiveness and sabotage our aspirations. Instead of exhibiting calm and steadiness under pressure, we become volatile and overreact to the slightest setback. Instead of appropriately challenging people's suggestions, we become distrustful and suspicious of their motives. Instead of being careful, we become overly cautious and hesitant to make any decision when an action is called for. See Table 12.1.

Derailers are not learned behaviors. They are ingrained personality traits. You're stuck with them. When stress rises, when anxiety hits a threshold, the impulses from your lesser self overpower the impulses from your more rational, mature, and relaxed self. You screw up, and you may not even realize you've done it. But those around you, whether your loved ones or your business colleagues, observe the derailment as clearly as a train going off the tracks. Your constructive behavioral train vanishes into an abyss, and it takes the passengers with it. Your colleagues, your reports, your family—they all get tossed around in the derailment.

Ron clearly exhibited one of the derailers: arrogance. This is a common one among hard-charging, competitive people. If you're one of them, you may recall times that, under stress, you let your natural confidence go over the edge to become hubris. In Ron's case, he required feedback to become acutely aware of the need to be more inclusive and open. He moderated his overweening style, determin-

Table 12.1. Leadership Strengths and Derailers

A strength . . .	. . . when taken to an extr... is . . .
Responsive	Volatile
Skeptical	Distrustful
Careful	Overly Cautious
Self-Sufficient	Aloof
Questioning	Passive Resistant
Bold	Arrogant
Creative	Mischievous
Expressive	Melodramatic
Imaginative	Eccentric
Conscientious	Perfectionistic
Dutiful	Pleaser

Source: David Dotlich and Peter Cairo, *Why CEOs Fail* (San Francisco: Jossey-Bass, 2003), xxii.

ing when to push his own ideas and when to exercise patience in bringing people along. By loosening his control and extending trust to his people, he became more effective.

In our coaching work, we run across people with the full selection of potential derailers, which show up both in their work and in their personal life. As another example, consider the case of Allison, a top operations executive at a global consumer brands company. Allison (introduced in Chapter Nine) had long run an operating division. She took satisfaction in delivering ever-better results, higher sales, better profits, and a solid pipeline of product improvements. If you gave her a defined task over a short period, she delivered every time. She was a star.

But Allison's boss moved her to a new job. As head of global branding, she became responsible for guiding, protecting, and strengthening the brand around the world. This took her from a world with few paradoxical problems to one full of them, a world where she often struggled with marketing directors and division presidents with demands to change products in ways contradictory to the global brand promise. Prompted by the added complexity and ambiguity, her stress and anxiety levels spiked, and her key derailer—being overly cautious—began to take a toll. To every new proposal, she would say, "yes, but . . ." For instance, the company had suffered a disastrous product launch in a new market five years earlier, and she would not agree to entertain a proposal in that market again. Her fear of failure started to overwhelm her ability to lead.

If you're caught derailing for this or another reason, what do you do? For most people, rehabilitation starts with awareness. Once you realize that you have a derailer or two—everybody does—you can build into yourself a sort of alarm system that starts flashing its lights and blaring its horn when you react to a paradox in a destructive way. Becoming aware, in some ways, is an easy first step, even though you—like Ron and Allison—may have to have someone help you. The next step is to acknowledge and accept the derailers. They are, after all, who you are. This can be hard, because the derailers are often strengths taken to an extreme—volatility, for example, is essentially responsiveness and enthusiasm on steroids.

But taking this step is easier when you know you're in good company: Everyone has a shadow side. Counterintuitively, acknowledging weaknesses and vulnerabilities, along with pinpointing how they hurt our effectiveness, actually makes us stronger in the eyes of others. After all, our colleagues and family already know what our derailers are. Only the act of admitting them may surprise people, since the nature of the derailers will be old news. We had one leader return home from learning about his derailers in one of our workshops, agog with his new insight, and his wife said, "I could have told you that over a cup of coffee."

Self-knowledge gives us authority and credibility—in addition to a better ability to manage paradoxes. We may have a cherished self-image. But we need to have compassion for ourselves and the vulnerabilities we wish we didn't have—and then embrace a modified, more vulnerable self-image.

Another key to managing derailers is knowing when they emerge. People differ in what stresses them. Some people have difficulty dealing with workload and deadlines. Some get overly anxious when they face a huge decision. Others have trouble working with people in authority. Still others react badly in the face of interpersonal conflict. Leaders need to know what their own hot buttons are and what situations push them over the edge before they can develop strategies for preventing derailment.

As another example, we coached the CEO of a large retail chain. He was a smart, highly analytical executive who loved data. His ability to absorb huge amounts of data and devise winning strategies had enabled him to turn around several companies. But he took his data hunger to an extreme, and it became a derailer of a special kind: His people feared approaching him without being prepared with encyclopedic detail, combat-ready for an intellectual competition with the boss. His people started to develop a sort of bunker mentality, which he regularly reinforced by telegraphing them the clear message: "You can never have enough data."

We introduced him to this derailer, and although he couldn't change his personality, we suggested he add new behaviors to mitigate his weakness and stop paralyzing the action of his staff. At a staff meeting, he opened up to his people: "I am more and more aware that my style may be hurting our effectiveness," he said. "I'm conscious that I overanalyze things to the point that you spend too much time preparing for me and too little time acting with your team. Tell me how you experience my behavior, and point out to me next time we meet the effects it has on you. I don't know how I should change, but I'd like to go on a journey with you to make myself better."

This was a remarkable multi-step process of acknowledgment, acceptance, and pinpointing how the derailer hurt other people. Two months later, his people said they were seeing a change. His initiative in asking for feedback on his behavior was, again ironically, helping him build his reputation as a leader. The parallels to your personal life are probably plain. You grow in the eyes of others as a strong human as you grow in self-knowledge, acceptance, and skillfulness as a collaborator.

Allison's development traveled along a similar path. With a better idea of her weaknesses and the knowledge that she could sabotage her own success, she positioned herself to push innovation rather than suppress it. She created special forums focused specifically on innovation, and she invited the company's best thinkers and outside experts to engage in open dialogue about extending product lines, discovering new products, and entering new markets.

Sometimes, in the case of overly cautious people, we simply ask, "What are you afraid of?" Or "What's the worst that can happen?" We then explore the consequences of not acting. In the end, leaders like Allison learn to recognize both assets and liabilities, which frees them to build on the assets and mitigate the liabilities. That's what Ron did—and he earned the rewards not only in helping the company deliver better results but in helping himself become a congenial colleague.

As an aside, note that stress doesn't just trigger derailers. It creates a barrier to raising people's consciousness of paradoxical problems in the first place. Because people face so many demands today, many leaders operate for days on end feeling overwhelmed. Their feet are held to the fire to achieve ambitious objectives, and at first glance, they think that managing paradoxes is tangential to their main work—especially for newer leaders who are less aware of paradox than more senior ones. When you talk to them about learning to manage paradox, they may look at you like you're oblivious to all the stress they're under. As Figure 12.1 shows, there is a fine line between learning and stress. You need to stay below the line, lest derailers get the better of you.

Overcoming Hindrances to Action

Learning to manage yourself as a paradox leader also means understanding your mental barriers to taking action—barriers that persist even after you make a decision. Some of these barriers are none other than derailers. A prolonged search for perfection, for example, can lull you into putting off action for months. A fear of failure or an

Figure 12.1. The Fine Line Between Learning and Derailing
Source: Adapted from John L. Luckner and Reldan Nadler, *Processing the Experience: Strategies to Enhance and Generalize Learning*, 2nd ed. (Dubuque, IA: Kendall/Hunt, 1997), 20.

excessive focus on what could go wrong, as in Allison's case, can become an unlimited excuse for delay. And the need to please others and avoid conflict can bring action to a standstill. By dealing with these derailers, you can help prevent them—and not just keep them from bringing things to a halt.

The danger of decision deferral is greater than it seems. The risk is not only that you will lose the time spent dithering. You will fail to act altogether. Research confirms something we all learn from experience: The more we put something off, the less likely we are to do it at all. A now classic experiment by psychologists Amos Tversky and Eldar Shafir demonstrated in the 1990s that, in effect, haste *prevents* waste (or at least timeliness does). They offered three groups of nearly sixty students each either five days to complete a questionnaire, three weeks, or no time limit. In return each student would earn \$5. Sixty percent of the five-day group responded, but only 42 percent of the three-week group—and just 25 percent of the indefinite group. The students were being offered easy money, but as Tversky and Shafir wrote, "Many things never get done not because someone has chosen not to do them, but because the person has chosen not to do them *now*."[3]

More recent research by a group of German researchers modeled data from a consumer survey of the German cell phone market. Consumers in this market were offered more than seven hundred plan options (of phones, fees, services, and price structures). The study looked at the effects of number, complexity, and comparability of features on people's behavior. The results revealed the source of consumers' tendency toward paralysis in decision making (that is, not picking a plan, delaying picking a plan, or sticking with the one they already had) as uncertainty over which alternative is best and "anticipated regret," or worry that you'll kick yourself later for making the wrong decision.[4] In our experience, uncertainty and anticipated regret influence not just coming to decisions on consumer choices but acting on paradoxical problems, owing to the much higher level of complexity and ambiguity.

Just knowing about the human tendency to defer decisions can help you get beyond it. We advise leaders to use another aid as well: an expanded circle of trusted advisers. If you keep the responsibility of pushing the start button all to yourself, you may come up short on the confidence to do so. But if you act with the backing of collaborators, you can move ahead more decisively. That said, in today's fast-moving world, you also have to learn to trust your instincts. Often you don't have time for an extra round of data gathering and review, in which case you need to remain mindful of the need to push aside the forces that encourage procrastination.

Along with deferring decisions, people are prone to inaction because of two other common biases. One is the omission bias, whereby people interpret the negative consequences of an event as less harmful if someone did not take (or omitted) action than if someone did take (or committed) action.[5] This bias operates even if we are aware of it. One study found that people hesitate to vaccinate a child even when the probability of the child getting the disease far exceeds the probability of death from the vaccine. The authors extrapolated these effects into the business world: "Consider a manager faced with a decision between investing in a new technology and sitting on the sidelines. Research suggests that investing and failing is more risky to the manager's career than failing to invest in a technology that proves successful elsewhere."[6] In both judgments of ourselves and of others, we are harsher when a bad outcome results from doing *something* than when it results from doing nothing.

Another strong determinant of failure to act is the status quo bias.[7] This bias refers to people's natural preference for the current state—when it is included as an alternative—even when they believe it's not necessarily the best choice. In addition to avoiding anticipated regret, psychologists speculate that the status quo bias arises from people's aversion to loss and the comfort they derive from having a familiar state of affairs.[8] People might also prefer the status quo because they feel less reason to justify their decision and accept accountability.[9] It's easy to recall instances in both work and private life where we stuck with the status quo, even though we somehow knew it wasn't the right alternative. Leaders need to beware of this.

Adding to the complexity of making the right decision is the tendency toward overconfidence. Most people have much greater confidence in their decisions than the facts would suggest. Leaders consistently overestimate their ability to succeed, whether making an acquisition, launching a new product, entering a new market, or picking a new member of their executive team. This tendency, documented like other biases we have mentioned in Daniel Kahneman's *Thinking, Fast and Slow*, bedevils even the best leaders. This is yet another reason for being inclusive when it comes to bringing others into your decision-making process, testing assumptions, and encouraging people to challenge your point of view.

The lesson is that acting to manage a paradoxical problem demands not just skilled decision making, but the courage—we have been calling it *guts*—to make things happen. Nobody is programmed to rush out and manage paradoxical problems, given they are so enmeshed in ambiguity. In fact, we could argue that we are actually programmed *not* to act. In the case of someone like Allison, this demanded that she overcome the programming of derailers as well as biases toward hesitation. Allison was a swift actor when her job was more defined, as when she was handed quarterly targets by the CEO. But when her challenge switched to handling the contradictions inherent in strengthening regional marketing needs at the same time as the global brand, she faltered.

One interesting factor that governs whether we give the final push to acting: general action and inaction goals. Experiments show that when people are primed to act, they often do so. In one set of experiments, people were exposed to a prime (a stimulus outside their awareness) in the form of a word game with either action words (for example, *go* and *active*) or inaction words (for example, *stop* and *rest*). The experiments were designed to induce actions as diverse as drawing, exercising, and political participation—and they did so, but only for the action group. Other experiments show that people primed with action words become more goal-oriented and more satisfied in completing goals.[10] We can infer that leaders play a key role in motivating others to action not only by their behaviors but also by doing nothing more than using action-related words more frequently when they communicate.

We can't help but refer back to a factor from Chapter Three that figures strongly in the hesitation to act displayed by many leaders in public life: the desire to appear consistent. We have argued (along with Emerson) that consistency in action, as opposed to consistency of purpose, can be destructive. The media and politicians, however, seem to assume the opposite. The press lampoons every possible inconsistency by our leaders. This contributes to the erroneous notion that changing your mind is poor leadership. Unfortunately, too few people distinguish between the consistency of purpose Emerson praised and the consistency of action he ridiculed. Leaders in all positions have an obligation to make the case for—and act on—this distinction. Until then, we will be haunted by the corpse of consistency, which discourages us from breaking from the status quo even when the wicked problems plaguing society demand it.

Spreading the Skills of Paradox Management

As you learn to manage yourself as a paradox leader, you owe it to those around you to spread the personal and collaborative skills widely. If you have not created an awareness of paradoxical problems at all managerial levels, right down to first-line supervisors, your people will become ensnared in conflicts without realizing why. They will default to either/or mindsets, and they will make bad decisions. This can turn people into victims and blamers. Confused by complexity and contradictions, people become passive: "There's no way I can win no matter what I do," they say, and lapse into indecision and inaction. They may also lash out at the company in frustration, blaming management for their bewilderment: "If senior leaders could just get their act together, I wouldn't have this problem; if they could just make things clearer, I could figure out what to do."

But of course things won't necessarily get clearer, not if it involves the persistent ambiguity of paradox. The only way to assuage hard feelings will be to help people understand that the forces of paradox demand that people value flexibility and open-ended problem solving. This is of course difficult if people remain confounded by the contradictions, angry at the inconsistency, and uncomfortable with the lack of closure.

Recently, in a major global health care products manufacturing company, we worked with a group of fifty high-potential leaders on developing enterprise leadership. We asked them each to describe in advance the enterprise challenges they faced. Their narratives, written independently, all described similar paradoxes. "How can we centralize in order to have the best possible service model at the best possible cost across the globe, while making sure we stay decentralized to bring the best solutions and price to all geographies?" "How can we bring affordable solutions across the lifespan of an individual, and in both developed and developing markets?" "How can we defy gravity and find $30 billion in new growth from new products while maintaining our core business?"

We pointed out to these leaders that these challenges cannot be addressed solely by a CEO or senior team. They require continuous reinvention and innovation by many people down through the organization. In other words, "it takes a village." It is imperative that leaders use multiple techniques to spread the skill of paradox management to their teams and organizations. This requires sharing the paradoxical challenge, role modeling, transparency, engagement, and training. Senior leaders need to communicate to young leaders the realities of paradoxical problems so developing leaders can grapple with the opposing forces within the safety of a development process.

The training program should follow from the skills and abilities we have already covered. First, if you're a top leader, you need to resist the impulse to deny paradox. You can't give in to the naysayers, who will paint your efforts to grapple with paradoxes as too complicated for others to understand or appearing weak and wishy-washy. People often glibly dismiss the existence of paradoxes for the sake of looking smart or decisive. Don't let them.

Second, you need to build and encourage a culture that embraces transparency, diversity, and reflection. As a leader, you need to model behaviors in which you encourage open conversations, include outsiders in discussions, and digest feedback from both inside and outside stakeholders before acting.

Third, you need to foster learning in yourself and others. As one executive told us, "Sometimes my role is education in order to manage paradox. . . . I believe in meeting people where they are and bringing them along. People may not know what they don't know."

Fourth, you need to reward effective paradox management—give encouragement, bonuses, and raises that reinforce the management of long-term contradictions, not just short-term moves to solve problems of the moment.

Fifth, you need to expand the use of the five tools we have covered: scanning the environment, scenario thinking, stakeholder mapping, dialogue, and conflict management. Most companies use these tools too little, because people see them as soft. But they are the tried-and-true implements in the toolbox of leaders who run high-performance companies that manage paradoxes to their advantage.

Fact is, you can simplify problems full of contradictions to the point where you create black-and-white choices. But that creates a dangerous illusion for employees, as if paradox doesn't exist at all. Instead, you should consider starting a conversation about paradox and keeping it going. Giving it a name—labeling what happens when managers are torn by contradictory forces—is a great starting point for awareness and reflection. It also helps people articulate their concerns in useful terms—so they're talking about managing paradox rather than solving problems.

As an example of the importance of spreading paradox management down through the ranks, consider our work with a major European technology company. After interviewing the top thirty people, we learned that the company faced a common paradox: how to build new businesses while maintaining the old ones. Both new and old demand cash. Both new and old demand management and R&D time and effort. The company was under intense pressure, however, because Chinese competitors had cut its margins from 20 percent to 5 percent. There was no time to lose.

The leaders had tried to refashion sales incentives to get people to sell new products and services, where margins were higher. But many people kept selling the old products, because familiarity made them seem a safer bet. Our advice was this: Don't leave managing the paradox to the people at the top. Educate everyone about paradox and let leaders down through the ranks manage it in the best way for their situation. Today, the company is embedding an understanding and the language of paradox at all levels of the organization. Leaders at all levels realize there is no quick fix to competitive challenges, and they must engage in building a better, more adaptable company that is sustainable over the long term. Customers will then pay more for new forms of value.

Western companies should see paradox management as a strength—the ability to adapt quickly and choose ever-changing ways to manage contradictory forces. True, paradoxes are messy. If you're a fastidious leader, you will be tempted to sweep them under the rug of corporate tidiness. But people in Western companies will be open to do the opposite, giving Western firms one distinct way to compete with growing Chinese competition.

The Complete Paradox Leader

What is the core secret to leading a company, business, or team faced with paradoxes? At the highest level, it means acting with a mixture of head, heart, and guts: Being analytical when you need to. Responding to human feelings and motives when you collaborate. Summoning the courage to act when challenged by both personal hindrances and perpetual ambiguity. This is what the three mindsets and five tools help you do, and this is what makes a complete leader today.

Without this, the analytical guru like Ron will fail. The soft-hearted people person like Danielle will stagnate. Gutsy autocrats who represent battlefront-style leadership will succeed only on occasion. In today's world, the people who flourish will bring all their paradox-management capacities together, working collaboratively with others to find fresh ways to resolve contradictions in an ever more complex world.

Above all, successful leaders will see paradoxes as opportunities instead of barriers. To be sure, we've all grown up in educational and business institutions that taught us to solve puzzle-like problems. We have learned to know them and master them. We feel comfortable as we take control, exercise consistency, and find closure with such problems. But complete leaders will move with energy beyond tame puzzle-like problems to the wicked paradoxical ones. They will jump over the line to make a difference in a world of uncertainty and ambiguity. They will not retreat from the challenge or give in to feeling depressed by the difficulty.

Of course, paradox management is not an end in itself. It is only a means to an end: Creating a nimble organization, an adaptable organization, an organization that succeeds where others ossify with outdated decision-making capabilities. When you get beyond thinking of paradoxes as illusions, and you master their mysteries with humility and energy, you will see them as the crucible for solving today's hardest problems. Organizations full of paradox leaders— people who can bring head and heart and guts into problem solving— will be the makers of our future. As Niels Bohr said, "How wonderful that we have met with a paradox. Now we have some hope of making progress."[11]

Complete Leader's Checklist for Chapter Twelve:
Developing Yourself

✓ Commit to lifelong learning, experimenting, dialogue, and behavioral change that take you outside your comfort zone.

✓ Cultivate awareness of your personal derailers, acknowledge them, and develop strategies to mitigate them. Self-knowledge gives you strength.

✓ Recognize your personal hindrances to taking action, overcoming human tendencies to defer, do nothing, and choose the status quo.

✓ Prime yourself and the people around you to act through the power of suggestion and exhortation.

✓ Spread the personal and collaborative skills of paradox management down through the organization, using role modeling, engagement, and training.

CONCLUSION

Managing Personal and Public Paradoxes

*I would rather be a man of paradoxes than
a man of prejudices.*
—Jean-Jacques Rousseau[1]

By now you might be thinking we have left a burning question unanswered: What makes someone a natural at managing paradox? Early in the book, we mentioned that one-third of leaders have no ability to see or manage paradoxes. Another third try to manage them but in a muddled way. And a final third are naturals. So where do you place yourself? And could you be a natural?

We must confess, we haven't done a study to establish what makes a natural. But we are certain a study would show that naturals come to grips with paradoxes in all parts of their lives. In the home. In the community. Within themselves. They don't pay attention to the paradoxes at work and ignore them everywhere else. And because they see and act on paradox in every walk of life—without thinking differently in different roles—they are better leaders.

Recall the executives from GlaxoSmithKline who took the trip to Kenya. Every night, they gathered and talked about their experiences. To be sure, they discussed the big picture of doing well by doing good—using the company to improve the lives of those in different parts of the world—but they also reflected on their own values and personal choices. One, almost unable to speak after seeing the ravages of malaria among patients on a hospital ward, resolved to have his family and children benefit at some point from similar eye-opening travel. Wrestling with the obvious paradoxes such experiences pose allows you to better deal with many gray areas in life. And that makes all the difference in skillful leadership.

In part that's because the paradoxes in the gray areas of everyday life mirror those in the office: how to work in the interest of yourself *and* the group, taking control *and* giving control, accepting individual accountability (ownership) *and* team accountability (ownership), practicing confidentiality *and* transparency, acting spontaneously *and* acting with plans. Using introspection to resolve these contradictions in your own life develops your skill and perspective for resolving them in the workplace.

We believe three particular personal paradoxes require resolution if you hope to function effectively within your organization. Confronting them and working your way through them gives you an increased capacity for managing in the short term and long term, developing people and increasing profits, and dealing with other paradoxes you and your employees will face.

The first is money versus meaning. The search for financial reward *and* life purpose mirrors the search in the organization to fulfill profit goals *and* corporate purpose. How you resolve one affects how you resolve the other. You might assume that many people see no paradox between money and meaning—the search for growth or profits is all there is. But we find that everyone struggles with this contradiction. At BlackRock, for example, people work in an industry that often pays outsized salaries and eye-popping bonuses. But leaders at the financial management firm still work in their own minds for meaning. While they earn money for the business, they also earn plenty for investors—firemen, teachers, and others on pensions. And they are proud they didn't fail these people during the 2008 financial crisis.

Because of that financial crisis, massive layoffs, and plunging assets, many people deferred their search for meaning while struggling to maintain their income and meet their obligations. Nonetheless, the search for meaning does not go away. Enjoying a meaningful life while also having material comfort is not a destination but a journey.

And during certain periods of one's life, or during certain cycles of the economy, one or the other becomes predominant. This illustrates well why every paradox demands constant revisiting.

The second personal paradox is the search for personal recognition versus enterprise success. You will always find your desire for personal accolades and achievements pitted against your willingness to sacrifice recognition to help the organization meet its goals. The question is this: How aggressively do you pursue your personal ambitions? How do you balance your desire to get ahead with your desire to serve the larger cause of the organization (or your function or team)? Are you willing to make sure customers are satisfied and their needs fulfilled, no matter who gets the credit? When should you cease being a collaborator? When are you too selfish?

Despite the opposing forces, you can find a way to act so that you strengthen the organization while also strengthening your personal portfolio of achievements. When you get a raise or a promotion, you will feel a bit hollow if you have not earned them after resolving the contradictions of self versus enterprise to your satisfaction. You may also find that over time, if you are not emphasizing the enterprise over your own ambition, your desire to be a leader will be thwarted by a lack of followers who truly trust and believe you are acting in their best interests.

The third personal paradox is perhaps the most difficult one to confront on a day-to-day basis, and that is work versus family. We face this one all the time, so much so that we have created a list of questions to help you think through the contradictions:

- What boundaries have you established regarding your personal and family time? Are there boundaries?
- What personal and family commitments are sacrosanct? Have you communicated the importance of these commitments to your colleagues?
- What rituals might you establish to assure your family of their importance? Might you adopt certain behaviors intended to shore up outward signs of commitment (say, dinner at home

three nights a work week, family movie night, kids join on one business trip per year)?

- How can time spent with family or hobbies enhance your performance at work (for example, healthy nutrition, exercise, reading, creative endeavors)?
- Do discussions with your family involve conversations about the why behind your work? Do your spouse and children understand that your work produces your ability to care for them? Do they understand the degree to which your work provides enjoyment and not simply frustration?
- To what extent do you allow others to integrate their work and life? While you might expect others to work on weekends, is it acceptable for them to leave during the day to attend a child's school function?
- Do your behaviors at work lead others to question their own ability to manage this common paradox? (Do you send late night e-mail messages that you expect immediate answers to? What about on weekends?)

We're all guilty of leaning too heavily toward work or toward family at points in our careers—workaholic parents who rarely see their kids are the classic example. The point here is to catalyze honest reflection about the way you're dealing with work and family. By taking the time to think long and hard about these questions, you will become a more agile manager of this paradox—and your practice, perspective, and skill will transfer to the workplace.

Living with the tension of paradoxes is unavoidable in any part of life today. The gray areas fill much more space than the black and white. As you deal with your personal and work paradoxes, you can't help but see how much the skill of managing paradox would help in our civic and political life. What would happen if 535 people in the U.S. Congress jumped over the line? What if they defined their role as serving the good of the nation while also meeting the needs of their constituents—and were more flexible and adaptable in how they undertook that challenge? What if they didn't argue over which was the one right solution, when in fact there are several? Or if they didn't see solutions to every problem as a way to win or a risk of losing? Or if they ceased forcing solutions into polarized either/or corners? How would this manifest in their leadership?

Citizens around the world are victims of leaders who will not look at the problems of the world with a grasp of the unique handling required by paradoxes. Instead, they are partisans of various political parties who try to checkmate each other. If only we could change this blinkered view, we would all be better off. Leaders could then acknowledge the need for paradox management. They could level with their constituencies that nobody has the single right answer—and no perfect one, either. They could admit they cannot fix most things once and for all like puzzles. They would instead declare they have to collaborate more intensively to find actions that ameliorate things now and demand a fresh look later.

If this were to happen, we would have leaders we all could consider role models: Leaders who demanded problem-solving control, yes, but also yielded to paradox-solving delegation. Who demanded consistency of values and purpose, but embraced flexibility in thought and action. Who demanded closure for tame problems, but who called for ongoing management of society's most wicked ills. These kinds of leaders would indeed include disciples of analysis, decision making, and execution. But they would also include masters of inquiry, collaboration, and action in the face of ambiguity.

Indeed, they would bring together paradoxical qualities to match the paradoxical challenges of our time. We would then have role models who would visibly and constantly strive to become complete leaders, integrating head, heart, and guts. In fulfilling the book's initial paradox, however, they would always consider themselves unfinished. They would wield the skills of a finished leader but retain a humility, a thirst for learning, and a sense of always becoming but never arriving. Finished and yet unfinished. These would be leaders who would deserve a place in the history books. They would exemplify what we view as naturals.

NOTES

Epigraph

1. Søren Kierkegaard (as Johannes Climacus), *Philosophical Fragments* (1844). See also online: http://www.religion-online.org/showbook.asp?title=2512.

Preface

1. Admittedly, there is only one answer that can be called "rational," but few people act on reason alone.

Introduction

1. John Steinbeck, *The Log from the* Sea of Cortez (New York: Viking, 1951).
2. This quote is attributed to Einstein, although not verified. A similar quote by Einstein, in scientific terms, is as follows: "It can scarcely be denied that the supreme goal of all theory is to make the irreducible basic elements as simple and as few as possible without having to surrender the adequate representation of a single datum of experience." For a discussion of the simpler quote's source, originally from the *New York Times*, see http://quoteinvestigator.com/2011/05/13/einstein-simple/#more-2363.

Chapter 1

1. Definition per http://www.merriam-webster.com/dictionary/paradox.
2. Other management authors divide problems into four or five categories. For more on this subject, see David J. Snowden and Mary E. Boone, "A Leader's Framework for Decision Making," *Harvard Business Review* (November 2007). See also online: http://hbr.org/2007/11/a-leaders-framework-for-decision-making/.
3. Horst W. J. Rittel and Melvin M. Webber, "Dilemmas in a General Theory of Planning," *Policy Sciences* 4 (1973): 155–169. See also online: http://www.uctc.net/mwebber/Rittel+Webber+Dilemmas+General_Theory_of_Planning.pdf.
4. For another take on this issue, note that psychologists distinguish between "well-defined" and "ill-defined" problems, and in turn suggest different ways to handle them. For example, see Gregory Schraw, Michael E. Dunkle, and Lisa D. Bendixen, "Cognitive Processes in Well-Defined and Ill-Defined Problem

Solving," *Applied Cognitive Psychology* 9, no. 6 (December 1995): 523–538. See also online: http://onlinelibrary.wiley.com/doi/10.1002/acp.2350090605 /abstract.

5. Rittel and Webber, "Dilemmas in a General Theory of Planning," 169.

6. Rittel and Webber, "Dilemmas in a General Theory of Planning," 169.

7. Russell A. Eisenstat, Michael Beer, Nathaniel Foote, Tobias Fredberg, and Flemming Norrgren, "The Uncompromising Leader," *Harvard Business Review* (July-August 2008): 51–57. See also online: http://hbr.org/2008/07/the -uncompromising-leader/ar/1.

8. Tobias Fredberg, Michael Beer, Russell Eisenstat, Nathaniel Foote, and Flemming Norrgren, "Embracing Commitment and Performance: CEOs and Practices Used to Manage Paradox." Working Paper 08–052: 13. See also online: http:// www.hbs.edu/faculty/Publication%20Files/08-052_18284f5a-c48b-45e9-acfd -8b3d3242514e.pdf.

9. Chris Dolmetsch, "Large-Size Soda Limits Should Be Reinstated, N.Y. Says," *Bloomberg Business Week*, June 11, 2013. See also online: http://www.bloomberg .com/news/2013-06-11/large-sized-soda-limits-should-be-reinstated-n-y -says.html.

10. Dave Luvison and Mike Bendixen, "The Behavioral Consequences of Outsourcing: Looking Through the Lens of Paradox," *Journal of Applied Management and Entrepreneurship* 15, no. 4 (December 2010): 28–52. (See page 41 in particular.) See also online: http://www.questia.com/library/1P3 -2253565871/the-behavioral-consequences-of-outsourcing-looking.

11. Eisenstat, Beer, Foote, Fredberg, and Norrgren, "The Uncompromising Leader," 57.

Chapter 2

1. Oliver Wendell Holmes, *The Professor at the Breakfast Table*, 1859 (a collection of essays first published in *Atlantic Monthly*). See also online: http://www .gutenberg.org/files/2665/2665-h/2665-h.htm.

2. Alison Mackey, "The Effect of CEOs on Firm Performance," *Strategic Management Journal* 29, no. 12 (December 2008): 1364. See also online: http:// onlinelibrary.wiley.com/doi/10.1002/smj.708/abstract.

3. Daniel Kahneman makes this same point. See Daniel Kahneman, *Thinking, Fast and Slow* (Farrar, Strauss & Giroux, 2011), 205.

4. Ellen J. Langer, "The Illusion of Control," *Journal of Personality and Social Psychology* 32, no. 2 (1975): 311–328.

5. Lauren A. Leotti, Sheena S. Iyengar, and Kevin N. Ochsner, "Born to Choose: The Origins and Value of the Need for Control," *Trends in Cognitive Sciences* 14, no. 10 (September 2010): 457–463; see p. 457. http://dept.psych.columbia .edu/~kochsner/pdf/Leotti_Born_to_choose_2010.pdf.

6. Leotti, Iyengar, Ochsner, "Born to Choose," 459.

7. Quotes in this section from Ralph Waldo Emerson's essay "Self-Reliance," published in 1841. See also online: http://en.wikisource.org/wiki/Essays:_First _Series/Self-Reliance.

8. J. Edward Russo, Kurt A. Carlson, Margaret G. Meloy, and Kevyn Yong, "The Goal of Consistency as a Cause of Information Distortion," *Journal of Experimental Psychology: General* 137, no. 3 (2008): 456–470. See also online: http://forum.johnson.cornell.edu/faculty/russo/The%20Goal%20of%20 Consistency%20as%20a%20Cause%20of%20Information%20Distortion.pdf.

9. A. W. Kruglanski and D. M. Webster, "Motivated Closing of the Mind: 'Seizing' and 'Freezing,'" *Psychological Review* 103 (1996): 263–283.

10. Arie Kruglanski and T. Freund, "The Freezing and Unfreezing of Lay-Inferences: Effects on Impressional Primacy, Ethnic Stereotyping, and Numerical Anchoring," *Journal of Experimental Social Psychology* 19 (1983): 448–468. See also online: http://www.sciencedirect.com/science/article/pii /0022103183900227.

11. A. W. Kruglanski, D. M. Webster, and A. Klem, "Motivated Resistance and Openness to Persuasion in the Presence or Absence of Prior Information," *Journal of Personality and Social Psychology* 65 (1993): 861–876. See also online: http://www.communicationcache.com/uploads/1/0/8/8/10887248 /motivated_resistance_and_openess_to_persuasion_in_the_presence_or _absence_of_prior_information.pdf.

12. Donna M. Webster and Arie W. Kruglanski, "Individual Differences in Need for Cognitive Closure," *Journal of Personality and Social Psychology* 67, no. 6 (Dec. 1994): 1049–1062. See also online: http://www.communicationcache.com /uploads/1/0/8/8/10887248/individual_differences_in_need_for_cognitive _closure.pdf.

13. Charles D. Bailey, Cynthia M. Daily, and Thomas J. Phillips Jr., "Auditors' Levels of Dispositional Need for Closure and Effects on Hypothesis Generation and Confidence," *Behavioral Research in Accounting* 23, no. 2 (Fall 2011): 27–50. See also online: http://aaapubs.org/doi/abs/10.2308/bria-50021?journalCode=bria.

14. Webster and Kruglanski, "Individual Differences in Need for Cognitive Closure."

15. Robert B. Cialdini, Melanie R. Trost, and Jason T. Newsom, "Preference for Consistency: The Development of a Valid Measure and the Discovery of Surprising Behavioral Implications," *Journal of Personality and Social Psychology* 69, no. 2 (1995): 318–328. See also online: http://osil.psy.ua.edu/~Rosanna /Soc_Inf/week9/PFC.pdf.

16. "Leading Through Connections: Insights from the Global Chief Executive Officer Study," IBM Institute for Business Value, May 2012. See also online: http://www-935.ibm.com/services/us/en/c-suite/ceostudy2012/.

17. Author interview with Jan Singer, Nike Inc.

18. Bailey, Daily, and Phillips, "Auditors' Levels of Dispositional Need for Closure and Effects on Hypothesis Generation and Confidence," 43.

19. Julia Q. Zhu, "Four Mistakes Behind Groupon's Failure in China," TechinAsia, November 4, 2011. Available online: http://www.techinasia.com/4-mistakes -behind-groupon%E2%80%99s-failure-in-china.

20. Tony Hsieh, *Delivering Happiness: A Path to Profits, Passion, and Purpose* (New York: Business Plus, 2010).

Chapter 3

1. Tony Schwartz, "Turning 60: The Twelve Most Important Lessons I've Learned So Far," *Harvard Business Review Blog Network*, May 1, 2012. See online: http://blogs.hbr.org/2012/05/turning-60-the-twelve-most/.

2. Thomas Sy and Laura Sue D'Annunzio, "Challenges and Strategies of Matrix Organizations: Top-Level and Mid-Level Manager's Perspectives," *Human Resource Planning* 28, no. 1 (2005): 39–48. See also online: http://connection.ebscohost.com/c/articles/17034559/challenges-strategies-matrix-organizations-top-level-mid-level-managers-perspectives.

3. Sy and D'Annunzio, "Challenges and Strategies of Matrix Organizations," 46.

4. Horst W. J. Rittel and Melvin M. Webber, "Dilemmas in a General Theory of Planning," *Policy Sciences* 4 (1973): 155–169; see p. 158. See also online: http://www.uctc.net/mwebber/Rittel+Webber+Dilemmas+General_Theory_of_Planning.pdf.

5. Dwight D. Eisenhower, quoted online at http://en.wikiquote.org/wiki/Dwight_D._Eisenhower.

6. For a summary of biases that relate to planning, see James H. Barnes Jr., "Cognitive Biases and Their Impact on Strategic Planning," *Strategic Management Journal* 5 (1984): 129–137. See also online: http://onlinelibrary.wiley.com/doi/10.1002/smj.4250050204/abstract. A more recent discussion of the consequences of biases in strategic planning includes T. K. Das and Bing-Sheng Teng, "Cognitive Biases and Strategic Processes: An Integrative Perspective," *Journal of Management Studies* 36 (6): 757–778. See also online: http://aux.zicklin.baruch.cuny.edu/tkdas/publications/das-teng_jms99_cognitivebias_757-778.pdf.

7. Daniel Kahneman, *Thinking, Fast and Slow* (New York: Farrar, Straus & Giroux, 2011), 204–205.

8. This passage is based on "Pop Quiz: Can Indra Nooyi Revive PepsiCo?" Knowledge@Wharton, March 28, 2012. See online: http://knowledge.wharton.upenn.edu/article/pop-quiz-can-indra-nooyi-revive-pepsico/.

9. Adrian Furnham and Tracy Ribchester, "Tolerance of Ambiguity: A Review of the Concept, Its Measurement and Applications," *Current Psychology* 14, no. 3 (Fall 1995): 179. See also online: http://link.springer.com/article/10.1007/BF02686907.

Chapter 4

1. Quote appears in Thoreau's letter to his friend Harrison G. O. Blake, dated November 16, 1857. Contained in *Letters to Various Persons* by Ralph Waldo Emerson and Henry David Thoreau, a classic now in print by various publishers.

2. Text excerpted from GlaxoSmithKline video, no longer available online. Accessed June 2013.

3. Commitments excerpted from GlaxoSmithKline website, accessed June 2013. See online http://www.gsk.com/responsibility/health-for-all/our-commitments

.html and http://www.gsk.com/explore-gsk/health-for-all/the-fight-against -malaria.html.

4. Data from GlaxoSmithKline website, accessed June 2013. See online: http://www.gsk.com/responsibility/health-for-all/access-to-healthcare.html.

5. John G. Taft, "How to Fix Financial Capitalism? Focus on Ethics," *Harvard Business Review* Blog Network, July 5, 2012. See online: http://blogs.hbr.org /cs/2012/07/how_to_fix_financial_capitalis.html.

6. Richard L. Leider, "The Purposeful Leader: A Purpose Checkup," in *Coaching for Leadership: Writings on Leadership from the World's Greatest Coaches*, 3rd ed., edited by Marshall Goldsmith, Laurence S. Lyons, and Sarah McArthur (San Francisco: Pfeiffer, 2012), 96.

7. Richard L. Leider, *The Power of Purpose: Find Meaning, Live Longer, Better*, 2nd ed. (San Francisco: Berrett-Koehler, 2010).

8. Credo is published on the Johnson & Johnson website. See online: https://www.jnj.com/sites/default/files/pdf/jnj_ourcredo_english_us_8.5x11_cmyk.pdf.

9. Reason.com, "Rethinking the Social Responsibility of Business: A Reason Debate Featuring Milton Friedman, Whole Foods' John Mackey, and Cypress Semiconductor's T.J. Rodgers," October 2005. See also online: http://www.biology.iupui.edu/biocourses/Biol540/pdf/WholeFoodsJohnMackeySR.pdf.

10. Information from Whole Foods Market website, accessed June 2013. See online: http://www.wholefoodsmarket.com/careers/our-mission-and-culture.

11. An updated version of the oath is here: http://mbaoath.org/about/the-mba-oath/. See also: http://mbaoath.org/mba-oath-legacy-version/.

12. Michael Porter and Mark R. Kramer, "Creating Shared Value: How to Reinvent Capitalism . . . and Unleash a Wave of Innovation and Growth," *Harvard Business Review* (Feb-Mar 2011): 62–67.

13. Jillian Goodman, J. J. McCorvey, Margaret Rhodes, and Linda Tischler, "From Facebook to Pixar: 10 Conversations That Changed Our World." Fast Company online, January 15, 2013. See online: http://www.fastcompany.com/3004348 /facebook-pixar-10-conversations-changed-our-world.

14. Mark Gunther, "Unilever's CEO Has a Green Thumb," *Fortune* 23 (May 23, 2013): 66. See also online: http://money.cnn.com/2013/05/23/leadership /unilever-paul-polman.pr.fortune/index.html.

Chapter 5

1. William Shakespeare, *Macbeth*, Act 4, Scene 3, lines 138–139. See online: http://www.shakespeare-navigators.com/macbeth/T43.html#136.

2. Johnson & Johnson News, "Johnson & Johnson Medical Companies Opens Innovation Center in China to Serve Emerging Markets," June 22, 2011. See online: http://www.jnj.com/news/all/johnson-johnson-medical-companies -opens-innovation-center-in-china.

3. See online video interview with Alex Gorsky, June 7, 2013: http://www .bloomberg.com/video/johnson-johnson-ceo-gorsky-on-strategy-for-china -Zr114bffTeqBdotyAlAEVw.html.

4. Bob Tita, "Illinois Tool Resists Pressure to Split," *Wall Street Journal*, August 31, 2012. See also online: http://online.wsj.com/article/SB10000 872396390444772804577621432056243146.html.

5. Charles G. Lord, Lee Ross, and Mark R. Lepper, "Biased Assimilation and Attitude Polarization: The Effects of Prior Theories on Subsequently Considered Evidence," *Journal of Personality and Social Psychology* 37, no. 11 (1979): 2098–2109. See also online: http://psycnet.apa.org/index.cfm?fa=buy.optionToBuy& uid=1981-05421-001.

6. David J. Malenka, John A. Baron, Sarah Johansen, Jon W. Wahrenberger, and Jonathan M. Ross, "The Framing Effect of Relative and Absolute Risk," *Journal of General Internal Medicine* 8, no. 10 (October 1993): 543–548. See also online: http://www.cuclasses.com/stat1001/lectures/classnotes/RR _FramingEffect.pdf.

7. Paul P. Baard, Edward L. Deci, and Richard M. Ryan, "Intrinsic Need Satisfaction: A Motivational Basis of Performance and Well-Being in Two Work Settings," *Journal of Applied Social Psychology* 34, no. 10 (2004): 2061. See also online: http://www.choixdecarriere.com/pdf/6573/Baard_Deci_Ryan(2004).pdf.

8. Sara L. Rynes, Barry Gerhart, and Kathleen A. Minette, "The Importance of Pay in Employee Motivation: Discrepancies Between What People Say and What They Do," *Human Resource Management* 43, no. 4 (Winter 2004): 381–394. See also online: http://onlinelibrary.wiley.com/doi/10.1002/hrm.20031 /abstract.

Chapter 6

1. Friedrich Nietzsche, *Twilight of the Idols* (New York: Penguin Classics, 1990), 54.

2. Clint Korver, *Framing*, unpublished monograph, 2004.

3. As quoted in John Berry, *Herman Miller: The Purpose of Design*, 2nd ed. (New York: Rizzoli International, 2004), 5.

4. Fast Company Staff, "'I No Longer Want to Work for Money.'" Fast Company online, February 1, 2007. See online: http://www.fastcompany.com/58514/i-no -longer-want-work-money.

5. Ap Dijksterhuis and Loran F. Nordgren, "A Theory of Unconscious Thought," *Perspectives on Psychological Science* 1 (2006): 95–109; see p. 107. See also online: http://www.alice.id.tue.nl/references/dijksterhuis-nordgren-2006.pdf.

6. Dijksterhuis and Nordgren, "A Theory of Unconscious Thought," 96, 102.

7. Dijksterhuis and Nordgren, "A Theory of Unconscious Thought," 96.

8. David Kiron, Doug Palmer, Anh Nguyen Phillips, and Robert Berkman, "Social Business: Shifting Out of First Gear," Report by Massachusetts Institute of Technology, Sloan School of Business and Deloitte LLP (Westlake, TX: Deloitte University Press: 2013), 5. See online at http://sloanreview.mit.edu/reports /shifting-social-business/?utm_source=WhatCounts+Publicaster+Edition& utm_medium=email&utm_campaign=Soc+Enews+-+July+16%2c+2013 &utm_content=Get+the+report.

9. Mihalyi Csikszentmihalyi, *Creativity: Flow and the Psychology of Discovery and Invention* (New York: HarperPerennial, 1996).

10. Paddy Miller, Koen Klokgieters, Azra Brankovic, and Freek Duppen, *Innovation Leadership Study* (London: Capgemini Consulting, 2012), 20. See also online: http://www.capgemini-consulting.com/innovation-leadership-study.

11. Michael A. West and Neil R. Anderson, "Innovation in Top Management Teams," *Journal of Applied Psychology* 81, no. 6 (1996): 690. See also online: http://psycnet.apa.org/index.cfm?fa=buy.optionToBuy&uid=1996–06918–005.

Chapter 7

1. Sir Francis Bacon, *The Essays and Counsels Civil and Moral of Francis Bacon*, 1597, newly written 1625. See full text online: http://www.luminarium.org/renascence-editions/bacon.html.

2. Based on observations by Jake Birchard working in Kakamega, Kenya, posted September 22, 2010. See blog post: http://jakebirchard.wordpress.com/2010/09/22/stoves-to-improve-lives/.

3. Bradley J. Olson, Satyanarayana Parayitam, and Yongjian Bao, "Strategic Decision Making: The Effects of Cognitive Diversity, Conflict, and Trust on Decision Outcomes," *Journal of Management* 33, no. 2 (April 2007): 218. See also online: http://www.buec.udel.edu/beckert/BUAD%20870%2012F/Presentation%202.pdf.

4. Daniel Kahneman, *Thinking, Fast and Slow* (New York: Farrar, Straus & Giroux, 2011), 186.

5. Bill Millar, "The Rise of the Digital C-Suite: How Executives Locate and Filter Business Information," *Forbes/Insight*, June 2009. See online: http://www.forbes.com/forbesinsights/digital_csuite/.

6. Michael Abebe, Arifin Angriawan, and Huy Tran, "Chief Executive External Network Ties and Environmental Scanning Activities: An Empirical Examination," *Strategic Management Review* 4, no. 1 (2010): 38. See also online: http://www.strategicmanagementreview.com/doi/pdf/10.4128/1930-4560-4.1.30.

7. William W. Maddux and Adam D. Galinsky, "Cultural Borders and Mental Barriers: The Relationship Between Living Abroad and Creativity," *Journal of Personality and Social Psychology* 96, no. 5 (2009): 1047–1061. See also online: http://www.esf.edu/international/documents/CulturalBordersandMentalBarriers_livingabroadandcreativity.pdf.

8. For a lengthy discussion of worldviews, see table 2, page 29, of Mark E. Koltko-Rivera, "The Psychology of Worldviews," *Review of General Psychology* 8, no. 1 (2004): 3–58. See also online: http://www.apa.org/pubs/journals/features/gpr-813.pdf.

Chapter 8

1. Johann Wolfgang von Goethe (translated by John Oxenford), *Conversations of Goethe* (London: George Bell & Sons, 1882), 223.

2. Margaret B. Glick, Thomas J. Chermack, Henry Luckel, and Brian Q. Gauck, "Effects of Scenario Planning on Participant Mental Models," *European Journal of Training and Development* 36, no. 5 (2012): 488–507. See also online: http://www.emeraldinsight.com/journals.htm?articleid=17036255.

3. René Rohrbeck and Jan O. Schwarz, "The Value Contribution of Strategic Foresight: Insights from an Empirical Study on Large European Companies," *Technological Forecasting and Social Change* 80, no. 8 (October 2013): 1593–1606. See also online: http://www.sciencedirect.com/science/article/pii/S004016251300005X.

4. Based on PricewaterhouseCoopers, "Managing Tomorrow's People: The Future of Work to 2020," 2007. See also online: http://www.pwc.com/gx/en/managing-tomorrows-people/future-of-work/pdf/mtp-future-of-work.pdf.

5. PricewaterhouseCoopers, "Managing Tomorrow's People," Appendix A3, 30–31.

6. Pierre Wack, "Scenarios: Shooting the Rapids," *Harvard Business Review* (November 1985): 139–150. See also online: http://hbr.org/1985/11/scenarios-shooting-the-rapids/ar/1.

Chapter 9

1. Plato, *The Republic*, 354c (Book I). See also online: http://www.aprendendoingles.com.br/ebooks/republic.pdf.

2. Donal Crilly and Pamela Sloan, "Enterprise Logic: Explaining Corporate Attention to Stakeholders from the 'Inside-Out,'" *Strategic Management Journal* 33 (February 27, 2012): 1174–1193. See also online: http://onlinelibrary.wiley.com/doi/10.1002/smj.1964/abstract.

3. Author interview with Ed Freeman, Darden School of Business, University of Virginia, August 14, 2013.

4. John Mackey, interview posted online January 12, 2011. See http://www.youtube.com/watch?v=z88g1DfXmu8.

5. Carrie Brownstein, "Quality Standards and the Multi-Stakeholder Process," Whole Story Blog, January 27, 2012. See blog online: http://www.wholefoodsmarket.com/blog/whole-story/quality-standards-and-multi-stakeholder-process.

6. We appreciate the pioneering thinking in this field by Ed Freeman and his coauthors. These thoughts are fully developed in: Edward Freeman, Jeffrey S. Harrison, and Andrew C. Wicks, *Managing for Stakeholders* (New Haven: Yale University Press, 2007), chapter 5.

7. Freeman, Harrison, and Wicks, *Managing for Stakeholders*, 117.

8. Freeman, Harrison, and Wicks, *Managing for Stakeholders*, 120.

9. "Company Network." See online http://www.ceres.org/company-network.

10. We take inspiration from Charles Green's "Trust Equation," another form but a similar concept. See online: http://trustedadvisor.com/articles/the-trust-equation-a-primer.

Chapter 10

1. Oscar Wilde, *The Picture of Dorian Gray* (New York: Signet Classic, 1962 [originally published 1890]), 55. See full text online: http://etext.lib.virginia.edu/etcbin/toccer-new2?id=WilDori.sgm&images=images/modeng&data=/texts/english/modeng/parsed&tag=public&part=all.

2. Mickey Connolly and Richard Rianoshek, *The Communication Catalyst* (Chicago: Dearborn Trade, 2002).

3. As cited in Chip Heath and Dan Heath, "The Curse of Knowledge," *Harvard Business Review* (December 2006). See also online: http://hbr.org/2006/12/the-curse-of-knowledge/ar/1.

Chapter 11

1. Gary Hamel, *Leading the Revolution: How to Thrive in Turbulent Times by Making Innovation a Way of Life* (Boston: Harvard Business Review Press, 2000), 25–26.

2. Carsten K. W. De Dreu, "When Too Little or Too Much Hurts: Evidence for a Curvilinear Relationship Between Task Conflict and Innovation in Teams," *Journal of Management* 32 (2006): 83. See also online: http://jom.sagepub.com/content/32/1/83.accessible-long.

3. Charlan J. Nemeth, Bernard Personnaz, Marie Personnaz, and Jack A. Goncalo, "The Liberating Role of Conflict in Group Creativity: A Study in Two Countries," *European Journal of Social Psychology* 34 (2004): 365–374. See also online: https://www.ilr.cornell.edu/directory/ja26531/downloads/Liberating_role_of_conflict_in_group_creativity.pdf.

Chapter 12

1. Carl R. Rogers (Howard Kirschenbaum and Valeria Land Henderson, eds.), *The Carl Rogers Reader* (Boston: Houghton Mifflin, 1989), 19.

2. Hugh McColl, Chairman and CEO, Bank of America, Presentation to Senior Executives, April 1999.

3. Amos Tversky and Eldar Shafir, "Choice Under Conflict: The Dynamics of Deferred Decision," *Psychological Science* 3, no. 6 (November 1992): 358–361; see p. 361. (Italics in original.) See also online: http://kie.vse.cz/wp-content/uploads/Tversky-Shafir-1992.pdf.

4. Frank Huber, Sören Köcher, Johannes Vogel, and Frederik Meyer, "Dazing Diversity: Investigating the Determinants and Consequences of Decision Paralysis," *Psychology and Marketing* 29, no. 6 (June 2012): 467–478. See also online: http://onlinelibrary.wiley.com/doi/10.1002/mar.20535/abstract.

5. I. Ritov and J. Baron, "Status Quo and Omission Biases," *Journal of Risk and Uncertainty* 5 (1992): 49–61.

6. Research as summarized in Margaret E. Brooks, "Management Indecision," *Management Decision* 49, no. 5 (2011): 683–693; see p. 686. See also online: http://www.emeraldinsight.com/journals.htm?articleid=1923562.

7. W. Samuelson and R. Zeckhauser, "Status Quo Bias in Decision Making," *Journal of Risk and Uncertainty* 1 (1988): 7–59.

8. S. Eidelman and C. S. Crandall, "Bias in Favor of the Status Quo," *Social and Personality Psychology Compass* 6 (2012): 270–281.

9. Brooks, "Management Indecision," 686.

10. Dolores Albarracin, Justin Hepler, and Melanie Tannenbaum, "General Action and Inaction Goals: Their Behavioral, Cognitive, and Affective Origins and Influences," *Current Directions in Psychological Science* 20, no. 2 (2011): 119–123; see p. 120. See also online: http://www.ncbi.nlm.nih.gov/pubmed/23766569.

11. As quoted in Ruth Moore, *Niels Bohr: The Man, His Science, and the World They Changed* (Cambridge: MIT Press, 1966), 196.

Conclusion

1. From Book II of *Emile, or On Education,* as quoted in Leo Damrosch, *Jean-Jacques Rousseau: Restless Genius* (Boston: Houghton Mifflin Harcourt, 2005), 238. Other translations are online. For example, see the translation by Barbara Foxley at Project Gutenberg: "You cannot avoid paradox if you think for yourself, and whatever you may say I would rather fall into paradox than into prejudice." http://www.gutenberg.org/cache/epub/5427/pg5427.txt.

ABOUT THE AUTHORS

David L. Dotlich is chairman and CEO of Pivot, one of the world's largest providers of customized executive development for top leaders of Fortune 500 companies: Walmart, Johnson & Johnson, GSK, Nike, Microsoft, KKR, Aetna, Best Buy, Deutsche Post DHL, AbbVie, Ericsson, and many others. Named one of the Top 50 Coaches in the United States, he is a former executive vice president of Honeywell International and advises CEOs and boards on talent, leadership, and strategy. He is coauthor of eleven best-selling books, among them *Head, Heart, and Guts*; *Why CEOs Fail*; and *Leading in Times of Crisis*. A former University of Minnesota faculty member and consultant to boards and CEOs on talent and strategy, he co-founded CDR International and Oliver Wyman Executive Learning Center, and served as president of Mercer Delta Consulting. He completed his MA and PhD at the University of Minnesota. He lives in Portland, Oregon, and New York City.

    Peter C. Cairo is a consultant who serves as an adviser to CEOs and boards on leadership development, executive team performance, and board effectiveness. He works with clients such as BlackRock, Colgate-Palmolive, GSK, Avon Products, ITW, PepsiCo, Thomson Reuters, Interpublic Group, KPMG, Boehringer Ingelheim, and the Carlyle Group. A noted author and speaker, he is coauthor of six books, among them *Head, Heart, and Guts*; *Why CEOs Fail*; and *Leading in Times of Crisis*. He is former chairman of Columbia University's Department of Organizational and Counseling Psychology, where he has taught for twenty years, and co-founder of CDR International and Oliver Wyman Executive Learning Center. He earned his BA at Harvard University and PhD at Columbia University. He lives in upstate New York.

Cade Cowan is a consultant and coach to senior executives on leadership development. The head of Pivot's leadership-development practice, he has led programs in thirty-one countries on five continents with firms ranging from Walmart to GlaxoSmithKline to Aetna. A leader in innovative practices such as immersion experiences and impact measurement, he formerly was director of all global learning at Coca-Cola University, Bottling Investments Group (BIG), building on his experience as director of global leadership development at Coca-Cola University and as program designer at GE's John F. Welch Leadership Development Center. He earned his MA in organizational and social psychology from Columbia University and BA in economics and finance from the University of Tennessee at Martin. He lives in Atlanta, Georgia.

For more information, please visit www.pivotleadership.com.

INDEX